ON THE SMALL SCREEN

ON THE SMALL SCREEN

New Approaches in Television and Video Criticism

Hal Himmelstein

PRAEGER

PRAEGER SPECIAL STUDIES • PRAEGER SCIENTIFIC

Library of Congress Cataloging in Publication Data

Himmelstein, Hal.
    On the small screen.

    Bibliography: p.
    Includes index.
    1. Television criticism.   I. Title.   II.   Video
criticism.
PN1992.8.C7H5   791.45'01'5   80-25141
ISBN 0-03-058343-8

    Grateful acknowledgment is hereby made to the following for
permission to use copyrighted material: Doubleday & Company, Inc. ,
for permission to use material from TV: The Most Popular Art, by
Horace Newcomb; copyright 1974 by Horace Newcomb. David Ross
for permission to use excerpts from a personal interview conducted
March 15, 1978 in Washington, D. C. The Long Beach Museum of
Art for permission to use excerpts from Southland Video Anthology,
by David Ross. The MIT Press, Cambridge, Massachusetts, for permission to use material from The New Television: A Public/Private
Art, edited by Douglas Davis and Allison Simmons; copyright 1977 by
Electronic Arts Intermix Inc. Douglas Davis for permission to reprint
material from Manifesto for the Everson Museum, 1972, and excerpts
from a personal interview conducted March 18, 1978 in New York City.
The Washington Star for permission to use selected excerpts from the
television reviews of Bernie Harrison; copyright by The Washington
Star. Harcourt Brace Jovanovich, Inc. , for permission to use excerpts
from Video Art, edited by Ira Schneider and Beryl Korot. Grove Press,
Inc. , for permission to use excerpts from Waiting for Godot, by Samuel Beckett; copyright 1954 by Grove Press, Inc. The New York Times
for permission to use excerpts from television reviews by John J.
O'Connor; copyright 1976/77/78/79, 1971/80, by the New York Times
Company.

Published in 1981 by Praeger Publishers
CBS Educational and Professional Publishing
A Division of CBS, Inc.
521 Fifth Avenue, New York, New York 10175 U.S.A.

For my wife, RoseAnne, and my parents,
Jack and Fanny Himmelstein

ACKNOWLEDGMENTS

I am deeply indebted to the following persons and institution for helping make this book a reality: to Charles Clift III, who encouraged me to begin the project and offered continual guidance and support—without his advice and personal concern, these pages would not be before you; to H. Gene Blocker, who provided numerous conceptual insights as the research for the book progressed; to Rich Kuhn of Cambria Press, who had confidence in my ability to persevere; to the five television and video critics who took time from their busy schedules to grant lengthy personal interviews; to Debra Skiver, who provided invaluable indexing and bibliographic assistance; and to the School of Radio-Television of Ohio University and its director, Drew McDaniel, who provided both encouragement and a lightened teaching schedule to expedite the book's completion.

Finally, I owe a special debt of gratitude to my wife, RoseAnne Spradlin, a dancer, painter, and TV crime drama afficionado, who shared with me her insights on television and contemporary art, and who put up with the abominable noise emanating from my 1940 Remington portable. Both she and the typewriter survived, and the crime dramas continue on late night reruns.

CONTENTS

ACKNOWLEDGMENTS   vii

INTRODUCTION   x

Chapter

1   TV CULTURE: ENTERTAINMENT OR ART?   1

    Art and Culture   2
    The Mass Culture—High Culture Debate   3
    Uncovering the "Art" in Television   12
    Notes   18

2   TELEVISION, VIDEO, AND THE CONTEXT
    OF CRITICISM   20

    The Critic Defined   20
    The Television Critic   25
    New Directions in Television and Video Criticism   33
    Notes   37

3   JOHN J. O'CONNOR: CRITIC "OF RECORD"   39

    O'Connor on Television   41
    O'Connor on Being a Television Critic   59
    Conclusions   62
    Notes   64

4   BERNIE HARRISON: FOUNDING FATHER
    OF THE "OLD GUARD"   66

    Harrison on Television   69
    Harrison on Being a Television Critic   80
    Harrison on His Readership   83
    Conclusions   84
    Notes   85

Chapter   Page

5   HORACE NEWCOMB:
      GURU OF THE ACADEMIC CRITICS   87

      Newcomb on Popular Television and Culture   91
      Newcomb on Being a Television Critic   105
      Newcomb on His Readership   108
      Conclusions   109
      Notes   111

6   DAVID ROSS: A SPOKESPERSON FOR ARTISTS' VIDEO   114

      Ross on Artists' Video   121
      Ross on His Role in the Video Community   133
      Ross on His Readership   134
      Conclusions   134
      Notes   135

7   DOUGLAS DAVIS: THE VIDEO ARTIST AS CRITIC   137

      Davis on His Video Works and His Writings about
        Video and Art   142
      Davis on His Role as an Artist-Critic   162
      Davis on His Audience and Readership   164
      Conclusions   167
      Notes   168

8   REDEFINING TELEVISION CRITICISM   171

      Questioning the Critics   173
      Notes   178

BIBLIOGRAPHY   179

INDEX   193

ABOUT THE AUTHOR   207

INTRODUCTION

> Criticism is . . . the context in
> which art works make it to the future.
>
> Nancy Marmer, "The Performing
> Critic," Art in America

In Act II of Samuel Beckett's Waiting for Godot, two garrulous old lifelong companions, Valdimir and Estragon, find themselves down and out, waiting to find some meaning in their lives. They stand on a country road, killing time, trying to relieve their boredom. They decide to call each other names:

> Vladimir: Ceremonious ape!
> Estragon: Punctilious pig!
> Vladimir: Finish your phrase, I tell you!
> Estragon: Finish your own!
> Silence. They draw closer, halt.
> Vladimir: Moron!
> Estragon: That's the idea, let's abuse each other.
> They turn, move apart, turn again and face each
> other.
> Vladimir: Moron!
> Estragon: Vermin!
> Vladimir: Abortion!
> Estragon: Morpion!
> Vladimir: Sewer-rat!
> Estragon: Curate!
> Vladimir: Cretin!
> Estragon: (with finality). Crritic!
> Vladimir: Oh!
> He wilts, vanquished, and turns away.

Crritic! To imagine that the mere mention of the word could conjure such feelings of baseness—a step below a cretin, or what's worse, an abortion! How can such a noble discipline as criticism receive such bad press? Is it justified? This volume will attempt to answer these questions as they relate to one particular type of criticism—that which focuses on television, our culture's most popular art form.

Television, or TV, catapulted into our culture over three decades ago. With it came major cultural displacements, especially in the areas of entertainment and leisure. Television legitimized popular entertainment to an extent never achieved by film, print, or even radio. People stayed at home more and the neighborhood shrank to the living room. It was inevitable that television's antithesis, video, would sooner or later arrive on the scene. Video became the domain of artists who were disenchanted with television's corporate control and its seeming lack of authenticity. These artists working with video are frequently engaged in making statements against popular TV both in their video works and in manifestos directed to a select art audience ostensibly intellectually above the masses of TV addicts in all pedestrian corners of our late twentieth-century electronic land.

As in the case with any art form, TV (and its video offspring) gave birth to a class of observers we call critics: self-appointed judges of the products and meanings of an art form. Those critics of television, unlike their fellow travelers engaged in evaluating the more traditional art forms of literature, theater, visual arts, music, and film, find themselves faced with a singularly challenging task— for they must examine not only works of television art in isolation, but they must also consider television's presence in the world as an economic institution of considerable influence; television as a technology constantly impacting on a substantial number of cultural issues including the directions and pace of social change; television as a barometer of the status of subcultural group relationships to a dominant culture's control of information processing and dissemination; and television as an institutional mechanism that encourages and constantly reinforces what cultural anthropologist Jules Henry aptly termed this country's "pecuniary philosophy"—advertising as the expression of an "irrational economy that has depended for survival on a fantastically high standard of living incorporated into the American mind as a moral imperative." To adequately address this broad range of ideas is a bewildering task. The task is made even more difficult when we realize that these television critics are not in the main writing for a readership of the so-called cultural elite who come to the critical dialogue with well-developed art-critical evaluative faculties.

Every art form produces not only individual works of art executed by persons referred to as artists or the creative community but also generates essays (some learned, some not so learned) written by critics in response to the appearance of those works of art. Today, in a growing number of cases, critics are themselves practicing artists who choose both to create works of art and to talk and write about art.

From the outset it must be recognized by the reader that no artist working in a particular art form—be that person a poet, novelist,

xi

painter, sculptor, composer, choreographer, architect, filmmaker, videomaker or whatever—holds an exclusive claim to the secrets of the soul or the wisdom of the ages. Therefore, no true hierarchy of the arts exists.

At the same time it must be recognized that within an art form there are individual works that for a variety of reasons stand above the remainder of works in that art form. There can exist "hierarchies of reputation" within art forms.

These hierarchies of reputation may take as their bases the cogency of a work in its interpretation of the conditions of man and his culture (content orientation or meaning); the "correctness" and salience of the work's formal structure; or, in the case of recent "formalist art," the existence of meaning in the formal structure of the work itself.

The task of uncovering and justifying these hierarchies of reputation within art forms ultimately falls to the critic—the skillful arbiter of significance in works of art. The critic helps us fine-tune our sensibilities so that we may better recognize what makes one work of art special and another work of art not so special. This responsibility is not to be taken lightly by the critic, or to be easily dismissed by those who would be spectators.

As long as the human imagination has been actively engaged in the creative process there have been persons who, with varying degrees of insightfulness, have busied themselves describing, interpreting, and evaluating creative products (often to the disdain of the products' creators). In some cases, a work of art deemed by knowledgeable observers to be significant has produced brilliant discussions of its meaning and formal correctness and salience (witness the volume of critical literature attaching itself to Melville's Moby Dick, Joyce's Finnegan's Wake, and Eisenstein's Potemkin); in other cases, a work of art deemed less than significant has spawned brilliant critical essays that transcend the limitations of the work which initially prompted the writing of the essays (a prime example is the school of auteur criticism of cinema that grew up in France and has achieved legitimacy in the United States through the writings of film critic Andrew Sarris).

In the final analysis, it is some combination of works of art and critical discussion about the works that produces a history of man's attempts to grasp the significance of his being. For this reason, it is incumbent upon those who seek a heightened awareness of their world and their places in it to closely examine critical approaches to art.

In the past three decades, television and video (a more personalized "television" existing and growing outside the boundaries of large, institutionalized commercial and public television broadcasting) have begun to grow as autonomous art forms.

Television, by common consent, has become the most pervasive popular art form in our culture today. And along with the creative products of television has grown a large body of television criticism. This criticism has consistently been demeaned for its lack of direction and sophistication when compared to the more established literary and visual arts criticism.

Video, which is still in its adolescent stages, has also given birth to a body of criticism that to date has been criticized for being parochial and defensive, primarily because most video practitioners and their supporters in print have attempted to summarily dismiss broadcast television as not worthy of serious critical attention. They generally have failed to acknowledge that video's artistic roots are firmly planted in the television soil. Video criticism, it is said, has been overly dogmatic and confused.

Are there no clearly defined critical approaches to television? Are television critics clearly lacking when compared with literary, visual arts, and contemporary film critics? Is video criticism parochial, dogmatic, and confused? These are a few of the questions this volume will address in the hope of shedding some light on the current status of television and video criticism, and of offering some suggestions for new directions in this critical realm. Above all else, the volume highlights the work of a variety of television and video critics who are, in their individual ways, facing up to the task of decoding television—the most ephemeral and perhaps our most socially powerful contemporary art form.

The five critics chosen for inclusion here, and the order in which they are presented, hopefully will provide the reader with a coherent structure in which to examine the true breadth of the emerging television and video criticism. I begin with the so-called "popular critics" or journalist-critics. John J. O'Connor of the New York Times is considered by many as one of the most influential television critics writing today, especially with television's network management and creative communities. Bernie Harrison of the Washington Star is one of the few remaining "original" television critics to combine reportorial and review in his columns. His career spans the history of television as a popular art and he thus brings a broad historical perspective to the discipline.

From these popular critics, I move to a discussion of academic critics, using Horace Newcomb as a representative example of the critical approaches taken by that group. Newcomb, himself a former newspaper television critic, is an excellent guide into the broader questions of television and culture.

Finally, David Ross, a museum video curator, and Douglas Davis, an artist working in video and a video critic, provide an alternative perspective to the role of television in our lives by introducing us to video—a more personalized form of television—and drawing comparisons between the television and video forms.

ORGANIZATION OF THE VOLUME

Chapter 1, "TV Culture: Entertainment or Art?," enters the conceptual thickets of trying to place television and video in the context of contemporary referents, namely art, entertainment, and culture.

Chapter 2, "Television, Video, and the Context of Criticism," offers one approach to talking about criticism in general and television and video criticism in particular, and the critics who write it or who have written it in the past.

Chapters 3 through 7 let the critics speak for themselves, rather than simply analyzing the critical writings of those individuals chosen for inclusion in the volume as representative of types of television and video critics. Each of these chapters examines the writings of one critic in the context of that critic's response to questions I asked him during lengthy personal interviews conducted in late 1977 and early 1978. Each critic's responses to questions about his critical writings, his perceptions of his role as a critic, and his perceptions of his readership provide clues to the questions posed above.

Chapter 8, "Redefining Television Criticism," offers possible new, alternative approaches to television and video criticism that might transcend the limitations of the existing criticism.

ON THE SMALL SCREEN

1

TV CULTURE:
ENTERTAINMENT OR ART?

What is television? In its most basic sense, television is the combination of electronically produced and transmitted visual imagery, music, speech, sound effects, and ambient "noise." These basic components of the television image/sound nexus can be infinitely manipulated to produce an endless variety of human communications.

But television is, of course, much more than this, and the "much moreness" is the ultimate arbiter of what we see and hear (and, more importantly, what we <u>do not</u> see and hear) on our home screens. Television is a powerful economic institution controlled by businesspersons whose responsibility (in the commercial realm) to their stockholders dictates that they make certain programming decisions which will result in their programs (the image/sound combinations) being viewed by the greatest possible numbers of people—the "masses." Television is an institutional mechanism that through the constant transmission of advertising messages tends to confirm and reinforce our society's continually escalating demand for goods and services promoting a higher standard of living through acquisitiveness. Television is a technology that impacts on numerous aspects of our communal culture including our perceptions of time and space: space simultaneously "shrinks" and "expands" as we are able to travel the world "live" via satellite broadcasts (the "global village" of Marshall McLuhan is as near as our television set and the cosmic village now extends to the surface of Jupiter); and time contracts as we can transport ourselves to the far corners of the earth in the time it takes to turn the knob on our television set and we can live through the cycle of a man's life in 90 minutes. Television is a cultural barometer measuring the status of minority subcultures in the larger culture according to their ability (or lack of ability) to gain access to television's transmission mechanisms and to thus make known their often unpopular or misunderstood but nevertheless important ideas.

But even beyond all these aspects of television there exists television's essential locus as a contemporary art form. This is the one aspect of television that has to date occupied center stage in the minds of those individuals called television critics.

Television is frequently referred to as our most "popular art." Indeed it is hard to argue against television's pervasiveness in our culture—almost every household in the United States and a great majority of households in other industrialized societies have at least one working television receiver, and current data suggest that the average American household's television set is operating nearly seven hours a day or almost half of our waking hours. But the term "popular art" has come to mean much more than television's pervasiveness or our seeming preoccupation with staring at the electronic cyclops. "Popular art" has taken on some rather ominous overtones as something lesser in quality than those traditional cultural products termed, in contrast, "high art." Television is even discussed in many circles as "subart" or "nonart" in comparison with the traditional creative products of literature, drama, music, visual arts, dance, and, yes, even film. Such a popular art/high art dichotomy is, in my view, much too easily arrived at and neither a reasonable nor a responsible approach to evaluating the creative products of television's creative community. Let's examine this area more carefully.

ART AND CULTURE

We must immediately confront two dichotomous pairs of phrases too frequently used by art critics to distinguish the television product from other creative endeavors, namely "mass culture" versus "high culture" and "popular art" versus "high art."

The problem begins with the presupposition that mass culture and popular art can only signify crass, formulaic, superficial works that correspond to a certain "level of taste" in the audience for such works; the audience for mass culture and popular art is said to be large in number and underdeveloped in its aesthetic sensibility. Such overgeneralized notions have led many culture commentators to incorrectly assume that television is and can only be the product of and for the mass culture and therefore a popular art form. Such a posture ignores the basic aesthetic designs and cultural significations in individual television works and the genres, or program types, they represent considered apart from their distribution contexts and in essence becomes a critique of the audience members rather than an evaluation of the works themselves. It should be recalled at this point that individual works of art in such traditional art forms as, for example, literature survive the ages while many if not most of their less "worthy" contemporaries fade away under critical scrutiny. The examples are, of course, too numerous to mention; nevertheless, the idea should not be easily dismissed.

THE MASS CULTURE—HIGH CULTURE DEBATE

From the 1930s through the 1950s a debate raged among academicians and literati over the nature and meaning of what had come to be called "mass culture" or "popular culture." Included in the mass culture category were television and other so-called "public" art forms (radio, film, and a variety of popular literature and popular music forms). While mass culture was never precisely defined, it seemed to refer to certain objects and events that engaged the attention of all strata of the population as opposed to those objects and events that were traditionally assumed to be the private domain of some ill-defined cultural elite. These latter objects and events were called high culture or superior culture to distinguish them from mass culture.

The most articulate participants in this debate over the nature and sociocultural significance of mass culture were Dwight Macdonald, Edward Shils, and C. Wright Mills. According to culture theorists James Carey and Albert Kreiling:

> Macdonald, in contrast to his political Trotskyism, led the conservative anti-populist and anti-bourgeois assault on popular culture in the name of the folk and the elite. Mills attacked the popular arts from the left, in the name of authentic democratic community and against the manipulation of political, economic, and academic elites who controlled the system of industrial production in culture. Shils in the name of liberal progress defended the center: taste was being neither debased nor exploited; artists were freer and better compensated and audience better entertained; artistic creativity and intellectual productivity were as high as they had been in human history. [1]

Macdonald, who drew upon the seminal writings of art critic Clement Greenberg, advanced the argument that "Mass Culture began as, and to some extent still is, a parasitic, a cancerous growth on High Culture."[2] Macdonald was forced to admit that even in the "old" art forms such as literature, music, painting, dance, and architecture there could be found numerous examples of mass culture. But he then made a critical distinction between these art forms and the more recently emergent art forms:

> Mass Culture has also developed new media of its own,
> into which the serious artist rarely ventures: radio, the
> movies, comic books, detective stories, science fiction,
> television. [3]

According to Macdonald's perspective, high culture has traditionally been the province of the serious artist "communicating his individual vision to other individuals"—an audience of intellectual and wealthy patrons, a cultural elite. Mass culture, in contrast, is the province of the individual artisan or team of artisans engaging in the "impersonal manufacture of an impersonal commodity for the masses."

To Macdonald, media such as television, film, radio, comic books, detective stories, and science fiction were initiated through a technological imperative that made possible the inexpensive reproduction and distribution of standardized artistic products in great quantities for consumption by a large group of persons who had become homogenized through the process of democratization.

Macdonald often used the "entertainment/art" dichotomy to distinguish mass culture from high culture: entertainment being the standardized mass culture product, art being the unique vision contained in each individual work of high culture. According to Macdonald, the barons of mass culture/entertainment drew the unique elements from works of high culture and standardized those elements making them easier for the masses to recognize and thereby appreciate. Thus, according to Macdonald and Greenberg, kitsch was created by including "the spectator's reactions in the work of art itself instead of forcing him to make his own responses."[4] Kitsch, said Macdonald, is a debased form of high culture rather than an elevated form of the traditional folk culture produced by the nonelite prior to their massification.

Macdonald concluded that mass culture is not only reinforcing the plebian tastes of the masses, but is wrecking the sacred province of the cultural elite who are dwindling under the pressure of massification as the intellectuals who comprised the once-strong elite are displaced by highly trained specialists who are themselves caught up in the mass production/mass consumption cycle.

Two weaknesses in Macdonald's basic arguments should be noted. First, Macdonald set up a "straw concept"—mass culture—which he then knocked down on the basis of the presumed level of taste of an audience, the "masses." Such an approach flies against the notion that each work of art should be judged on its own merits as to both its formal structure and its handling of the symbol systems or cultural myths internal to the work and reflecting back on the culture in which the work was created. Instead, Macdonald produced generalized statements about art forms without citing representative works in

those art forms that might contradict the very notion of the "mass-
ness" of the art forms themselves.

Second, Macdonald greatly overgeneralized when he argued
that serious artists rarely ventured into his so-called mass culture
"entertainment." Macdonald chose to ignore a number of film artists
who were initially recognized for their work in other art forms before
they became filmmakers and who as filmmakers made significant contributions to the enhancement of the filmic art. Examples of such film
artists include the Russian filmmaker Sergei Eisenstein, who began
work as a director of Soviet theater and later became a noted filmmaker and film theoretician; Jean Cocteau, who began as a theater
actor, and was a successful poet, novelist, dramatist, and essayist
before becoming a highly respected filmmaker; and, more recently,
American experimental filmmaker Jordan Belson, who was a widely
exhibited painter prior to his extensive involvement with film. These
are but a few who immediately come to mind. Macdonald's argument
would also exclude such television writers as Gore Vidal, a successful novelist before he began writing teleplays; Paddy Chayefsky, a
successful playwright who concurrently wrote teleplays; and Robert
Alan Arthur, also a successful playwright and teleplay writer. These
writers are frequently mentioned as having made significant cultural
contributions through their notable television work.

In an apparent attempt to shore up the crumbling walls protect-
ing what he called a cultural elite, Macdonald failed to properly as-
sess culture, namely, experience cast up by an individual or individuals in symbolic forms that are capable of being apprehended by other
individuals. Such symbolic forms may heighten our awareness of con-
tinuities or discontinuities in our personal environments and our
broader cultural contexts; they may also entertain us, providing us
with diversion from the harsher everyday "realities" of living in the
world while at the same time establishing their own set of realities
by their very presence in the world. Heightened awareness and entertainment are, in this cultural context, not mutually exclusive.

Edward Shils, like Macdonald, noted that in Western societies
today there has occurred a loosening of the power of tradition. Shils
interpreted this to mean that individuals in these societies have a
greater variety of choices of personal experience than in any other
period in recorded human history. Shils wrote that the choices today
are more personal, and not dictated as much by tradition, scarcity,
or authority as in the past.

Shils noted the virtues of this "mass society":

The new society is a mass society precisely in the sense
that the mass of the population has become incorporated
into society . . . . most of the population (the "mass")

now stands in a closer relationship to the center than has
been the case in either premodern societies or in the earlier phases of modern society. [5]

As the masses become integrated into the society's center—its
central institutions and the value systems that legitimize those institutions—their perception of cultural events is heightened. According
to Shils:

> The classes consuming culture may diminish in number,
> their taste may deteriorate, their standards become less
> discriminating or more debased. On the other hand, as
> the mass of the population comes awake when its curi-
> osity and sensibility and its moral responsiveness are
> aroused, it begins to become capable of a more subtle
> perception, more appreciative of the more general ele-
> ments in a concrete representation, and more complex
> in its aesthetic reception and expression. [6]

Thus Shils granted what Macdonald most feared—that the cultural elite (or what Shils here terms "the classes consuming culture")
may well become fewer in number and less discriminating in their
preference for certain works of art. However, Shils, using an argument that attached importance to greater numbers (i.e., the "masses")
as a means for measuring the significance of taste in a society, rejected Macdonald's notion that art is doomed through the growth of
mass culture. Thus, a basic and very important distinction between
the two arguments becomes apparent: Macdonald argued that mass
culture will continually decline in taste level as fewer products of
high culture become available for imitation, while Shils argued that
mass culture will continue to rise in taste level as more individuals'
consciousness levels are raised by their exposure to art forms of
which they had previously been unaware.

Shils devised a tentative three-category paradigm of culture
levels, which he wrote were "levels of quality measured by aesthetic,
intellectual, and moral standards."[7] The levels were differentiated
as superior or refined culture, mediocre culture, and brutal culture.
Superior culture was characterized according to the seriousness of
its subject matter based upon some standards of truth and beauty.
This culture, Shils suggested, was produced by a "high intelligentsia"
with international ties and was consumed primarily by intellectuals
(e.g., university teachers and students, members of learned profes-
sions, artists, writers, journalists, and higher civil servants). Mediocre culture was characterized as not measuring up to the standards
of superior culture—it was less original and more reproductive. It

also occasionally operated in novel genres not yet incorporated into superior culture. This culture, according to Shils, was produced by a "mediocre intelligentsia" and was consumed by the "middle class." Brutal culture was characterized as being more elementary in its symbolic elaboration (i.e., containing more directly expressive actions with a minimum of symbolic content). It lacked the subtlety and depth of penetration of either superior or mediocre culture. It continued traditional cultural patterns with little consciousness of their traditionality. Brutal culture was produced by what Shils termed the "brutal intelligentsia" who had no connections with superior culture and was consumed by the members of the industrial working class and the rural population. Shils added that there was an intermixture of the three cultures in the newspaper, on television, and in film, although one would most likely find mediocre culture prevading them.

It must be clearly recognized that Shils was himself leery of claiming that his culture categories were rigid. For example, he was quick to note that even in the brutal culture category there would be an occasional individual work that reached the limits of superior culture. In fact, in a perceptive footnote to his discussion, Shils made a frank admission as to the limitations of his culture paradigm:

> I have reservations about the use of the term "mass culture," because it refers simultaneously to the substantive and qualitative properties of the culture, to the social status of its consumers, and to the media by which it is transmitted. Because of this at least three-fold reference, it tends to beg some important questions regarding the relations among the three variables. For example, the current conception of "mass culture" does not allow for the fact that in most countries, and not just at the present, very large sections of the elite consume primarily mediocre and brutal culture. It also begs the important questions whether the mass media can transmit works of superior culture, or whether the genres developed by the new mass media can become the occasions of creativity and therewith a part of superior culture. Also, it does not consider the obvious fact that much of what is produced in the genres of superior culture is extremely mediocre in quality. [8]

Thus, while Shils was arguing in support of the effects of mass culture in raising the aesthetic, social, and moral consciousness of the so-called masses to some higher level than they had previously enjoyed, he was not foolish enough in his polemic to establish rigid boundaries of culture classification that would preclude consideration of individual works of art as something other than representative of

certain classes of culture. Nevertheless, his argument is not sufficient even given this limited flexibility—for by and large he was still
matching genres with culture classes, means of transmission, and
presumed taste levels of audiences.

C. Wright Mills concentrated his criticism of mass media and
mass culture on the notion that the media themselves are the tools
used by the modern elite in their efforts to manipulate the masses.
Mills wrote:

> The means of opinion-making, in fact, have paralleled in
> range and efficiency the other institutions of greater scale
> that cradle the modern society of masses. Accordingly, in
> addition to their enlarged and centralized means of admin-
> istration, exploitation, and violence, the modern elite have
> had placed within their grasp historically unique instru-
> ments of psychic management and manipulation, which in-
> clude universal compulsory education as well as the media
> of mass communication. [9] [Italics added.]

According to Mills, the result of this elite manipulation of the
masses is the impersonalization of life itself:

> As they now generally prevail, the mass media, espe-
> cially television, often encroach upon the small-scale
> discussion, and destroy the chance for the reasonable
> and leisurely and human interchange of opinion. They
> are an important cause of the destruction of privacy in
> its full human meaning. That is an important reason why
> they not only fail as an educational force, but are a ma-
> lign force: they do not articulate for the viewer or listen-
> er the broader sources of his private tensions and anxie-
> ties, his inarticulate resentments and half-formed hopes.
> They neither enable the individual to transcend his nar-
> row milieu nor clarify its private meaning. [10]

Mills here provides some insight into what works of art might
be expected to provide an audience, namely, an articulation of the
broader sources of the audience member's "private tensions and an-
xieties, his inarticulate resentments and half-formed hopes." As the
audience member begins to apprehend the work's significations, he
should be able to transcend his private world and become aware of a
broader cultural milieu as it relates to his own environment. Thus
works of art can serve a culturally integrative function in the sense
of promoting better understanding of our culture.

The difficulty with Mills's statements about mass culture (like those of Macdonald and Shils) is located in his sociological overgeneralizations. By producing a blanket indictment of "mass media" as tools for cultural manipulation by an elite, Mills refused to grant the possibility that artists are producing culturally significant "liberating" works of art in such media. Those same works of art that promote cultural understanding may at the same time act as a freeing influence—one may better understand the culture in which he lives and thereby reject elements of that culture as not meeting his personal needs.

Shils at least recognized the need to consider the individual work of art and its apprehension by a spectator in some larger cultural context. Yet he, like Macdonald and Mills, was never able to get heart of the issue. The major limitation of the mass culture/high culture debate is that it tells us little or nothing of the aesthetic designs of works of art as representative examples of genres or of their interpreted symbolic or mythic significance in the culture in which they are produced. Rather, the debate assumes that some highly ambiguous changes in individuals' lives are brought about through their exposure to certain art forms; these changes are described as "modification of levels of taste" and "manipulation of one group of people by another." These limiting notions divert our attention from the central problem, which is to uncover how works of art are integrated into people's understanding of the symbolic forms or "myths" that comprise the shared experience of which the works are a significant part.

Unlike the sociologists Macdonald, Shils, and Mills, aesthetician Abraham Kaplan has provided us with some specific criteria that we might apply to individual works of art to determine into which area of the high art/popular art dichotomy the works might fall. While Kaplan's criteria are on the whole plausible, it should be recognized at the outset that they, as in the case of any paradigm, are subject to modification as new directions in art creation are explored.

Kaplan distinguished art (or high art) from popular art by noting that popular art may be said to be "mass art"—art that "is mass-produced or reproduced, and is responded to by vast numbers of people."[11] However, Kaplan quickly qualified this definition by noting that the specification of the origin and destination of works of art

> . . . does not of itself determine just what it is that is being responded to. There is no fixed a priori relation between quantity and quality, and especially not between quantity and certain specific qualities as distinguished from worth in general.[12]

Kaplan believed that popular art forms have their own formal structures and meanings, and as such are not bastardizations of high art or the products of external social forces. To support his contention, Kaplan divided the elements distinguishing art from popular art into three general classes: form in the work of art itself, the relationship between the work of art and the spectator confronting the work, and the social functions of the work of art. A schematic representation of Kaplan's high art/popular art criteria follows.

HIGH ART	POPULAR ART
FORM	
1. Provides a form with cultural significations.	1. Provides a formula, but gives us nothing to which to apply it.
2. All elements in the work are significant.	2. A few elements in the work are singled out as carriers of meaning, while the remaining elements are merged into an anonymous mass.
3. Fill-in by the spectator is called for.	3. The work is predigested (i. e., self-completed).
4. The work is a cognitive challenge to the spectator due to its ambiguity.	4. The work is intolerant of ambiguity.
5. The work is illusory without being deceptive.	5. The work rings false.
6. In the work, reality is transformed from represented subject to expressive substance.	6. The work takes over the shapes of reality, but not the form.

RELATIONSHIP BETWEEN THE WORK
OF ART AND THE SPECTATOR

7. Emotion or feeling is expressed by the work.	7. Emotion or feeling is associated with the work.
8. Feeling is drawn out of ourselves by the work, creating a fulfilling aesthetic experience.	8. Feeling is consummated in the work, but without the spectator's aesthetic fulfillment.
9. The work creates an intense awareness (i. e., sensibility) in the spectator.	9. The work creates superficial feelings (i.e., sentimentality) in the spectator.
10. The work enlarges the spectator's apprehension of a "world."	10. There is too little of substance that requires a spectator's understanding of the work and its cultural significations.
11. The work produces spectator empathy or identity with its substance.	11. The work produces spectator self-centeredness.

12. The work helps the spectator transform ugliness in the work into meaning.

12. The work helps the spectator escape ugliness.

13. The work dares to disturb the spectator.

13. The work seeks to relieve the spectator's anxiety.

14. The work heightens our aesthetic perception or response so that we become self-stimulated when faced with the work itself.

14. The work produces our recognition of its substance, but this is a mere reaction to the work.

15. The work raises us to "divine objectivity."

15. The work is too subjectively human.

16. The work presents to immediate experience the values of a culture in factual form.

16. The work assures us that the facts as presented support our prejudged values.

17. The work is wish-fulfilling in itself.

17. The world depicted in the work is wish-fulfilling.

18. The work transforms reality only to enable the spectator to better apprehend it.

18. The work strips fantasy of the qualities of creative imagination.

19. The work posits a vision of reality and at the same time evokes a pleasurable experience in the spectator.

19. The work evokes a pleasurable experience only.

20. The work calls for enough aesthetic distance by the spectator to give him perspective and enough wisdom to enable him to see himself in perspective (i. e. , object-ification).

20. The work calls for little or no aesthetic distance.

21. The work shows us the limits of our powers in the world.

21. The work turns its back on a world it has never known.

SOCIAL FUNCTIONS OF THE WORK OF ART

22. The work appeals to a common denominator—"the universality of art."

22. The work appeals to a "distinctive majority taste" and is indicative of the status quo in culture (i. e. , imitation of previously successful forms).

Kaplan's criteria offer us one approach that differentiates works of art according to certain specific characteristics of the works them-

selves. However, Kaplan's high art and popular art categories are so
meticulously constructed that they preclude the probability of any single work of art satisfying all the prerequisites he established for "high
art"; on the other hand, many works of art, including some of those
commonly classified as "popular art," could seemingly satisfy many
if not most of those prerequisites. Despite such limitations, Kaplan's
approach is valuable as a reference against which one can compare
evaluations of works of television art.

Since one major concern of this book is the examination and
evaluation of television and video as culturally significant art forms,
one of Kaplan's conclusions about his high art/popular art dichotomy
is relevant here:

> For audiences, art is more of a status symbol than ever;
> its appearance in the mass media is marked by a flourish
> of trumpets, as befits its status; the sponsor may even go
> so far as to omit his commercials. I am saying that even
> where popular art vulgarizes yesterday's art, it might an-
> ticipate tomorrow's—baroque once meant something like
> kitsch. I am willing to prophesy that even television has
> art in its future. 13

UNCOVERING THE "ART" IN TELEVISION

It may well be that occasionally a work of purely television art
as Kaplan defined the term (as opposed to a work conceived in another
art form merely transmitted through the television medium) makes its
way to the home screen; and there is no reason for us to doubt that
from the countless hours of television weeds to come, at least a few
if not many orchids will emerge to take their proper places in the history of this art form. But for many careful observers of the television
scene, such preoccupation with separating television programs into
Kaplan's two categories is at best tangential to what they perceive to
be the central questions of television's "expressive substance." These
questions recently have focused on the nature of the "world" presented
on television programs.

Among the most significant recent approaches to the presentation
of a world on television are those of television as "dream"; television
melodrama as a self-reflexive device; television's elaboration of our
culture's mythologies; and television fiction as anthropology. Each of
these approaches is worthy of serious consideration.

The notion of television as dream was somewhat tentatively first
advanced by Peter H. Wood, professor of history at Duke University. 14
Wood provided an interesting thesis: television may constitute part of

the collective dreamlife of our culture. Both television and dreams are highly visual, both are highly symbolic, both involve a high degree of wish fulfillment (fantasies or hallucinatory experience), both appear to contain a large amount of disjointed and trivial material, both contain powerful content which is quickly and easily forgotten, and both consistently use materials drawn from recent experience.

According to Wood, television may be linked to a larger consciousness, a "collective subconscious," which includes both the creative community and the viewers—"a TV society purposefully and unconsciously creates its own video world and then reacts to it."[15] This dreamlife is actualized through dramatization that is often condensed with little or no prior exposition, and contains a variety of ambiguous verbal and visual symbols that latently point to a world—our subconscious world, a world of strong fears and desires.

The story line, or manifest content, is of little or no real importance in such an analysis. Of real importance, according to Wood's interpretation, is the latent content—the disguising of a culture's needs and wishes in an <u>acceptable</u> television form. By employing conventional plot formula, for example, we can insert these manifestations of our collective dreamlife, and like a dream, we can feel safe and comforted when we awaken from the dream.

If, as in psychoanalysis, we as a collective culture can work through this dreamlife by employing our cognitive mental processes to interpret the television programs we watch, we may be better able to understand the meaning of our contemporary world.

Wood's hypotheses are of course speculative and are yet to be thoroughly tested by the critical community. Yet they offer one interesting approach to "creative" television viewing that sidesteps traditional questions of artistic worth.

A similar approach to examining the world created in television was advanced by David Thorburn, an English professor at Yale University. In an essay entitled "Television Melodrama,"[16] Thorburn examined television melodrama as a self-reflexive device in which consistent references to its own history and repeated reassuring conclusions and moral allegories presented in topical contexts are, for the audience, "the <u>enabling conditions</u> for an encounter with forbidden or deeply disturbing materials."[17] For Thorburn, melodrama (which includes the television genres of made-for-television movies, soap opera, fictional lawyers and doctors programs, Westerns, mysteries, and adventures) is above all else a market commodity employing stereotyped formulas and expounding "the conventional wisdom, the lies and fantasies, and the muddled ambivalent values of our bourgeois industrial culture."[18] Yet it is precisely these characteristics of melodrama that Thorburn feels highlight its importance as a cultural artifact. For melodrama's basic aesthetic of reassurance enables the audience member to deal with the central value conflicts of the culture in which the melodrama is produced.

A central characteristic of melodrama's self-reflexivity is what Thorburn termed a "multiplicity principle," a principle of plot development whereby a particular melodrama continually employs a number of stories and situations previously created in other melodramas. Such formulaic plot structuring is both reassuring to the viewer and enables both the creator and viewer to disregard long establishing sequences and instead to focus on the moral and emotional heightening of intense value conflicts. While this emotional heightening and conflict are not often encountered in the "real" world by most viewers, they nevertheless reveal, albeit on an exaggerated scale, the underlying truths of the culture that they represent; or, to refer to Peter Wood's notion of television as dream, television melodrama is an aesthetic mechanism that actualizes our culture's dreamlife.

One specific way in which television explores the culture's dreamlife is through its exploitation of mythology. John Cashill has written an illuminating essay on the subject of television advertising's exploitation of our culture's mythology that with little effort can be expanded to encompass the broad range of television genres. [19] In Cashill's estimation, myths are a series of beliefs having a very real force in a culture. American mass media barons have been perceptive enough to put our communal myths to work in selling products—who can forget the Davy Crockett T-shirt and assorted paraphernalia?

Cashill's account of these televised "working" myths tells us much about ourselves and our general belief systems. Consider the myth of "manifest destiny," or the United States is the most powerful nation on earth (i. e. , "buy this product to keep America strong" or the White Man pushes Westward overcoming the American Indian's savagery and backwardness in the process)—this myth is frequently unveiled when we rattle our sabers in the face of presumed external threats to our country's security.

Then there is the myth of "the compelling need for absolute cleanliness," or sex will not be yours if your husband's shirt collars are black; but if you, through the miracle of . . . , make them white again, you will once again be the object of love.

The myth of "the frontier" or freedom, virility, and ruggedness associated with the American West has been with us on television from the mythical Matt Dillon through the now-expurgated Marlboro man and numerous contemporary cowboy-type he-men. This myth was transposed to the urban ghetto in a flood of television police detective series; "McCloud" literally melded the two frontiers by establishing the cowboy/policeman central character.

One of the most eye-opening myths exploited by television in the 1960s is the myth of the "middle landscape"—a mythic "country" place where order, sanity, and compromise prevail over turmoil, the space between the frontier and the megalopolis. This myth evolved through numerous series of the period, most notably "The Beverly Hillbillies," "Green Acres," and "Petticoat Junction." The myth served a useful function during a period when the United States was mired in the morass of the war in Vietnam—it gave us respite from the chaos of the times, both at home and abroad. The myth can still be seen at work today with lesser power in "The Waltons" and "Little House on the Prairie" and in commercials for Hush Puppies and Country Time Lemonade, to name a few. It is a dream of our urban dwellers to return to a more peaceful, less complicated time and place—the remembrance of the womb.

Another pervasive myth, the myth of "the puritan ethic," or "God helps those who help themselves," is useful as a reinforcing agent in a culture whose drives for success and acquisition of goods is well-documented. This myth is found throughout television programs and advertisements.

The myth of "distrust and resentment of anything intellectual" is one employed most notably in political advertising—the old saw "A man of (or for) the People" has repeatedly proved successful in the political trenches; a virtual unknown named Carter rose to the national spotlight on the wings of this myth. A man named Nixon crashed because in part he was not able to convey the "good 'ol boy" aura to his constituency.

Last, there is the myth of "individualism," which, claims Cashill, is the one hope if we are to survive intact the onslaught of all the other myths transmitted through our contemporary media. This myth holds that one, through the exercise of individual choice, can apprehend and accept or reject the exploitative appeals of televised myths as they mesh or do not mesh with personal needs.

Perhaps the exploitation of our mythologies is a result of a subconscious dreamlife such as the one discussed by Peter Wood from which we have yet to awaken. Putting mythology "to work" does not necessarily imply any sinister plot on the part of program producers to con or harm us. Television, after all, is by and large safe and reassuring, and the tapping of mythologies to sell products or peace and security would seem to be an unconscious attempt above all to preserve societal structures which, in the past at least, have proved to be workable ordering mechanisms. But we must always be willing to question whether certain myths are harmful to our general cultural well being. Returning to Cashill's account of myths, one in particular should give us pause for such questioning—the myth of the "middle landscape."

In his essay "Fiction As Anthropology: Images of the South in Popular Television Series," Horace Newcomb lays bare this middle landscape myth and highlights the dangers of blindly accepting the mythic construct. [20] The middle landscape, that "country" place between the rugged frontier and modern magalopolis, the place where order prevails over chaos and fear, has taken many televised forms. Among these forms is that dealing with the American South, a region inhabited by characters with certain sets of values and attitudes that are "Southern" and therefore are made to appear different from mainstream American values.

One manifestation of "Southern" is that of the hillbilly, the "inferior native ethnic" who is to be laughed at for his provincialism. The symbols of the hillbilly stereotype as employed throughout popular culture include shabby dress, malapropisms, gullibility, and shiftlessness. Such symbols are clearly employed in the highly popular television series "The Beverly Hillbillies." However, equally strong symbols exist in that series which tend to shift the focus of the myth of the middle landscape to those areas of the larger culture outside the South. For example, the notion of "the moral superiority of rural wisdom" is juxtaposed with the contemporary decadent urban value structure to produce a condemnation of the larger American culture. Ultimately, however, Southerners in this and similar series are portrayed as children, and not as members of the adult population of the country or the culture. Such a manifestation of the myth is obviously not a healthy one for the larger culture.

In "The Waltons," a fictional series of a more recent vintage that employs the myth of the middle landscape, we find a different symbolic approach taken. The conflict of urban and rural value systems frames the themes of many episodes of "The Waltons." However, the myth of the middle landscape as presented through the vehicle of the series provides a characterization that includes the value of hard work, the wisdom of elders, and the notion that "strength, endurance, tolerance, honor, humility, simplicity, kindness and mutual support serve as the basis for a successful life and not merely as opportunity for comic encounter or for cynical remarks."[21] This view is much closer to the purity of the middle landscape myth as defined above. The melodrama as a genre seems to offer more flexibility for the sensitive exploration of the myth than does the situation comedy form, which by its very formula must rely on zany characterizations to draw out laughs.

We should remember, however, that the myth can and has been exploited by the creative community in ways that speak ill of the ease with which we can slip into thinking of our fellows in unflattering stereotypes.

Essayists such as Wood, Thorburn, Cashill, and Newcomb are quite willing to grant that television is a popular art that employs formula, is frequently sentimental, often focuses on exaggerated incident or action at the expense of subtle characterization, makes sensational appeals to the audience's emotions, and ends with the central characters living happily ever after. Yet these reassuring qualities of popular art as entertainment are not necessarily "bad"; rather, they offer clues to the deeper meanings of our communal cultural lives—what we are and what we may become—clues embedded beneath the surface structure of reassurance.

These approaches to the evaluation of the world presented to us through television are noteworthy for their ability to discount television's popular culture "weaknesses" as conceived within traditional aesthetic parameters and instead to focus their attention on television's reflection of our commonly held myths and symbols—one key link to understanding the culture in which television works are conceived and produced.

On the other side of the art/entertainment question as it relates to television lies the domain of video, television's younger brother. Video can be distinguished from television in part by its adherence to art's traditional concept of the personal expression, of the individual artist's (or small group of artists') struggle against the ordering principles established by a culture's dominant institutions.

Those who create video works are often the first to claim that television is a dominant cultural institution that does not allow those with individual "vision" access to its high technology production mechanisms—a statement not without merit. They are also quick to condemn contemporary television as mindless pap, a natural outgrowth of a production and distribution system that is governed not by the creative community itself but rather by unsympathetic administrators, businessmen, and lawyers who are constantly wary of regulatory scuffles ensuing from the production of controversial material.

Video works produced in response to these guiding concepts frequently take the form of parodying television content, or of demonstrating how on an extremely low budget the artists can one-up television by doing something worthwhile, or of showing their disdain for commercial television's use of the advertisement's time signature—a "linear succession of logically independent units of nearly equal duration," the video of "boredom."[22]

Video often uses deliberate repetition, sexual explicitness, and occasionally candor on social issues to break the taboos of television. When done well, it can be highly effective as an alternative, subcultural voice. In the case of community video documentary such as that produced by Downtown Community Television (John Alpert and Keiko Tsuno) and at numerous public access cable channels throughout the United States, the use of relatively inexpensive video technology by individuals sensitive to their community's problems and needs can and has acted as a unifying force within the community—the portapak picks up where the front porch left off, providing an arena for discussion of neighborhood interests.

Video as employed in the art community and in the social community has been evaluated according to traditional aesthetic conceptions of worth and has often been found to be wanting. However, as is the case with television, perhaps different perspectives need to be employed in the evaluation of video works, especially as the works set themselves against the institutional domination of the television industry. The significance of video must be seen primarily as personal statement in a larger cultural sense. Traditional production values are of far less significance than questions of access to our culture's most pervasive means of communicating, although "good" production values can obviously enhance the impact of the video message.

Is television art or entertainment? We began with that question, and the answer must be that it is both. It is entertainment inasmuch as it pleases us and provides us respite and reassurance. And it is art, both in its television and video forms, inasmuch as it opens up our world to new perspectives. But whereas we can assume a passive viewing posture in the entertainment viewing experience, it is necessary for us to actively look through television's surface structures to unearth the latent meanings of its symbols. Who, after all, ever implied that the spectator's experience with art does not require work?

To help us with our spectator's "work" in this area, we must turn to individuals who have spent a good portion of their professional lives examining art and who have endeavored to act as learned teachers and guides through the art experience—those whom we call critics.

NOTES

1. James W. Carey and Albert L. Kreiling, "Popular Culture and Uses and Gratifications: Notes Toward an Accomodation," in The Uses of Mass Communications: Current Perspectives on Gratifications Research, eds. Jay G. Blumler and Elihu Katz (Beverly Hills, Calif.: Sage Publications, 1974), p. 225.

2. Dwight Macdonald, "A Theory of Mass Culture," in Mass Culture: The Popular Arts in America, eds. Bernard Rosenberg and David Manning White (Glencoe, Ill.: Free Press, 1957), p. 59.

3. Ibid.

4. Ibid., p. 61.

5. Edward Shils, "Mass Society and Its Culture," Daedalus 89 (Spring 1960): 288.

6. Ibid., p. 291.

7. Ibid.

8. Ibid.

9. C. Wright Mills, The Power Elite (New York: Oxford University Press, 1956), pp. 310–11.

10. Ibid. , p. 314.

11. Abraham Kaplan, "The Aesthetics of the Popular Arts," The Journal of Aesthetics and Art Criticism 24 (Spring 1966): 352.

12. Ibid.

13. Ibid. , p. 364.

14. Peter H. Wood, "Television as Dream," in Television as a Cultural Force, eds. Richard Adler and Douglass Cater (New York: Praeger, 1976), pp. 17–35.

15. Ibid. , p. 25.

16. David Thorburn, "Television Melodrama," in Television as a Cultural Force, eds. Richard Adler and Douglass Cater (New York: Praeger, 1976), pp. 77–94.

17. Ibid. , p. 80.

18. Ibid.

19. John R. Cashill, "Packaging Pop Mythology," in The New Languages, eds. Thomas H. Ohlgren and Lynn M. Berk (Englewood Cliffs, N. J. : Prentice-Hall, 1977), pp. 79–90.

20. Horace Newcomb, "Fiction As Anthropology: Images of the South in Popular Television Series" (Paper presented at the University of South Carolina Conference on Visual Anthropology and the American South, Columbia, S. C. , October 1977).

21. Ibid. , p. 16.

22. David Antin, "Video: The Distinctive Features of the Medium," in Video Art, (University of Pennsylvania, Institute of Contemporary Art 1975), p. 67.

2

TELEVISION, VIDEO,
AND THE CONTEXT OF CRITICISM

    As long as man has created products of the human imagination there have been others who have focused their attention on discussion of these products. These observers of the cultural scene have been given the dubious title "art critics." Theirs is not the most enviable position among professions since they frequently find it necessary to attack either verbally or in writing not only the creative products themselves but also those people who create the products—the artists. Failure to do so would be inauthentic. These art critics face another problem, for they must also address their commentary to an audience or readership all of whom will not be in agreement with their judgments. Thus the adage "you can't please all the people all the time" is one the art critic must live with daily as he goes about his work. Any art critic worth his salt must take some small pleasure in being the perennial curmudgeon; otherwise he would forever suffer the sting of self-doubt.

    It is unfortunate that the term art critic has been bandied about so loosely in recent times. The term has come to signify everything from an erudite scholar formulating elaborate though obscure treatises on the meaning of the jump cut in the third scene of a particular epic film tracing the history of the peasant revolt in Upper Volta to the public relations operative writing for the daily gazette about Tom Brokaw's late night parties and how they have produced dark circles under his eyes that makeup can hardly hide at eight o'clock in the morning.

THE CRITIC DEFINED

    The contemporary overuse of the word critic has cast in obscurity the original significance of the term. If we travel back in time via a trusted guide, the Oxford English Dictionary, we will find the term critic employed in its more pristine state. The Oxford defines a critic as "one who pronounces judgment on any thing or person; especially one who passes severe or unfavorable judgment. . . ." The definition is then further narrowed to "One skillful in judging of the qualities and merits of literary or artistic works . . . . a professional reviewer of books, pictures, plays and the like." The words critic and criterion are derived from the Greek krit, meaning a standard or test. Thus a critic is a person who skillfully applies some standard or test to something from which he produces a judgment regarding that thing.

One recent view of a critic is that he is someone who states his opinion about something with precision; one whose analysis penetrates to the "heart of the matter"; one whose opinion itself possesses "its own truth, its own significance apart from the works that may have prompted the original critical responses." Time vindicates the critic's judgment. His opinion is significant for what it tells us about "a work's character and intentions and the larger perspective—social, cultural, historical—in which that work may be seen and better understood."[1]

Another view of the critic comes from John Simon, himself a film critic. Simon wrote of the attributes of the critic:

> With cogency, suasion, passion, and charm, he induces
> us to think, to widen our horizons, to open yet another
> book, to reconsider a snap judgment, to see something
> from a loftier vantage point, in historic perspective, and
> using more and truer touchstones. Good criticism of any
> kind—of movies, ballet, architecture, or whatever—makes
> us think, feel, respond; if we then agree or disagree is
> less important than the fact that our faculties have been
> engaged or stretched. Good criticism informs, interprets,
> and raises the ultimate questions, the unanswerable ones
> that everyone must try to answer none the less. [2]

The truly skillful judge must therefore possess a combination of attributes, including the analytical techniques of a scholar, the insights of an intellectual, and the eloquence and expressive power of the best of stylists. While these lofty qualities can serve as goals for those who pursue the critical profession in its various guises, it will help to put criticism in perspective as it operates in the workaday world of the practitioner.

Poet Bruton Connors once described what he called the "applied" critic as the middleman between artist and audience, a sort of public relations officer explaining the work to the uninitiated. [3] The so-called applied critic is most at home in the role of journalist who must be, according to Nigel Gosling of the British newspaper the Observer, "first and foremost a reporter." In such role he performs a distributive function, often providing the public its first acquaintance with a work of art via his critical review. After he reports the existence of the work, he may analyze and evaluate it, acting "as instant advisor to some reader who may be considering whether to spend money on it or not." Because of deadline pressures he is often forced to make a rather hasty judgment on "a complex work that may have taken years to create—a judgment of whose limitations he is constantly aware, and which is further open to editorial cuts. . . ."[4]

The life of the journalist who would be critic is not an easy one. Speaking from experience, Irving Wardle, former theater critic of the London Times, wrote:

> There are inescapable journalistic conditions, of course,
> and sometimes they take over completely. I always asso-
> ciate them with West Croydon railway station where I
> have scribbled many a notice on winter nights, assessing
> Ibsen and O'Neill to an accompaniment of crashing fruit
> machines. At times like this, with one eye on the clock
> and the phone box, all you've got left is the actor's prayer,
> "Oh God, let me be barely adequate."[5]

Alas! The deadline and the snap judgment are the bane of the journalist who pursues the critical venture. The mouth from which comes the critical pronouncement often also contains a foot. As Wardle put it, the journalist who would be critic "cannot refrain from ap-plying what he sees to his own life and judging what he sees by his personal values."[6] To do this on such short notice leaves the journal-ist open to grand failures of rationale; however, and fortunately for his readership, this critic is willing to take a chance even though he risks being proved incorrect.

In contrast to the conscientious journalist-critic is an ilk com-monly known as the "reviewer." Wardle had a word or two to say of this person:

> [He] never makes a fool of himself. He is detached, wit-
> ty, well informed, sceptical; he often has a nice turn of
> phrase . . . . he may think a show good or bad, but ei-
> ther way it's not going to keep him awake at night. . . .
> London's commercial management want . . . the review-
> er, who has always provided them with free advertisement
> and who often goes to the trouble of dropping in phrases
> suitable for quotation on the posters.[7]

Many among the potential audience are aware, if unconsciously, of the tactics of many reviewers. We see a poster for the latest blockbuster film and read "a magnificent accomplishment—Joe Doakes, Pomeroy Tribune." In the backs of our skeptical minds we may envision the entire passage from the review that reads something like "Epic' could have been a magnificent accomplishment had it not been for the directing, acting, and camerawork in the final scene." Many of us suspect such chicanery from a reviewer; but, on the other hand, I would guess many of us do not.

Richard Kostelanetz, a noted art critic, has less kind words to write of the reviewer, calling him a "pseudocritic":

> No one can become a functioning critic overnight; and those who try, such as newspapermen, generally embarrass all concerned by educating themselves in public. In general, fly-by-night critics tend to have no real purpose, which means not only no credo but also no consistency of either interest or opinion. [8]

While the journalist must struggle to bang out meaningful commentary to meet a deadline and fight to keep his editors from annihilating his prose, the academic who pursues the art criticism discipline has substantially more temporal flexibility in evaluating art works; and the luxury of time allows this observer to subject his target to thorough analysis. Also, whereas the journalist in general must write to a diversified readership, many of whom are unfamiliar with the work in question, the academic, whose topic is frequently quite narrow, has a captive audience of fellow travelers. This critic, according to Nigel Gosling, is

> . . . usually a hard cover performer [who] starts from a special premise. . . . He will take the sculpture of Donatello or Rossini's operas or the novels of Fielding and subject them to new analysis and appraisal. He can assume that his readers are already interested in the topic (otherwise they wouldn't be reading the book), and roughly familiar with it. He does not have to inform—he explains and persuades. He is both deeply sunk in his subject and detached from it. [9]

This academic critic has a major advantage over the journalist in that he does not have to participate in the producer-consumer relationship that day-to-day affects the contemporary world of art salesmanship. However, this distancing factor may sometimes prove a hindrance, for this critic's writings may become anachronistic by ignoring contemporary reassessments of traditional evaluations of art works.

It is precisely these contemporary reassessments of artwork that provide the impetus for acceptance of new styles of art making and conversely the rejection of previous styles. The critic plays a predominant role in this process. Richard Kostelanetz addressed the role of the contemporary art critic along such lines when he wrote:

> Serious, consistent critics can be divided into conservatives and radicals. The former prefer works that formally resemble the milestones of the past; they relish acknowledgment of traditional artistic verities and the fulfillment of expectation.
> Radical critics, by contrast, prefer works that are formally unlike anything they have seen before. [10]

It is apparent that both journalists and academics can be "serious and consistent" critics. Yet some may be conservative in their approaches to art while others might be thought of as radicals. Not only do critics differ in their basic preferences for styles of art, but they also differ in their basic approaches to participation in the art community itself. Kostelanetz continued:

> Radicals are more inclined than conservatives to do their own creative work, to become cultural middlemen (agents, anthologists, curators), to write polemical critiques of cultural dissemination . . . radical critics tend to be closer than conservatives to the creative processes of contemporary art . . . their biases make them aware of first-rate work that does not enter the cultural marketplace . . . they inevitably wonder why the art they admire is not earning its just rewards. . . .
> . . . Conservative critics, by definition, are those who continually object to the emerging avant-gardes.
> . . . A "critic" unresponsive to innovation is ultimately not a critic but a caretaker. [11]

Thus there is a wide variety of types of practitioners whom we call critics—the journalist who is "serious and consistent" in his writings but who faces the severe pressure of a publication deadline and perhaps even editorial control of his essays; the journalist who "plays it safe" and often falls into the "reviewer's" trap of becoming a shallow publicity agent for works he is discussing; and the serious and consistent academic who has the luxury of time to perform an indepth and sometimes even cogent analysis of art. In addition, both the journalist and the academic may fall into the snares of conservatism, ignoring contemporary art styles that reflect back upon previous styles and subsequently change contemporary assessments of those styles, while other journalists and academics may dive into the contemporary art scene and with guns ablazing defend and advance the avant-garde efforts in an art form and thereby attempt to stretch the boundaries of both contemporary art making and art discourse.

It does not suffice, therefore, to simply talk about criticism as a discipline populated by a particular type of individual with strictly defined attributes. Criticism, in a practical sense as discussed here, is a multifarious discipline encompassing numerous approaches to discussing art.

THE TELEVISION CRITIC

Art criticism that focuses on a popular art form such as television must also confront a complex world of art making, high finance, and the possibility of the medium's significant cultural and social ramifications affecting all walks of life, for all of these attributes accrue to the television phenomenon. Television, once merely a gleam in Philo T. Farnsworth's eyes, is the most pervasive form of information and entertainment loose in the world today.

Television entered the world with a majestic and somewhat utopian pronouncement from one of its founders, David Sarnoff, Chairman of the Radio Corporation of America. On April 30, 1939, the National Broadcasting Company, a subsidiary of RCA, telecast the dedication ceremonies of the RCA Exhibit Building at the World's Fair. Sarnoff, standing before a television camera whose images were projected to the exhibit's visitors on television monitors, spoke of the great potential of this new medium:

> It is with a feeling of humbleness that I come to the moment of announcing the birth in this country of a new art so important in its implications that it is bound to affect all society. It is an art which shines like a torch of hope in a troubled world. It is a creative force which we must learn to utilize for the benefit of all mankind. [12]

Television had been introduced in Great Britain three years prior to the World's Fair exhibit, but the "troubled world" of which Sarnoff spoke erupted into World War II, halting temporarily television's development in both Great Britain and the United States. Following the conclusion of the war in 1945, television reappeared on the scene and began its meteoric rise to world prominence. Television had no boundaries. It was to become something much more than Sarnoff's "art which shines like a torch of hope." And the art critic who would have to tackle the electronic cyclops would not be able in good conscience to restrict his evaluations of the medium to the artistic products flickering on the phosphorescent tube.

It has been over four decades since Sarnoff's remarks at the World's Fair, and one conclusion seems irrefutable in today's developed societies—television is now or is rapidly becoming omnipresent. Marshall McLuhan has gone so far as to suggest that "the medium is the message" as well as the massage. [13] (Italics added.) According to McLuhan, the content (visual and aural information) transmitted via communications mediums such as television is ultimately of less significance to our culture than is the very presence of such communications mediums, especially electronic communications mediums. McLuhan noted that the presence of mediums in our lives "shapes and controls the scale and form of human association and action." [14] He has even postulated that these mediums affect such abstract cultural manifestations as defining personal or private space. Certainly such "noncontent" notions as the increasing institutional centralization and personal decentralization or alienation in our society—effects frequently attributed to the pervasiveness of television in our culture— are directly relevant to any serious evaluation of television. The practicing television critic would be accused of tunnel vision were he to completely ignore such potentially significant sociocultural ramifications of his subject. Yet this is but one piece in the television puzzle.

One cannot ignore the "content" that McLuhan too easily glosses over but that nonetheless bombards viewers nonstop, 24 hours a day, every day of the year. It rolls on, an electronic river carrying all of us downstream at its own inexorable, fluid pace. In its most basic sense, the content of television is a structured combination of images and sounds in various configurations presented to us via airwaves and cables through a boxlike piece of furniture located in a living or working space. The images and sounds carry with them some meaning that is essentially an articulation, whether intended or not, of our culture's values, symbol systems, and myths. The viewer is invited to transcend his or her immediate "personal" environment and to share in the broader cultural life-style presented in the television content. The images and sounds may be combined in such a way as to produce "serious" drama or "diversionary" entertainment, or in a way that promotes consumption of products and services by tapping the viewer's as yet uncharted motivational reserves. Yet, in all these cases, the myths of the culture are exposed, if not always explored in depth, and the culture's symbol systems are employed to elicit predictable patterns of viewer reaction. The television critic must also be aware of these mythic and symbolic dimensions of his subject if he is to do it justice.

Obviously television is not an art form that is easily evaluated. Broadcast television is an intricate structural web of program genres or types. David Littlejohn, professor of journalism at the University of California—Berkeley, observed that

> Television . . . is "everything." It includes not only almost all the other arts (drama, film, music, dance, visual design of many sorts), but also various forms of journalism. In this latter role, it is expected to cover local, national, and international politics; wars and disasters, presidential speeches, inaugurations, and national funerals; and almost anything else that passes as a news event. It also presents popular sports, classes (at many levels and in many subjects), intellectual (and non-intellectual) discussion, quiz shows, game shows, and other diversions; and innumerable advertisements. It is a complex, profitable, and much-regulated industry. It is an even more complex technology. [15]

One could add comedy (domestic, situation, monologue, sketch), various melodramatic forms (mystery, adventure, Western, professional, soap opera), and a variety of televised religious offerings to Littlejohn's list without exhausting the incredible range of broadcast television program types. And one could then move to cable television and its recent forays into two-way interactive programs that directly, if somewhat coldly, involve the viewer as participant in the program.
Have we exhausted the wide panorama of television programs? Not by a long shot, for we have yet to mention that alternative to traditional television—a form that is referred to as "artists' video," and is itself a complex of varied works in a variety of formats. Allison Simmons elaborated on this area:

> In the United States . . . a number of artists . . . found the camera and portable recording deck—as well as the TV set itself—inviting tools for work oriented in many different directions, from street documentation to the recording of performances to the use of videotape itself as the performance (or "canvas") of the work. Crude "video synthesizers" were invented by engineer artists, allowing virtually anyone to manipulate dials and create colorful, radiant abstractions for display on nearby TV monitors. Monitors themselves were altered, painted, stacked, arranged, or assembled as see-yourself sculpture (with cameras installed inside them). [16]

While much of the early artists' video work was exhibited in small galleries or a select few art museums around the world and was seen by a relatively miniscule number of art afficionados, today public television has opened its doors at least a crack to these artists and has showcased a number of these alternative video works in a few series such as "Video Visionaries." A minority of the general viewing public and some adventurous journalist-critics have taken notice of these happenings in the expanding contemporary world of television and video.

So we must ask specifically about television and video critics how one person can be expected to adequately undertake such a tortuous critical adventure through this elaborate maze of programs, culture, myths, symbol systems, social and economic institutions, and technologies? We might further question what characteristics this insightful wizard need possess. One answer to these questions was supplied by Washington Post television columnist Lawrence Laurent in 1962:

> This complete television critic begins with a respect and a love for the excitement and the impact of the combination of sight and sound—pictures which can be viewed, and words which can be heard, by millions of people at one time. . . . [He] must be something of an electronics engineer, an expert on our governmental processes, an esthetician. He must have a grasp of advertising and marketing principles. He should be able to evaluate all of the art forms; to comprehend each of the messages conveyed, on every subject under the sun, through television. . . .
>
> He must be absolutely incorruptable, a firmly anchored man of objectivity in a stormy world of special interests and pressure groups . . . . he should stand above the boiling turmoil while he plunges into every controversy as a social critic and guardian of standards. . . .[17]

There we have it—the genius of the contemporary era. Now we must look at reality—human beings with human foibles, time limitations, editors, program access limitations, and the like. In other words, we must survey the practitioners, those men and women who do the actual work of looking at and listening to television and reporting their findings to us, the viewers in need of some critical guidance.

The most available criticism of television entertainment programming is found in the television pages of most major newspapers and many general circulation magazines. These columns are generally written either by individuals employed by the respective publications or by syndicated columnists. These publications rarely allow for much in-depth analysis of television. Most newspapers, for example, restrict their television columns to about 600 words.

As early as 1958, nearly 80 percent of American daily news-papers of over 50,000 circulation had television editors (a percentage higher than that for business-finance, real estate, garden, education, and art editors). [18] Twenty years later, nearly all large dailies had a full-time television editor. Furthermore, readership studies indicate that the television page is the second most avidly read section in news-papers. [19] Thus there is a substantial demand for information about television.

Of those television critics writing for newspapers and magazines, those writing for syndication reach the greatest number of potential viewers and thus have significant potential for impacting on the tele-vision scene. Syndicated television columnists such as Rick Du Brow of United Press International have been in a favorable position to in-fluence a large number of viewers who constitute the massified audi-ence for the products of popular art. Such a viewer-oriented, populace-centered criticism is important if one is to bring to a broad spectrum of viewers a basic, clearer understanding of what television is and what it could become, what it does for us and to us.

On the other hand, there are a few critics writing for certain general circulation publications who seem to have more impact on tel-evision's administrative and creative communities than their breth-ren. One rather loosely documented study of the relative influence of various television critics around the United States found that "the most influential critics in the country, without question, are the ones whose opinions reach the ears of the policy-makers in New York and Los An-geles."[20] Names that immediately come to mind are John J. O'Connor of the New York Times and Michael Arlen of The New Yorker maga-zine. These respected publications can be found in most anterooms of network television executive suites. The Times is often called our "newspaper of record," and its television criticism must be consid-ered in that context.

Influence of another type may be equally important—the influence of the television critic in the hinterlands on local station managers' programming decisions. This "outback" criticism may in many cases more adequately address the needs of the individual local community culture.

Although there has been much discussion of the assumed influ-ence of television columns in major daily newspapers and wire ser-vices, little hard evidence is available to either support or refute these assumptions. Laurent once noted that "no one has ever estab-lished a connection between favorable (or even unfavorable) reviews and the success of a television series. A contributory relationship? Perhaps, but a shaky relationship at best."[21]

A recent study of the correlation between a television critic's assessment of a television series and the length of time that series remained on the air concluded that program reviews "probably have little effect on determining the success or failure of the television programs in terms of longevity."[22] Such a conclusion could be interpreted as an argument against the influence of some higher critical judgment on the general viewing audience. On the other hand it may be that television critics writing for general circulation publications have not attempted to raise the level of the general audience's aesthetic sensibilities. Addressing the latter possibility, critic Ernie Kreiling has claimed:

> . . . American newspapers have failed to develop a significant body of informed, penetrating and effective criticism of television . . . [and] . . . have been duped into serving as the industry's principal means of promotion and exploitation. [23]

In the same vein television critic Richard Burgheim, writing in Harper's magazine, noted that

> Most of the newspapers' TV reportage today amounts to little more than reprinted press releases, minutiae of gossip, and fawning profiles of the stars. Most embarrassing of all is perhaps the question-and-answer drivel. . . .[24]

These are overgeneralizations of the lack of quality writing in newspaper television columns. There are some newspaper television columnists who, although they cannot meet many of Laurent's critical quality criteria, do nevertheless often present cogent evaluations of television programs, programming decisions, and regulatory matters. According to an editorial for the Journal of Broadcasting written by its editor John Kitross, "There are a scant dozen frequently read newspaper and magazine critics of high quality. A few senior writers are infrequently found in books and magazines."[25] While the numbers can be disputed, the overall dearth of important television criticism in mass circulation publications cannot. But there are the bright spots or, as TV critic John Leonard once remarked in another context, there are "nosegays among the weeds." Among these nosegays past and present can be counted Lawrence Laurent and Tom Shales of the Washington Post, Bernie Harrison of the Washington Star, Jack Gould (who wrote for the New York Times), John Crosby (who wrote for the New York Herald Tribune), John J. O'Connor (presently writing for the New York Times), and John Leonard (who until recently wrote about television as well as literature for the New York Times). But the list of highly regarded newspaper television columnists does not extend much further although, as we shall see, there is movement at this moment toward greater involvement of talented young critics working the television beats of major metropolitan dailies.

Charles Steinberg offered a possible explanation as to why there have been so few examples of good writing about television in American newspapers. Steinberg criticized the hiring practices of newspapers as contributory to the scarcity of cogent writing about television. In 1973, Steinberg mailed two related questionnaires to television columnists in major cities across the United States asking them to provide information about their backgrounds as writers, their perception of social responsibility in their professional role, and their perception of the amount of "influence" they believed they had over relevant government agencies, broadcasting industry executives, and television viewers who read their columns. The results of the Steinberg survey provided an interesting portrait of the newspaper television columnist in 1973. Less than one-third of the respondents viewed their function primarily as "critic." Only about one-half of the respondents covered the television beat exclusively, while one-fourth had numerous assignments other than television coverage. Two-thirds of the respondents had no previous experience or preparatory training in television, either professionally or academically. Two-thirds of the respondents were arbitrarily assigned to cover television by their managing editors. [26]

In addition to these problems of perceived role, background, and experience, numerous observers of the television criticism scene have pointed to the columnist's lack of time and space brought on by the deadline and the need to fill up the television page with trivia to attract the average reader. The ultimate result of these pressures is the 600-word column filled with industry-prepared public relations handouts on programs and stars.

In contrast to the writing about television in daily newspapers, various limited-circulation magazines have, by many accounts, offered the most highly respected commentary on television over the years. According to one observer, "Weekly magazines like The New Yorker and The New Leader offer an opportunity for a greater degree of specialization, a more concentrated focus, a more personal style."[27]

David Littlejohn, in his survey of television criticism appearing between 1949 and 1974, studied not only daily newspaper columns, but also writings about television in general-interest magazines and American and British periodicals of specialized interest. [28] Among the magazines included in Littlejohn's "reading list" were Commentary, The Nation, The New Republic, The New Yorker, The Atlantic Monthly, and Saturday Review—publications considered by many observers to appeal to a more "culture-concerned" readership. Many of the essayists writing about television for these publications are considered by Littlejohn to be the best representatives of an articulate television criticism. Included among these writers past and present are Michael J. Arlen of The New Yorker, Neil Compton of Commentary, Robert Lewis Shayon of Saturday Review, and Paul Goodman and Reed Whittemore ("Sedulus") of The New Republic.

Littlejohn perceptively highlights the plight of the daily newspaper columnist writing about television in comparison to the television critic writing for the weekly or monthly magazine and the "intellectual" critic:

> There are worlds of difference between the working conditions of the TV editor of a large daily newspaper, the television critic of a weekly or monthly magazine (who may be asked to contribute to only occasional issues), and the intellectual who offers his thoughts on television in a single essay or book. The daily TV critic (whose work is typically subject to the greatest amount of outside abuse) works under an extraordinary set of pressures his more leisured counterparts know nothing of: daily deadlines, 600-word limits, the obligation to fit a paper's existing style, Newspaper Guild regulations, publishers' hiring habits, and the pressing expectations of hundreds of thousands of local readers to be informed regularly on new shows, new seasons, new stars, and current issues. [29]

In most discussions of television criticism, little thought has been given to the "intellectual" to whom Littlejohn refers as one whose evaluations of television are to be found in a single essay or a book. Littlejohn mentions some individuals whom he would place in the category of "intellectuals" writing about television. Included in this group were literary critics and cultural historians such as Daniel Boorstin, Nat Hentoff, Richard Hoggart, and Gore Vidal, all of whom have written intelligent essays on television at one time or another; film and drama critics such as Hollis Alpert, Paulene Kael, Dwight Macdonald, Richard Schickel, and Kenneth Tynan who have also written about television; and music critics such as Irving Kolodin who have written essays about televised musical events such as opera and symphony concerts.

Another oft-neglected group of people writing about television are the creative people themselves. Stephen Hearst, Controller of the British Broadcast Corporation's Radio 3, focused on these types:

> Whereas the cinema has given birth to a vast body of literature . . . television has not as yet been a like source

of literary fertility. Some textbooks, a few trendy novels,
the beginning of serious sociological television investigations [have been published]. . . .

Granted that important movie-making began about
forty years before television came of age, the contrast
between the literature of the cinema and that of television
cannot be explained by the time gap alone. In the field of
daily or weekly criticism there is at least no dearth of
activity . . . . such criticism . . . ought to require . . .
insight, illumination, and background knowledge against
which the average viewer can pit his own impressions and
opinions . . . . only a handful of professional critics whose
knowledge of the medium equals that of the producers has
ever provided such insight . . . .

Partly in reaction to the absence of informed comment on television programmes, television practitioners
have of late themselves begun to draw conclusions from
their experience in print. [30]

We would be wise to take into consideration the writings of those
individuals who normally have not been included in discussions of television criticism—namely "practitioners" in the art form and "intellectuals" who do not regularly write television essays but who bring
to the discussion of television a broad perspective developed through
a consideration of cultural history and/or art forms other than television.

In addition to a need for the writings of these types of individuals, one observer has noted the need to develop a "television scholar-
ship" that concentrates on "the preservation and compilation of primary resources: scripts, kinescopes, films, videotapes, reviews, and
interviews with those who have been directly involved with the programs."[31] Such a role would likely fall to the "academic-type" critic
who functions primarily as a synthesizer of an existing but scattered
body of information about television. Indeed at various colleges and
universities around the country such collation of broadcast materials
is presently being undertaken. In the private sector, institutions such
as the Museum of Broadcasting in New York City, founded in 1976 by
William S. Paley, Chairman of the Board of CBS, have begun collect-
ing, preserving, and providing access to a growing collection of land-
mark television programs and public-events coverage.

NEW DIRECTIONS IN TELEVISION AND VIDEO CRITICISM

In spite of the comparatively weak status of television criticism,
there does seem to be a movement beginning on a variety of critical

fronts that in the long run may provide all interested persons—readers
of newspaper and magazine criticism, artists engaged in exploration
of the art form, and scholars interested in compiling an accurate and
meaningful history of television—with a discourse about television that
is both more conceptual and more lucid than that of the past.

On the so-called "popular TV" front, a number of journalists in
1978 formed their own critics' organization, the Television Critics
Association. On the journalist-critics' semiannual visits to Hollywood
(which are increasingly being funded by the critics' newspapers rather
than by the networks as has traditionally been the case), the critics
seem to be gaining the upper hand in their battle to get at the hard
news of programming decisions and at the same time avoid being
snowed by the networks' extravagant publicity stunts. According to
Richard M. Levine, writing about television in New Times, "In heated
exchanges the minority of younger, more vocal critics attempted to
hold television executives responsible for the shows they put on the
air—a frustrating but vigorous game that might be called "Pin the Tale
on the Donkey."[32] Rena Pederson, Television Editor for the Dallas
Morning News, is a member of the Television Critics Association
(TCA) and an example of the young critics who are university trained
in the discipline of television criticism and who seek responsible positions as television critics with major dailies. Pederson spoke to the
Broadcast Education Association in 1979 about the new television criticism emerging from major American newspapers:

> Let me take you back a little bit now. Television criti-
> cism—probably when it originally started most newspa-
> pers and magazines didn't know what to do with it, and
> often people were put in positions of being TV critics that
> didn't bring to it a background of broadcasting or neces-
> sarily hard news reporting. Some of them were reporters
> or fine arts writers, but sometimes there would be in-
> stances where somebody would be a secretary or a TV
> listing person who typed up the TV listings, and the job
> was expanded to include some program notes and features
> and interviews. Sometimes it would be some guy from
> sports who didn't want to go out of town all the time and
> follow the baseball games, and so he got stuck doing the
> TV coverage. It was a plum job. You got to go out of town,
> you got to go on some trips to Hollywood, and in those
> days the network interview sessions were called "junkets"
> because there were a lot of cocktail parties and a lot of
> free time, and a lot of free tickets to plays. But in the
> last two to five years there has been a metamorphosis,
> an evolution or revolution in TV criticism in that people

began to have an awareness that TV perhaps was not the family hearthplace, the electronic hearth, your friend, your glowing warm companion, but there were some threatening aspects of TV. They began to look at it more seriously. In response to this their newspapers began to take it more seriously as TV became news. You have more people going into the field who come to it from a repertorial background who majored in broadcasting in colleges. Generally these people are younger, but not necessarily so. The result has been a more fractious, aggressive, contentious lot which in some instances, like in any movement, has perhaps swung too far in one way. But, I think, there is a levelling off now, and it's a very healthy, aggressive climate that is perhaps good for the reader and the viewer and the networks. I think the networks were frightened by the movement, and a little turned off, but the response that I have gotten most often from the people that I deal with on the network level is that it has been a healthy thing for them. [33]

What Pederson calls "the movement"—the Television Critics Association—now has procured financial support from the Markle Foundation and is able to set up its own extensive interview sessions with members of television's creative community in addition to its semiannual sessions with network programmers and independent producers in Hollywood. The Association also publishes a bimonthly TCA Newsletter that contains interviews with network executives, producers, writers, and directors, news of upcoming TCA events, letters from the TCA to network management, letters from the creative community and network management to the TCA regarding its activities, and a sampling of critical opinion from TCA members. The TCA has even formed its own speaker's bureau to provide TCA members as speakers at "major broadcast and journalism events."

The Television Critics Association is indicative of the markedly increasing concern with how and why television programming decisions are made. Yet the TCA was not the first step in this critical direction. The TCA's thrust clearly rests on the initiatives of the so-called maverick TV critics of the past two decades, including Michael Arlen of The New Yorker, Gary Deeb of the Chicago Tribune, Ron Powers, formerly of the Chicago Sun-Times, and Tom Shales of the Washington Post. These intelligent young television critics developed their critical postures toward our culture and its television during the 1960s—the decade of disillusionment. Their writings about television reflect a certain skepticism regarding television's ability to transcend its economic imperative and pecuniary psychology and to establish authentic cultural links with its vast audience and numerous sub-audiences.

On the more esoteric art critical front, a new publication has emerged from the New York Sohoites. Called TV Magazine this fledgling project promises to bring to an interested national readership news of new artists' video projects, profiles of artists working with video on an independent basis, articles on research and development of new technology, and, most important, theoretical essays on a software level dealing with both the formal aspects of television and video and the cultural ramifications of the art form.

Academicians in increasing numbers are being awakened to the fact that television can be a legitimate subject for theoretical discourse. Genre studies by academicians such as Horace Newcomb,[34] David Thorburn,[35] and Robert Alley[36] are beginning to convince academicians that they should reconsider television as a significant art form in its own right with its own set of artistic criteria.

It is apparent that critical movement in these directions is long overdue. The viewers deserve a more serious journalistic approach to television as an art form and as a powerful economic and political institution; there is a need for the general recognition of the more esoteric individual video works that help define new directions the art form can take; and there is a need for an organic theoretical approach to television and video as art forms that have unique discernable characteristics.

A new television and video criticism is now emerging that focuses on these areas. Academics, with access to videocassette and soon to video disc libraries are beginning to reevaluate television's history. Artists working with personalized video are slowly if painfully gaining access to computerized editing facilities and Public Broadcasting production and postproduction facilities and are thereby facilitating a nexus of television the public art and video the personal, private art; and, equally important, these artists who are bridging the artistic gap are also writing about their bridges. And finally, the audience's main link with the products of TV pop cult, the television critic/journalist writing for the daily newspaper and weekly or monthly magazine, has joined with comrades to take on the vast commercial television empire on its own turf.

In the chapters that follow, I will examine the lives and work of a few select prominent contemporary television and video critics presently writing in the United States. Each critic brings his own unique perspective to the critical confrontation, and by the very nature of each critic's role as a practitioner, the critical approaches differ in focus and substance. Yet all the critics carefully examined in the following chapters seem to possess a common trait that makes their work significant—the "respect and . . . love for the excitement and the impact of the combination of sight and sound" that Lawrence Laurent so aptly noted almost 20 years ago.

NOTES

1. Saul N. Scher, "The Role of the Television Critic: Four Approaches," Today's Speech 22 (Summer 1974): 1.

2. John Simon, Private Screenings (New York: Macmillan, 1967), p. 4.

3. Bruton Connors, "Criticism Pure or Applied?" Twentieth Century, no. 1032 (1967): 10.

4. Nigel Gosling, "The Critical Tightrope," Twentieth Century, no. 1032 (1967): 11.

5. Irving Wardle, "Growth of a Critic," Twentieth Century, no. 1032 (1967): 12.

6. Ibid. , p. 13.

7. Ibid.

8. Richard Kostelanetz, "The Compleat Critic," Twentieth Century, no. 1032 (1967): 17-18.

9. Gosling, "Tightrope," p. 11.

10. Richard Kostelanetz, "An ABC of Contemporary Reading," in Esthetics Contemporary, ed. Richard Kostelanetz (Buffalo, N. Y. : Prometheus Books, 1978), p. 365.

11. Ibid.

12. Allison Simmons, "Television and Art: A Historical Primer for an Improbable Alliance," in The New Television: A Public/Private Art, eds. Douglas Davis and Allison Simmons (Cambridge, Mass. : MIT Press, 1977), p. 3.

13. Marshall McLuhan, Understanding Media (New York: Mc-Graw-Hill, 1964).

14. Ibid. , p. 9.

15. David Littlejohn, "Thoughts on Television Criticism," in Television as a Cultural Force, eds. Richard Adler and Douglass Cater (New York: Praeger, 1976), pp. 150-51.

16. Simmons, "Television and Art," p. 10.

17. Lawrence Laurent, "Wanted: The Complete Television Critic," in The Eighth Art, Robert Lewis Shayon et al. , (New York: Holt, Rinehart and Winston, 1962), p. 156.

18. Patrick D. Hazard, "TV Criticism—A Prehistory," Television Quarterly 2 (Fall 1963): 59.

19. Charles Steinberg, "The Compleat Television Critic," Television Quarterly 11 (Winter 1974): 6.

20. George Condon, "Critics' Choice," Television Quarterly 1 (November 1962): 24.

21. Lawrence Laurent, "A Critic Looks at Reviewing," Journal of Broadcasting 11 (Winter 1966-67): 16.

22. Maurice E. Shelby, Jr., "Criticism and Longevity of Television Programs," Journal of Broadcasting 17 (Summer 1973): 285.

23. Ernie Kreiling, "The Kreiling Thesis," The Bulletin of the American Society of Newspaper Editors, September 1, 1965, p. 1.

24. Richard Burgheim, "Television Reviewing," Harper's, August 1969, p. 100.

25. John Kitross, "Criticism," Journal of Broadcasting 11 (Winter 1966-67): 2.

26. Steinberg, "Compleat Television Critic," pp. 8-9.

27. Scher, "The Role of the Television Critic," p. 5.

28. Littlejohn, "Thoughts on Television Criticism," p. 149.

29. Ibid., p. 154.

30. Stephen Hearst, "Writing About Television," Times (London) Literary Supplement, 12 November 1971, p. 1418.

31. John L. Wright, "The Focus of Television Criticism," Journal of Popular Culture 7 (Spring 1974): 889.

32. Richard M. Levine, "The Medium of Record Finally Catches On," New Times, 7 August 1978, p. 57.

33. Address by Rena Pederson to members of the Broadcast Education Association attending a panel "Are Television Critics Doing Their Homework?," Broadcast Education Association annual convention, Dallas, Texas, 25 March 1979.

34. Horace Newcomb, TV: The Most Popular Art (Garden City, N. Y.: Doubleday, Anchor Press, 1974).

35. David Thorburn, "Television Melodrama," in Television as a Cultural Force, eds. Richard Adler and Douglass Cater (New York: Praeger, 1976), pp. 77-94.

36. Robert S. Alley, "Media Medicine and Morality," in Television as a Cultural Force, eds. Richard Adler and Douglass Cater (New York: Praeger, 1976), pp. 95-110.

3

JOHN J. O'CONNOR:
CRITIC "OF RECORD"

John J. O'Connor, television editor of the New York Times, is perhaps the most influential individual writing about television on a regular basis in American daily newspapers today. His columns probably have a greater impact on television's management and creative communities than do those of most other critics, in part because his words appear almost daily in what has been called our country's "newspaper of record."

O'Connor writes about television in the best tradition of Jack Gould, who wrote about radio and television for the New York Times from 1944 to 1971, Lawrence Laurent of the Washington Post, and John Crosby, who wrote about radio and television for the New York Herald-Tribune from 1946 to 1961. He has carried on Gould's in-depth coverage of events occurring at New York's, and, many would argue, the nation's major public television outlet—WNET-TV. He consistently commends the "best" works of public television while at the same time encouraging public television programmers to focus their energies on producing more significant indigenous programs, thus reducing the Public Broadcasting System's top-heavy reliance on imported British Broadcasting Corporation (BBC) fare. He also frequently lambasts public television's seeming reluctance to allow independent producers access to its high technology facilities. Like Laurent, O'Connor makes an effort to keep his readership informed on the larger institutional questions regarding television, such as regulatory issues and the imbalance between huge commercial broadcast network profits and the paucity of public television funding. Like Crosby, O'Connor does not nesitate to come down hard on those programs he considers to be "trash," often providing his readership with suggestions on ways to improve the programs. While his writing style does not exhibit the wit of Crosby's, O'Connor's writing is nevertheless well-organized, concise, and logical.

One aspect of O'Connor's work that is highly unusual for a daily television critic is his concern with alternative personal video statements by video artists. Having a location in midtown Manhattan near much of this video activity makes such a focus more feasible than it would be for many other journalist-critics.

Still, a lack of time and space due to deadline pressures and competition with program listings for column inches ultimately frames O'Connor's essays, as is the case with any television critic writing for a daily paper. In spite of these limitations, he has to date made a significant contribution to intelligent critical writing about television. We will examine that contribution shortly, but first some background on the man behind the words.

O'Connor was born in 1934. He received a Bachelor of Arts degree in drama from Yale University in 1957 and a Master's degree in drama from Yale in 1958. Between 1958 and 1960, O'Connor taught at City College of New York, and in 1960 he joined the staff of the Wall Street Journal as a copy editor. He continued in that position until 1965, when he convinced the Journal that it should create a position for an arts editor. Using as an example the Financial Times of London, a business publication that also covered the arts, O'Connor managed to garner support for his idea, and in 1965 he became the Journal's arts editor, reviewing theater, film, dance, opera, books, and occasionally a television work.

Early in 1971, the New York Times approached O'Connor at the Journal. O'Connor described the contact:

> They came to me, actually. They liked my stuff in the Journal, and they had three jobs. . . . One was the daily book reviewer. John Leonard was going up to the Sunday book review section of the Times. Another was a roving cultural correspondent, going around the country, which was not for me—travelling all the time. And the other just happened to open up at that time with Jack Gould, who was both the critic and the correspondent-reporter . . . he became ill and had to give up something and decided to give up the reviewing part. So the reviewing aspect just opened up at that time. Thinking it over, I thought, well, that I'd be most interested in television.

In March 1971, O'Connor began writing about television for the New York Times. While he had written an occasional piece on television for the Wall Street Journal during his stint as arts editor there, his move to the Times marked his first real in-depth involvement with television.

O'CONNOR ON TELEVISION

O'Connor's move to the New York Times was prompted by two things. According to O'Connor,

> One was, I thought it was time. I was doing too much at
> the Journal, it was impossible for me. Again it was a
> seven . . . day job. They [the Times] offered me a hell
> of a lot more money. And the Journal actually came up
> half way in trying to meet that offer, and it was a very
> pleasant place to work for, the Journal. So I left with
> some reluctance, but, as it turned out I thought I'd have
> more time for myself just focusing on one area—but I
> picked the wrong area because television is unending—it
> just goes on and on and on.

O'Connor zeroed in on the problems of this "on and on and onness," confronting the daily television critic. When I asked him, for example, if he would like to devote more review time to what he consider- ed worthwhile avant-garde video works, he responded:

> Well this is the problem for the daily . . . newspaper
> critic. I'd love to do more, but it is impossible. I can
> only watch so many hours a day, and I'm bombarded just
> keeping up with the commercial networks. I have a ma-
> chine at home now that they deliver the programs to me
> and pick them up as I'm finished, so that they bring any-
> thing. I don't know, when I go home there are cassettes
> just stacked outside my door. It could take me twelve
> hours a day to watch them all. So there's just so much
> coming out of the machine . . . that it's impossible to
> get around to. Of course, public television I watch a lot.
> Two independent stations—I think I rarely go into inde-
> pendent stations. . . . And there are two factors work-
> ing, pushing me toward the network product, or the pub-
> lic television network . . . . one is that the daily critic,
> unlike the weekly or monthly critic, somebody like Mi-
> chael Arlen who can lean back and look at something and
> do a long take out on one program—watch one program
> and then do a long piece on it—the daily critic is also—
> one of his functions, her functions, is to be a kind of con-
> sumer guide. Readers expect it. . . . The other is that
> you really need a large staff to really cover the area ade-
> quately at all and to get time to go to these. I think video
> is fascinating. I've met a lot of people doing a lot of inter-

esting work. I just don't do it. Every once in a while like a "VTR" I'll try to get something out on that, but I rarely get to the museums, the Whitney, the Museum of Modern Art, and they're being neglected.

The television critic writing for the daily newspaper cannot even cover the entire television waterfront, and he certainly does not have the luxury to often venture into the esoteric, as important as those works may be. These are the parameters within which the daily critic must work, including what O'Connor termed the function of the "consumer guide"—trying to deliver as much copy as is possible to a readership interested in what is coming up on television that night and whether or not it will be worth watching. This is often called the pre-reviewing function of the critic. Pre-reviewing highlights both a major weakness of the daily critic and a major strength—the weakness lies in the critic's need to crank out a program preview with great haste, thus prohibiting prolonged contemplation of that program and its deeper structures; the strength lies in the contemporaneity of the preview—viewers are supplied with knowledgeable commentary that will help them make informed viewing decisions. O'Connor believes his readers both want and need this type of pre-review information, and he takes this part of his work quite seriously. O'Connor talked to me about the significance of the pre-reviewing function:

> . . . when I came to the job . . . ABC and CBS were allowing pre-reviewing. You could do it if you wanted. But very few critics were doing it. Jack Gould didn't like to do it. But when I came I decided, well, the hell with it. I mean I felt ridiculous reviewing most of the stuff the day after and you couldn't see it any more. And again, going back to this consumer guide kind of function, part of my function, I thought rightly or wrongly I'm writing for a readership that would tend to be more selective in their viewing, would want to know if there was something special on that night or two nights from now. So that when I started doing it, then the other editors got on their critics' backs and said: "Look, the Times is pre-reviewing." It went that way, and then gradually NBC's reluctance to do it was worn down. I think finally they gave up with "The Execution of Private Slovik"—[it] was the first one they allowed.

O'Connor added that there are some restrictions in the program distribution mechanism that prohibit access to all programs for pre-reviewing:

. . . there may be an occasional clinker that [producers] really don't want to get out and they'd rather not have you look at or see—I think that's rare. I think what happens is usually in the production process, producers tend to hold on to it till the last, the very last minute. They're always tinkering, they're always fixing it, there's always that one scene that's going to turn the dud into a fantastic success. This is a very natural thing, I think. . . . right now I just watched Marlo Thomas and "It Happened One Christmas," and they called me up saying . . . "please don't say that I had seen those takes because Marlo Thomas says that they weren't color corrected." She has a new set of tapes that she insists that I watch because the hues were off slightly. People . . . tend to get a little bit mad about this kind of thing. I think in many cases [the networks] don't get them until the last minute. In fact I know that they don't go out because they send them out to their af- filiates and sometimes they don't go out until that night at midnight the day before the show's actually going on the air. But that's really not all that much of a problem. In fact, in most cases they <u>want</u> a notice in the <u>Times</u> even if it's a bad review. It's better to be noticed than to be ignored. . . . Some people have the idea that if they're not mentioned in the <u>Times</u> they don't exist. . . . It's a strange thing. I mean I've had people call me up and say why didn't you—producers, actors, or somebody—how come you didn't review my . . . I said, well I was busy, I didn't have enough room, and all this kind of thing. I said . . . in a way you're lucky because I hated the damn thing. They didn't <u>care</u>.

What exactly are these pre-reviews that the producers, direct- ors, and actors are clamoring for? O'Connor's pre-reviews focus generally on highlights of a single program, providing viewers with reasons they might enjoy or not enjoy viewing it. Rarely does he have either the time or the space in these brief discussions of programs to situate the program in the larger context of its genre. It seems likely, however, that even a brief discussion of a program acts as a legitimiz- ing mechanism for both the program's creators and the newspaper's readership. A representative example of O'Connor's pre-reviewing style is this discussion of Bette Midler's December 1977 television special:

Bette Midler comes to network television tonight with her very own special, on NBC at 10 o'clock, after years of do- ing guest-star stints on other shows. . . .

The question of the moment: Can the performer who started up the road to fame playing in a baths establishment catering to homosexuals find fortune on prime time "family" television without compromising her talent for being outrageous? The answer . . . is yes—to an extent, but a surprisingly rewarding extent.

Describing Midler's audience appeal, O'Connor continued:

Carving out her distinctive niche between the kooky vulnerability of Barbra Streisand and the calculated "red hot mama" brassiness of Sophie Tucker, Miss Midler becomes a human projectile of almost irresistable energy.

O'Connor then cited evidence in the program for Midler's popularity with the larger audience.

Miss Midler is still dizzy camp. Her opening number, set "on a peaceful island somewhere in the South Pacific," has the friendly natives hauling in a giant shell. Out steps the Divine Miss M in skimpy bathing suit to join the gentlefolk in a rousing rendition of "Oklahoma!"

However, O'Connor was not all kudos. He evaluated the special in sufficient depth to establish an opposition between its "successful" and "unsuccessful" elements:

But there is some compromise and, reverting to the typical other side of the outrageous coin, Miss Midler dabbles rather heavily in sentimentality. [1]

His consumer-guide function fulfilled, O'Connor must move on to similar evaluations of other upcoming programs. What is omitted from his evaluation of Midler's special and from similar pre-reviews is a discussion of how this particular program stacks up against other specials in the musical-comedy-variety form—a genre analysis.

The reviewing function of the daily television critic is similar to that of his counterparts in weekly or monthly general-circulation magazines. The review, although written after the fact (i.e., following the airing of a particular program), can be useful to the viewer for three reasons: first, it can either corroborate the viewer's opinion following the viewing experience; second, it can highlight the general quality or lack of quality of a series or serial and thereby help the viewer determine whether or not to pursue future episodes of the series or serial; and third, it can stimulate the viewer's awareness of a program he may have missed the first time around but may be able to catch on its second play.

O'Connor's longer Sunday pieces reflect a greater evaluative depth on the whole than his weekday pre-reviews. An excellent representative example of the Sunday edition review is O'Connor's discussion of the PBS series "Live from Lincoln Center." He began his discussion of the series by explaining the new video techniques used to enhance live performances, both for the viewing audience and the audience in the theater. While he praised these new techniques, O'Connor also cautioned "that there is something more essential than advanced technology in the overall process. And that, simply enough, is substance."[2] That substance takes two forms when performance works are realized for a home-viewing audience. First is the actual performance itself, and second is the manner in which the performance is recorded, including both the performance "on stage" and the activities during the intermissions. In a single column, O'Connor focused on these elements as he compared two "Live from Lincoln Center" productions—the New York Philharmonic with Van Cliburn as guest soloist and the American Ballet Theater's "Swan Lake"—with the CBS television network's recording of the Bolshoi Ballet's "Romeo and Juliet."

About the New York Philharmonic concert, O'Connor wrote "The Philharmonic concert was uninspired, most notably in Mr. Cliburn's playing." In contrast, O'Connor wrote of "Swan Lake": "American Ballet Theater's production of the dance is splendid. Miss Makarova, superbly partnered by Mr. Nagy, is a great Odille/Odette."[3]

In regard to the use of video in these productions, O'Connor wrote of the Philharmonic concert that ". . . efforts to fill the intermission breaks were singularly awkward." He wrote at greater length about "Swan Lake":

> . . . with "Swan Lake" all of the right elements seemed to fall together effortlessly. . . . The performance and the excitement of the theatrical event was encompassed fully in the extremely intelligent television direction of Kirk Browning. And the intermissions, set back stage with Dick Cavett as a very effective host, were models of how a performance can be broadened and illuminated. Among the unusually informative "guests" was Miss Makarova, on the run between acts and managing to project great eloquence and charm while wrapped in bulky leg warmers.[4]

O'Connor contrasted the effective use of video for "Swan Lake" with the inappropriateness of video as used in the Bolshoi's "Romeo and Juliet":

As danced for television, the production was flawed. The immense Bolshoi stage and the spectacular scope of the ballet itself proved too unwieldy for the cameras. Getting a broad picture of the entire scene meant that the dancers were reduced to moving dots. A closeup of one detail often excluded several equally important details. Only the uncluttered solos and duets, plus the great Prokofiev score, survived intact. [5]

O'Connor also criticized CBS's use of Mary Tyler Moore as hostess for the Bolshoi production:

CBS, however, was not confident enough to put performance first. The network framed the event in the presence of one of its own stars, evidently hoping that people who don't like dance might tune in to catch a glimpse of Mary Tyler Moore. When commercial television dabbles in limited-audience "culture," it will try anything. That's fair enough. But this particular effort only managed to leave Miss Moore looking silly, if not downright incompetent. [6]

In his concluding remarks on the "Live from Lincoln Center" series, O'Connor cautioned against limiting the performances to those with "mass audience" appeal:

One program danger is looming at the moment: the possible temptation to concentrate on the more obvious "blockbusters." . . . In fact, in the New York area, "Swan Lake" registered a quite impressive 13 percent share of the total sets in use during that time period. But, superstars and blockbusters aside, the television project has an obligation to all the artistic elements at Lincoln Center, to the small chamber concert as well as to the massive opera production. The central point is quality, not the size of the audience for any one production. [7]

O'Connor's review of "Live from Lincoln Center" illustrates his tendency, in a review format, to explore in depth the complexities of a program by placing the program in both a genre and an institutional context. Such an expanded consumer-guide function seems appropriate to O'Connor, in large measure due to his perception of the level of sophistication of his readership. I asked O'Connor who he felt reads his reviews, to which he responded without hesitation:

For the most part, a very intelligent audience. I think it

is . . . the more educated New Yorker, suburban, and from all over the country . . . and for the most part selective viewers, people concerned, activist types, and of course the producers and actors and all those people. Read the credits. I'm lucky in that sense in that I never have to write down. I just assume I'm writing for an intelligent, fairly intelligent readership, whereas if I were writing for the Daily News I would have a different approach. I'd have to have a different approach.

O'Connor indeed has a nationwide audience. His pieces appear regularly in a large number of dailies via the New York Times Service. His analyses reach as far as Canada and Puerto Rico. His perception of his readership as "more educated" and "selective" in their viewing habits allows him the latitude to delve into the complex realm of genre study, and his perception of his readership as "activist" permits his sometimes lengthy discussion of institutional strictures affecting telecommunications. These forays into a comprehensive criticism are most likely to appear in his Sunday pieces in the "Arts and Leisure" section of the newspaper.

Let us focus now on O'Connor's treatment of genre. While he often examines individual works of television art in their genre contexts, O'Connor tends to limit his comparisons to current works, which precludes his evaluating genres in their historical contexts. In his nine years as a writer about television for the New York Times, O'Connor has firmly and consistently maintained that the great majority of programs aired on commercial broadcast television are "trash." In one of his first columns for the Times, he commented that "Television, conservatively speaking, is at least 90 percent trash." He added:

Obviously there is no denying the trash—the inane situation comedies, the insane game shows, the insipid interviews, the overblown specials, the commercials bordering on downright fraudulence. A reviewer new to the medium and determined to spend (for a while) most of his working hours in front of the tube, gets the picture quickly. [8]

However, O'Connor did not wish at that time to impulsively relegate broadcast television in the United States to the status of a "lower" cultural form. He wisely noted that while he believed television was mostly trash, "most people will hesitate to admit that precisely the same can be said about theater, films, recordings, books, and yes, even newspapers." [9]

I asked him if he still felt the same about television programming in general after seven years of writing for the New York Times.
He replied:

> Oh, I think there are a lot of examples [of good programs]
> still around, that if you choose selectively, very selec-
> tively, that you can get as much out of television as you
> can out of going to the theater regularly or going to films
> regularly. Public television of course is still doing the
> most in this area, and dramas . . . tonight . . . you've
> got a very fine drama in "Abide With Me" with Cathleen
> Nesbitt, and "I, Claudius". . . . is fairly good. . . . So
> I'm still convinced, yes, that there's an awful lot. At the
> same time . . . I think that television has gone down sev-
> eral notches with the success of ABC and kiddievid pro-
> grams.

When O'Connor writes about "quality" productions on television,
he most often cites such genres as "serious drama, a concert, an
ambitious documentary, or imaginative experimentation."[10] Of these
genres, he seems to feel most comfortable with enunciating criteria
in the "serious" television drama form. Given his extensive theater
background, such a preoccupation is not unexpected. While there is
no single essay he has written for the New York Times that compre-
hensively sets forth his criteria for "quality" drama on television, a
group of criteria do emerge from a variety of columns he has written.
Included among the primary elements that O'Connor believes delineate
"quality" drama on television are superior acting; interesting concepts in the teleplay; plausible, complex characters; and strong visual and audio production elements.
    An analysis of several of O'Connor's columns provides illustra-
tive examples of criteria he has established for serious television
drama. For example, O'Connor hailed the return of "The Forsyte
Saga" to PBS:

> . . . given a whale of a story, splendidly acted, the home
> audience was afforded a glimpse of what television could
> be. A new yardstick had been created and the old formu-
> las just didn't measure up.[11]

According to O'Connor, the teleplay, another primary element
in the television drama form, includes both concepts or story ideas,
and their execution through script writing. O'Connor noted that "Interesting concepts don't necessarily evolve into successful productions."[12] He documented this viewpoint in a review of a Swedish pro-

duction entitled "Brecht—On the Run from My Fellow Countrymen."
The drama, shown on PBS in 1977, was a portrait of the German playwright Bertolt Brecht as a refugee in Sweden in 1939. O'Connor commented:

> It was a fascinating and ironically productive period in the
> playwright's life, but this production is unable to bring the
> biography to satisfying dramatic form. . . . the actors be-
> come little more than talking heads. The talk goes on in-
> cessantly about experimental theater being a home for free-
> dom. . . . And on, and on—into a form closer to a some-
> what tedious lecture than to a drama, epic or otherwise. [13]

Interesting concepts are integral to O'Connor's formulation of
criteria for serious television drama: "Drama has limited mileage in
terms of the mass audience. . . . it is risky, precisely because it
seeks to explore beneath superficialities, precisely because it may
prod and disturb. "[14]

The best dramatic writing, according to O'Connor, is that which
creates plausible, complex characters acting out their lives in meaningful, complex situations in which the characters' actions are tempered by ambiguities, as in life. O'Connor found these dramatic elements coalescing in "Live Your Life":

> Written by Anna-Maria Hagerfors, this terribly moving
> treatment of death and life was given an almost documen-
> tary-like sense of reality by Gun Jonsson, the director.
> . . . Hardly a moment seems superfluous as Nina, a 45-
> year old Stockholm woman, is followed from the first
> signs of her illness to death from a brain tumor, only
> months later, in the arms of her husband and three chil-
> dren. . . . Refusing to be noble, Nina fights against bu-
> reaucratic insensitivity and narcotizing sedatives. She
> leaves her family on her own terms. They are not pretty,
> but they are strangely comforting and touching. [15]

O'Connor has also noted that strong visual and audio production
values can greatly enhance a well-acted, well-written television drama. An example is found in his pre-review of the BBC dramatic series production of "The Pallisers":

> The story begins in the early 1860's and traces the for-
> tunes of an aristocratic British family through two dec-
> ades. . . . The novels and the TV adaptation offer won-
> derfully detailed etchings of manners, fashion, and Par-
> liamentary maneuvering.

He added: " 'The Pallisers' is unusually lavish even by the remarkably high standards of the BBC. The first episode . . . offers a splendid collage of visual settings. "[16]

Thus, an analysis of a variety of O'Connor's columns dealing with what he would categorize as serious television drama reveals a relatively coherent delineation of genre characteristics. These columns provide an in-depth look at the aesthetic foundations of the genre, if not a strong historical perspective of the genre's development as a television form.

O'Connor's writings about the comedic genre seem less assured. In 1971, as he began writing about television for the New York Times, O'Connor commented that comedy programs "are a depressing lot, but then 'All in the Family' manages to be remarkably entertaining in the sensitive area of unabashed bigotry. "[17] In a 1976 review of that year's new television season O'Connor claimed:

> Not surprisingly, the new programs are at their best—or, if you will, their least objectionable—in the area of situation comedy, a format particularly suited to the medium. Also not surprisingly, the most promising candidates for survival have been created and tailored at the factories of Norman Lear and MTM (Mary Tyler Moore) Enterprises. [18]

While O'Connor offers no specific elaboration as to why comedy is "a format particularly suited to the medium," he does from time to time point to the Norman Lear comedies as important because they take chances by examining the absurdity of some contemporary value systems while still having fun and providing the audience with entertainment. When "All in the Family" recently died a rather poignant death and was transformed into "Archie Bunker's Place" on CBS, O'Connor noted that the spin-off was "in just about every respect, a first class disaster." The old Archie apparently was somehow a more relevant character than the new Archie in terms of his representation of one part of our cultural fabric. O'Connor observed that "over the years, the lovable bigot routine gradually gave way to more serious, surprisingly touching explorations of blue collar life. . . . Carroll O'Connor . . . consistently demonstrated an ability to achieve marvellous affecting performances while portraying a near stereotypic character." However, after ten years on the air, "the bigotry doesn't work as a comedic device. . . . The clever pacing, the crispness of the scripts, the skill of the performances have all disappeared. "[19]

These comments raise an interesting, if unstated, possibility: if the gestures of the comic remain consistent, and the essential thematic structure of the comedy remains essentially unchanged, why does the transition produce unsatisfactory results? Perhaps the departure of supporting characters from the "All in the Family" series sapped Carroll O'Connor's creative energies. Perhaps the familiar surroundings of the Bunker household became etched in the viewer's subconscious and a move to a different setting such as the bar in the spin-off series produced some cultural dislocation for viewers. Or perhaps, as O'Connor hinted, the serious treatment of the frustration of the blue-collar life-style was critical to the original show's success. In the latter case, we may have witnessed the fusing of two genres— the true comedy-melodrama, in which the fine line between the two forms is obscured and the viewer each week is taken on a roller coaster ride through the absurdity and glory of a family's everyday existence. As Lear himself once said, the Bunkers live at the ends of their nerves, yet through the shouting and conflict emerges a humanness that reaches the audience, and that the audience understands. That humanness may be validated by the intimacy of television's small screen and its placement in the living room. Our living rooms and the living room tableau of "All in the Family" merge and the empathic bonds between performers and audience are sealed.

Although O'Connor classifies comedies such as "All in the Family" as "situation comedies," perhaps they are more accurately thought of as domestic comedies with relevancy. As Horace Newcomb, another insightful observer of television art has pointed out, these comedies (including "All in the Family," "M*A*S*H," and "Maude") focus on setting rather than some absurd situation (as is the case with situation comedy); feature the family unit itself as the cultural device that produces order from chaos; and permit the entrance of the ambiguities of the world existing outside the specific setting into the internalized interactions of the family members. [20]

In a culture that was beginning to face up to the contradictions inherent in bigotry and prejudice of all kinds, a culture that was living through events such as the trauma of busing school children to achieve racial balance in schools and the Equal Rights Amendment controversy, it makes sense that the domestic comedy with relevancy as presented through television would strike a responsive chord in our national sensibility. We could examine our foibles safely through personification. Archie and Hawkeye are the sad clowns who draw out emotions and help us reach inside ourselves for answers.

One hopes that O'Connor will address these issues in a future lengthy essay. To date, such an essay has not been forthcoming. Nevertheless, O'Connor has at least talked around the issues if he has not zeroed in on the more substantive aspects of the comedic genre.

One area of the critical dialogue upon which O'Connor has frequently focused is the relationship of television to the larger cultural terrain, including commentary on the institutional constraints on the television production process. This is especially evident in his discussions of the relationship of institutional constraints to the question of access of independent producers to the high technology facilities of television broadcasters.

In discussing institutional strictures in a television production context, O'Connor has, in numerous columns, juxtaposed the performance of commercial broadcasters and public broadcasters in the United States. In the process, he inevitably concludes that those types of programs which commercial broadcasters will not take the risk to produce and air must be produced and aired by public television. However, O'Connor is quick to point out that public television in this country is severely underfinanced and therefore must rely heavily on imported fare:

> . . . much of the quality on public television is imported—
> "Masterpiece Theater," etc. —but that situation is just
> about unavoidable without more money being pumped into
> the system. [21]

In addition to the lack of money, PBS is often faced with the additional problem of having strings attached to the meager funds it does receive from the government and other sources. When I asked O'Connor about the problems with public broadcasting funding support, he commented:

> . . . you have to have some system where . . . you can
> do major projects. You have to have the money to do that.
> . . . I think also one of the problems in funding now is
> that there are so many, especially with the government
> or foundations, there are so many strings attached—like
> "The Best of Families" . . . that's on now [1977]. It's
> ass backwards. It's drama ass backwards. Instead of an
> idea growing out of a dramatist's mind, the idea was de-
> termined by foundations saying wouldn't it be interesting
> to have all this authentic furniture, and we could hook all
> of this to real historical happening, and <u>then</u> we'll hook
> the characters on to this . . . . It just doesn't work; . . .
> there's got to be a pool of money with no strings attach-
> ed, of open money. And when something comes along, a
> major project, it can be funded and done by the artistic
> people.

In one of his 1977 columns, O'Connor recommended a restructuring of the PBS funding mechanism that would continue present sources of funding and add commercial broadcast network contributions to the funding pool. This proposal anticipated the approach to be taken in the U. S. House of Representatives Communication Committee's proposals for rewriting the 1934 Federal Communications Act. O'Connor observed:

> Undoubtedly, the sources of programming dollars should continue to be diversified to insure insulation against undue pressure from any single entity: Federal, state and local financing; foundation grants; corporate underwriting, and individual viewer donations. But other sources might also be found. One that has long been mentioned, but then neatly and almost mysteriously shelved, is the well-stocked profits pot of the commercial networks. . . .
> . . . the commercial side is capable of contributing heavily to the public side. That contribution could be voluntary, cleverly leaving the networks free to pursue "lowest common denominator" saturation on a full-time basis. Or, more likely, a financing formula, devised with every concern for fairness, could be imposed on the networks. [22]

Yet, even if public television had such an ideal funding situation, additional problems involving the distribution of those funds would almost certainly arise. In fact, O'Connor has devoted many column inches to a discussion of the continuing problem of public television's distribution of its production monies. This problem says much about the difficulties independent producers encounter in attempting to gain access to public television's program production and distribution apparatus. Why blame public television for the access woes? Perhaps because it is the last resort for independent producers whose project ideas are summarily dismissed by the commercial television networks, which rely most heavily for the bulk of their product on the "majors" (MCA/Universal, Twentieth Century-Fox, Paramount, United Artists, Columbia, MGM, and Warner Brothers—traditionally successful Hollywood film companies who have moved into telefilm production) and a few hand-picked independent producers such as Norman Lear and Quinn Martin with successful TV series track records.

O'Connor highlighted the importance of the truly independent producer in the commercial television arena in a 1978 column:

> In the popular arts, economic structure dictates product. That is the basic lesson being brought home again by the current revival of public and governmental interest in the dollars-and-deals whirligig of Hollywood. The focus so far has been on the major studios and a relative handful of theatrical films born of incredibly complex and highly suspicious contract arrangements. But it shouldn't be for-

gotten that these same studios . . . are the primary suppliers of programming to television. Purely in terms of quantity, those studios have a stranglehold on television. . . . The result may be an irritating pattern of imitation and production blandness, but the participants are evidently more concerned with minimizing risks than taking chances.

One key source of new ideas or more ambitious concepts is the independent producer. . . .

How does the independent compete with the majors? In a word, cautiously—by being as judicious and reliable as possible. . . .

. . . [the independent producer's] survival on the fringes is essential to the industry as a reasonable alternative to the over-researched and computerized pap. [23]

O'Connor here speaks to the problems facing the independent producer attempting to gain access to commercial television's exclusive club of program suppliers. Another issue is the independent's need for access to public television, the supposed "alternative" production and distribution outlet. As O'Connor has written on numerous occasions, all is not right in public TV land. Writing about the 1979 documentary "Home" produced by Global Village's John Reilly and Julie Gustafson, O'Connor focused on the successes and failures of public TV's relations with independents:

[Reilly and Gustafson] are prominent members of a diverse group of producers, scattered throughout the country, who are trying to break through the access barriers of both commercial and public television.

Public television, for its part, is bearing the brunt of protests by independents. Less powerful and less well-financed than the networks, the system is more vulnerable to assorted pressures.

This is particularly true at WNET-TV, Channel 13 in New York City, as O'Connor observed:

. . . clearly, WNET/13 is responding to angry complaints from several quarters. Highly organized pressures are one reason. But another is the fact that independents have provided the station with some of its best productions. From the early efforts of the TVTV group in covering political conventions to Downtown Community TV's portraits of Cuba and New York's Chinatown to Susan and Alan Raymond's

"The Police Tapes," the independents have been winning
both audiences and awards for public television. The second Carnegie Commission report [on the future of public
broadcasting in the U. S.] . . . and even the Corporation
for Public Broadcasting have recognized the importance
of these contributions. Things in general should be looking up for the independents; yet, curiously, more dissatisfaction is heard rumbling across the country. [24]

Examples of access problems abound. While Reilly and Gustafson's "Home" took 16 months to shoot and produce, it took the
producers two-and-one-half years to raise enough money to do the
project. In that instance, financing predominated over actual access
to production and postproduction editing equipment necessary to accomplish the project. Financing problems also played an important
role in an earlier independent project for PBS, but in that case the
financing difficulties seemed more closely tied to political issues.
The project was "Visions," a series aired on PBS in 1976 that was
produced by KCET-TV in Los Angeles and featured the teleplays of
writers new to television. According to "Visions" Executive Producer
Barbara Schultz, the series was originally scheduled for 36 original
productions with no strictures on length, made over a three-year period and aired weekly. However, the Corporation for Public Broadcasting soon cut back on funding, and the series was trimmed to 24
productions. O'Connor commented on the series:

> With its emphasis on the writer, its determination to give
> the writer's concerns top priority, "Visions" is sprinkled
> with language, themes and certain anti-establishment pos-
> tures that would hardly be welcomed on commercial tele-
> vision. Perhaps they have proven too sensitive for even
> public TV. [25]

What of the present and future of independent producers' ability
to gain access to public television production and distribution mechanisms? The direction of access is cloudly to say the least. In two recent essays, O'Connor surveys the difficulties raised by the access
issue. Writing about the tendency of public TV in recent years to
"play it safe" in its programming approach, O'Connor argues:

> Something is rotten in public television. . . . the distres-
> sing symptoms are scattered throughout the system. . . .
> public television has become the ward of the Establish-
> ment—of corporations that serve as key underwriters, of
> station boards consisting of influential members of the com-

munity, of politicians who can be instrumental in obtaining various governmental fundings, and of executives preoccupied with financing difficulties rather than with programming. It is hardly surprising, then, that the overall thrust of the system is toward "safe" products, the kind unlikely to provoke discomforting controversy. . . .

. . . the system has become a repository for nicely reassuring, non-minority, middle-class values and attitudes. Diversity of content is being sacrificed to policies of bureaucratic protectionism. . . .

. . . "What is not broadcast" directly concerns the newly militant independent producers who are either unable to penetrate the system or, upon getting in, are embittered by unexpected problems—inadequate financial compensation, arbitrary editing, poor scheduling or skimpy publicity. . . .

. . . Perhaps the central problem is insensitivity. If black viewers were pointedly neglected with the preemption [during the 1980 pledge week] of "American Short Story," [Ernest J. Gaines' "The Sky Is Gray," a story dealing with the problems of being black in the South] Irish-Americans could complain about Channel 13's deletion, in the weekend preceding St. Patrick's Day, of a "Camera Three" half-hour starring the Chieftans, the acclaimed Irish folk musicians. . . .

And so public television moves forward, dipping back into the past for Marlene Dietrich festivals and the like, and largely restricting the present to up-scale cultural events or Grand Ole Opry celebrations.

. . . Public television cannot keep insisting on serving only one part of the public, the part willing and able to make contributions and thereby exert varying degrees of control over content. [26]

When independent producers are able to get at least limited access to public TV, there is no guarantee the executive gatekeepers will not step in to ax a controversial production. O'Connor highlighted this problem in an essay on the new series "Independent Focus," which features works by 24 independent film and video producers:

. . . the setting of programming priorities has always thrown public television into a turmoil, and the next decade will probably bear witness to more of the same backbiting and infighting.

Meanwhile . . . the system continues to search anx-

iously for programming, producing some of its own and
acquiring much from outside sources. . . . And that
means having to come to terms with the increasingly vocal demands of independent producers. . . . There are
hundreds, perhaps thousands, of smaller producers working in film or video. Some charge that television's doors
are simply shut to new or controversial ideas. Others
have had their work broadcast, primarily on public television, but feel that the financial arrangements have been
woefully inadequate, putting them in the position of sub-
sidizing the system. . . .

WNET-TV in New York City has been reasonably open to independents
in the past few years. The latest example of WNET's access policy is
its coordination of the "Independent Focus" series. However, this series has opened another access controversy. O'Connor cited:

For the WNET project [Marc Weiss, who is assembling
the series] demanded and got an advisory panel of seven
persons to help in the selection of works. Channel 13 believes that this is the "first peer review panel for an acquisition series on public television."
. . . While the lineup reflects a variety of styles
and attitudes, the dominant thematic direction is clearly
sociopolitical. These are films making statements about
people and movements, many of them involving minori-
ties. . . .
But even this much of an advance in relations between the station and independents has created new and
serious tensions. It seems the advisory board's decisions were not final. Four of its recommended films
were vetoed by Channel 13 executives. . . . One of the
rejects was "A Comedy in Six Unnatural Acts," which
satirizes the stereotypes of lesbians held by the general
public. . . . Lesbian delegations have already taken their
protests to WNET's corporate offices, noting that the film
has been widely shown and reviewed favorably in Europe.
At last report, a coalition of several groups—women,
blacks, Hispanics, homosexuals and assorted filmmakers—was preparing to protest the rejection of all four
films and to demand that the role of the peer-review panel
be defined in terms of what power it has. [27]

There is a collision looming between public television executives
who are seemingly taking their service down a path similar to that of

the commercial networks in their search for larger audience and greater financial solvency and the independent producers who are trying to reach smaller specific minority audiences with programs more relevant to special group interests. Perhaps the goals of these two groups are not mutually exclusive. At a time when public television is trying to stand on its own as a viable, meaningful program service, the clash of ideologies may provide a healthy atmosphere for redefining the long-range goals of the service. But we must all be more than a little wary of the historical strength and persuasiveness of the dominant culture's ideology and not forget about the minority cultures' voices in the wilderness that deserve a public hearing. O'Connor, much to his credit as a writer about television, is one who apparently is not willing to permit those voices to disappear without a battle.

If public television's doors are closed to much of the work of independent film and video producers, they must turn to other distribution outlets for dissemination of their works. These outlets include both cable access channels now springing up around the country and traditional art gallery and museum exhibitions. Both these outlets are better suited to the esoteric work of artists aimed at specific minority audiences.

John O'Connor stands virtually alone among the group of television critics writing for general circulation newspapers in his coverage of such experimental video productions. One possible reason for O'Connor's focus on these works is that most avant-guarde video activity of some consequence is either produced in New York or is produced elsewhere and exhibited in New York on WNET-TV or in video gallery/theaters such as The Kitchen or Anthology Film and Video Archives. Thus, O'Connor has relatively easy access to these productions. It is not always convenient for him to get out and view these works because of his already heavy viewing load from regular broadcast productions, but he has shown in the past the motivation to at least make his readership aware of ongoing avant-garde video activities he considers to be significant.

Among the more esoteric video productions O'Connor has reviewed are Ed Emshwiller's "Pilobolus and Joan," shown on WNET-TV in 1974, the Image Union's coverage of the 1976 Democratic Convention in New York City for Manhattan Cable entitled "The Five Day Bicycle Race," and Video Free America's drama/documentary "The Continuing Story of Carel and Ferd," shown at The Kitchen in 1972.

Although O'Connor has said good things about those avant-garde video productions he believes offer significant contributions to the general television art form, he has held firm to his position that avant-garde video, like avant-garde film, has and will continue to have a very limited audience. When I asked him to elaborate on this conviction, he responded:

. . . I think it's <u>not</u> a popular thing. It's fine for Global
Village or some place like that to show it. Or have it in
the Paley museum over here [The Museum of Broadcasting in New York City] and have them available for people.
. . . A lot of it is experimental and a lot of it is boring.
There's people discovering the new electronic toy, and
they're fascinated by the images that they can create. It's
very reminiscent of . . . Cinema 16 of years ago that used
to show these little artsie films to small groups of people
who'd go, and their eyes would be <u>glazed</u> by the time there
was an end to all this nonsense. But it's important. I mean
out of all this comes certain developments that are then
absorbed into the mainstream. That's where it's important. So . . . you have a group like Downtown Community
TV, John Alpert's group, down in Chinatown, going to Cuba on their own and finally getting their material out on
Harrison Salisbury on Channel 13. And then they just recently did a thing on hospitals, medical care on Channel
13, WNET, that was excellent. As a narrow documentary
it was fantastic—good stuff, straightforward documentary.
So they've been absorbed. And the same with Michael Shamberg and TVTV. Michael Shamberg could be the next head
of CBS News. He's no longer the avant-garde.

The "mainstream" is obviously crucial to O'Connor, for that is
the locus of the great majority of his readership. It is important, however, that he notes the significance of the esoteric work as an influence on the mainstream. The notion of the esoteric eventually becoming the conventional mainstream standard is a fact of life in all the
arts, and this process of assimilation ultimately hinges on the avail-
ability of highly specialized dissemination mechanisms such as those
video galleries and cable access channels mentioned by O'Connor.

The preceding discussion of O'Connor's writings and conversations about television illuminates his wide-ranging focus on television
art. Yet one must not ignore the motivations that underlie the critic's
posture. Thus we must finally turn to O'Connor's perception of his
role and influence as a writer about television. Does O'Connor perceive himself in the role of critic "of record"?

O'CONNOR ON BEING A TELEVISION CRITIC

O'Connor is quick to note that his primary role as a writer
about television is that of an "objective" commentator on television
works and the organizations and individuals who create and show the

works to audiences. He separates this evaluative function from the function of a "reporter" who, according to O'Connor, must constantly interview those people who are intimately involved in the day-to-day activities of program production, distribution, and/or regulation. When asked about his role as a writer about television, O'Connor responded:

> When I came [to the New York Times], it was with the condition that I would not combine the job of reporter and critic and I think . . . there's the possibility of an inherent conflict of interest between the two functions. Not only that you might play off one against the other, the critic and reporter saying . . . you give me an exclusive and I'll review your program. . . . But a reporter has to deal differently with the industry. A reporter has to cultivate contacts, do a lot of socializing . . . and meet people on a different level than a critic. . . . I try to stay as independent as possible. I don't want to interview, do celebrity interviews. I don't want to know about it.

O'Connor feels his position as a writer about television for the New York Times gives him a certain amount of power to influence the directions of television in this country. However, he adds that this power rests more with his newspaper than with himself. His awareness of this power has to a degree tempered his writings:

> . . . the Times has never told me . . . what even to review or not to review. I'm strictly on my own. . . . The Times does have a clout . . . I mean it's not John O'Connor who has clout, it's John O'Connor writing for the Times that has clout, and I do tend to shy away from being overly vicious towards somebody, because it wrecks careers. I mean it can make programs in some cases, and it can destroy programs. Mr. Paley likes to read nice things about himself in the Times. He pays very close attention to reviews. . . . I've got that kind of exposure that I'm not going to be flip, I try not to be overly flip about what I'm writing about. . . . I just got a thing from a California Congressman. That article on suggesting that commercial networks give some money to public television—he entered that in the Congressional Record. . . . I'm also on a news service [New York Times News Service], and I'm picked up by sometimes as many as between 90 and 120 papers from San Juan to Canada, so I've got a kind of national audience which also skews the type of things I will review.

O'Connor is not so brash to believe that either his own personal influence or that of the New York Times is all-pervasive. In fact, he admits, there are many instances in which what he says will have little, if any, impact on the success or failure of a program. He told me specifically:

> . . . the Times is read. It has that impact. . . . and people get very upset about what they see or they're delighted . . . about what they read in the Times about television. And I know it's read in Washington, I know it's read in the Corporation [for Public Broadcasting]. They do pay attention to what's been said. And they worry about what being said. . . . the producer of "Family" for instance . . . said that my reviews saved the series. . . . I mean, there's [only] so much influence you can have. "All In The Family" at its height—I could have written a bad review of "All In The Family" week after week after week and it wouldn't have made the slightest difference; you know it still would have been a hit. But there are marginal things that I know you can feel the impact, or the smaller programs, the video programs. . . . I get letters from readers saying "Oh thank you; I never would have turned this on." So that kind of influence. I'm thankful, you know, who the hell wants the influence of opening and closing a show, which I think is going out anyway. I don't think the Times has the influence it used to have on Broadway or films . . . to make or break a film. I don't think anyone does that any more. There are too many other media things happening around.

Finally, O'Connor talked with me about specific instances in which his columns have produced strong reactions from readers:

> . . . the final Elvis Presley special . . . was made just about five weeks before his death. And I wrote . . . a fairly short piece . . . saying how pathetic it was. . . . I didn't mean it viciously, I mean it was pathetic that he had reached the stage of his career and looked dreadful. He was kind of puffy and fat and a belly hanging over and he could hardly bend and . . . I found it painful to watch. . . . The Elvis Presley clubs around the country bombarded me with letters and pictures they'd taken of Elvis and every kook in the country who had seen all of his concerts. . . . Tony Brown of "Black Journal" mounted a letter writing campaign against one of my reviews. I called

him a racist. This was after I had given him many good
reviews. . . . But he had some bunch of—they were discussing religion and the whole theory that Christianity
was black, Christ was black and all this. It was just tak-
en for granted. . . . They were making all of these . . .
offhand remarks very casually, and I just happened to
tune in to it at home and I wrote an article saying what
the hell was he talking about and what is he supposed to
be up to and all this. He called a press conference the
next day and denounced me as a tool of the Zionist press,
and then had a letter writing campaign set up with a group
called Friends of Black Journal and they sent several hun-
dred letters, but I'm not influenced by that kind of thing,
so you just roll with it. I mean half my mail is telling me
that I'm an idiot and half is telling me that I'm a genius,
so it evens itself out.

Thus O'Connor perceives his influence as a writer about television stemming in large measure from his position with an influential newspaper, the New York Times, and a widely distributed news
service produced by the Times. While he believes he has the power
to influence the success or failure of certain "marginal" programs
or video works (i. e. , those about which the audience was either previously unaware or about which they have yet to form a solid judgment), he also recognizes that a program that has won substantial
viewer loyalty will not likely be affected by any negative evaluations
he may make.

CONCLUSIONS

A few years ago David Littlejohn criticized that

John O'Connor's appointment to fill the other half of
[Jack] Gould's role, as TV critic, marked a distinct im-
provement in this function. O'Connor writes better, thinks
more interestingly, and seems less committed to televi-
sion-as-it-is. On the whole, however, he seems hesitant
to judge and fits in perhaps too easily with the Times' un-
exciting gallery of careful, relatively unadventurous critics past and present, all of whom have been read by producers with an attention beyond their due. [28]

An evaluation of O'Connor's writings about television supports
Littlejohn's contentions that O'Connor is indeed more articulate, a

more interesting theoretician, and more of an activist than was Gould. However, Littlejohn's assessment of O'Connor as "hesitant to judge," and a "relatively unadventurous" commentator is questionable.

Generally, this survey of O'Connor's writings about television for the New York Times since 1971 finds him to be instead relatively quick to judge, especially when his judgments are directed at the productions aired on commercial network television. Until recently, O'Connor was more cautious in his evaluations; the past two or three years has seen him become more and more upset over public TV's reluctance to admit and encourage the work of some of the more esoteric independent television producers.

Littlejohn's notion that O'Connor is "relatively unadventurous" can be countered by an examination of O'Connor's writings about video experimentation in which he praises those video works he believes to be breaking new aesthetic ground in the art form. Not only does he praise such work, but he also advocates the production of additional experimental work that would build on the existing works.

O'Connor is articulate and obviously well-versed in the aesthetic of drama, and when dealing with this form he is on firm footing. He seems equally confident about his analyses of "popular" television genres such as comedy, action-adventure, entertainment specials, and advertisements. His evaluations of these popular genres occasionally have drifted into what might be called a "culture elitist" stance, rejecting the genres on the whole as unworthy of serious consideration, whereas we shall see later that these genres can be mined for deeper structures that tell us much about the culture in which they are produced.

While O'Connor has singled out and frequently given positive evaluations of avant-garde video works, he has not to date attempted to situate their significance in the overall avant-garde video movement or to explicate parameters for the movement. Further, he has not to date adequately discussed the unique characteristics that separate television from other art forms such as film or theater, nor has he delineated how, for example, certain combinations of television, film, theater, and dance might open new aesthetic vistas hitherto unexplored. That is not meant to single O'Connor out from the pack—for such theoretical explorations have to date been very scarce in the dialogue about television.

While O'Connor is generally an insightful writer about individual works of television art and has obviously concerned himself with exploring many of the larger questions regarding the pervasiveness of television in our cultural life, the pressure of three or four deadlines a week plus the demands of his readership for timely information have prevented him from writing more profound essays on television. An evaluation of his columns to date suggests that he is indeed intellectually capable of writing such essays. One would hope that in the near future, he will find the luxury of time to begin to tackle the very difficult conceptual questions he has raised about television in our lives.

NOTES

1. John J. O'Connor, "TV: Divine Miss M, Boundless Energy," New York Times, 7 December 1977, p. C30.

2. John J. O'Connor, "'Live from Lincoln Center' Has Found Its Focus," New York Times, 11 July 1976, sec. 2, p. D21.

3. Ibid.

4. Ibid.

5. Ibid.

6. Ibid.

7. Ibid.

8. John J. O'Connor, "There's Gold in That There Trash," New York Times, 28 March 1971, sec. 2, p. D21.

9. Ibid.

10. John J. O'Connor, "Why Can't the Networks Help Support PBS?" New York Times, 30 October 1977, sec. 2, p. D35.

11. John J. O'Connor, "The Granddaddy of 'Em All, 'The Forsyte Saga,' Returns," New York Times, 3 July 1977, sec. 2, p. D21.

12. John J. O'Connor, "Scandinavian TV Argues Well for Imported Fare," New York Times, 17 July 1977, sec. 2, p. D25.

13. Ibid.

14. John J. O'Connor, "New Play Series Long on Talent, Short on Funds," New York Times, 17 October 1976, sec. 2, p. D31.

15. O'Connor, "Scandanavian TV," p. D25.

16. John J. O'Connor, "Trollope's Novels Stylishly Serialized," New York Times, 30 January 1977, sec. 2, p. D29.

17. O'Connor, "There's Gold," p. D21.

18. John J. O'Connor, "Competition Makes Networks Go Rigid," New York Times, 26 September 1976, sec. 2, p. D29.

19. John J. O'Connor, "Has Archie Run His Course?" New York Times, 23 September 1979, sec. 2, p. D35.

20. Horace Newcomb, TV: The Most Popular Art (New York: Doubleday, Anchor Press, 1974), pp. 42-43.

21. O'Connor, "Why Can't Networks Help?," p. D35.

22. Ibid.

23. John J. O'Connor, "The Importance of the Independent," New York Times, 19 February 1978, sec. 2, p. D31.

24. John J. O'Connor, "The Squeeze on Independents," New York Times, 4 November 1979, sec. 2, p. D39.

25. O'Connor, "New Play Series," p. D31.

26. John J. O'Connor, "Should Public Television Be Playing It Safe?" New York Times, 23 March 1980, sec. 2, pp. D35, D38.

27. John J. O'Connor, "Public TV and Independents—Wary Partners," New York Times, 27 January 1980, sec. 2, p. D31.

28. David Littlejohn, "Thoughts on Television Criticism," in Television as a Cultural Force, eds. Richard Adler and Douglass Cater (New York: Praeger, 1976), pp. 158-59.

4

BERNIE HARRISON:
FOUNDING FATHER OF
THE "OLD GUARD"

Bernie Harrison, television editor of the Washington Star, is somewhat of a grandfather among journalists in the television-reviewing profession. He ventured into the thickets of television reviewing when the medium was very young and "live," and like many of his notable contemporaries such as Jack Gould, John Crosby, Lawrence Laurent, Harry Harris of the Philadelphia Inquirer, and Dwight Newton of the San Francisco Chronicle, he stayed with the medium as it "matured." Few individuals have a better perspective from which to judge the changes television has undergone during the past 34 years.

Harrison was born in Washington, D. C. in 1916. He graduated from Wilson Teachers College in Washington in 1938 with a Bachelor of Science degree in education, majoring in history. Between 1937 and 1939, Harrison wrote a radio column for the Washington Morning Herald. From 1939 until 1941 he was the Herald's education editor, and from 1941 until 1943, when he enlisted in the army, wrote film and theater criticism for the Washington Times-Herald. Upon his return from the war in 1944, Harrison resumed his post as film critic for the Times-Herald, and between 1950 and 1954 wrote a television and radio column for the paper. When the Times-Herald was sold to the Washington Post in 1954, Harrison moved over to the Washington Daily News to write a television and radio column for that paper. In 1955, he joined the Washington Evening Star and since then has written about television for that daily newspaper (now called the Washington Star).

Remaining on the TV beat for 30 years and writing about the medium for three dailies during that time has required a greater than normal amount of dedication. When I asked Harrison how he became interested in writing about television in the first place, he responded:

> . . . I was as interested in [television] as the ordinary
> person was. I had come across television in a nearby

restaurant when I went out to dinner at night, watching
shows while I was at dinner, . . . and as I watched it I
found some very interesting shows that I enjoyed, and
so it was a very easy thing to move into the concept of
writing about something that is part of your life. And
while I didn't quite buy all of the dreams of the dreamers for television, I had read about it. I had read Jules
Henry's book Culture Against Man. It's one of the great
books, and he really lined up everything for us . . . so
I thought, well, I worked for a newspaper—I'd be happy
to work any place for a newspaper . . . we're not what
we used to be, television has replaced us in many cases—
but I loved working for a newspaper, and this was a new
assignment, and I took it on with that sort of interest and
enthusiasm. We hadn't developed color yet. We had a
whole lot of problems to lick. But I liked it. I saw mostly
the potential. I didn't see the harm yet. . . . I think the
years have borne out Mr. Henry. I sometimes refer to
[Culture Against Man], and I hope that somebody will go
to the library and pick it out and look at it. . . . It just
thrills you when you come across something exceptional.
And every now and then even in television today you run
across that.

Jules Henry's book, which Harrison so justifiably praised, was
written in 1963 and predicted the ascendency of a "pecuniary philosophy" in our industrialized society—a state of mind in which the desire
to acquire goods would predominate over traditional human values
such as meaningful interpersonal relationships. Thus, we as individual members of the society would come to place greater importance
on wanting more and more than on being more and more. In our interview, Harrison linked that idea to television's historical development:

> . . . I think that we have been fighting a losing battle as
> long as we have only commercial television. . . . Radio
> went down the tubes long before television did. In 1938
> [the Federal Communications Commission] had to come
> out with a Blue Book about all of the problems, because
> [radio] had settled down into the same sort of program-
> ming ruts. Of course, they promised faithfully this
> wouldn't happen with television, but it did. General Sarn-
> off promised it, but Sarnoff was important enough to have
> "NBC Opera" on five or six shows per season. He was
> important enough to see to it that these shows were done.

. . . For a while we thought the magazine concept of advertising would eliminate the individual advertiser who controlled everything, but television today is all magazine [advertising]. Very few individual sponsors can afford one show. And that was really not the answer. And that is why Pat [Weaver, former president of NBC] went to "The Today Show," "The Tonight Show," and "The Home Show" hoping to get away from that sort of sponsor-agency control of content. You see . . . some solutions were really not solutions. They were temporary things and the problem was basic. We needed a whole new way of backing shows, of putting programs on the air in which business was not the fundamental concern. . . . the profits in it are <u>incredible.</u> How much money does William S. Paley want? As Edward R. Murrow said in 1958, which I keep referring to quite often, "Where is it written in stone that the profits have to increase every year?"

Despite Harrison's obvious frustration with many of the directions commercial television has taken in the United States over the years, he has chosen to continue writing about it. When I asked him why, he was quick to answer:

. . . part of our function is to educate the public into realizing that we're being shortchanged if that's all we're going to get. . . . there's a better way to deal with this great, marvelous medium. What it can do for us is incredible, but it's not [doing it]. . . . even in public television, which in many cases has forgotten its function of education, of teaching, of bringing us to master teachers. There is no reason why great teachers should be available only to students at whatever. Let's <u>see</u> them. So this is the whole aspect of it. If I have helped people understand that, then we've contributed something.

Harrison thus drew what he perceived to be the fundamental battle lines between the TV entrepreneurs on the one hand, and the television critic as advocate for cultural uplifting through televised "education" broadly defined on the other hand. Ultimately Harrison's focus on the inside battles between television's creative and management communities frames much of his more significant commentary on the medium. We will examine Harrison's writings about television in terms of that critical theme as well as the notions he has developed over the years about the value of popular television entertainment in our culture.

HARRISON ON TELEVISION

Harrison, like most journalists writing for daily newspapers on a regular basis, has always had to confront the pressures of both limited space for his columns and the daily deadline. However, unlike writers such as John O'Connor who have colleagues on their paper's TV beat who handle the nuts and bolts repertorial work, Harrison is representative of the vast majority of television critics who have run one-person operations (although in recent years Harrison has had a small staff of reviewer-reporters working for him at the Star). The multipurpose critics write the program reviews, do the personality interviews, and dig into the behind-the-scenes machinations of the television industry. Because of the necessity of performing this variety of tasks, the actual program pre-reviews and reviews of these television critics must invariably suffer to some extent. Such critics on the whole are referred to as reviewers by those who concern themselves with classifying types of criticism. John L. Wright, writing for the Journal of Popular Culture, aptly described the characteristics of and the dilemma confronting the television reviewer:

> . . . all of us deal with the What of entertainment programs. We flip through the TV Guide making viewing judgments on the basis of capsule plots and anonymous stars. If we wish to make more informed decisions about our viewing, however, we must rely on the reviewer. . . . the most available criticism of entertainment programming is found in the columns of the reviewers employed by most major newspapers and many magazines. Reviewers are as divergent in quality and style as the programs they view. Many TV reviewers rely solely on network press releases and industry rumor for their information. Some reviewers may be co-opted by the networks. And the pressures of time and space sometimes lead even the best of reviewers to a simple "I liked it" or "I didn't like it" backed up with a few quick observations about the theme of a particular show or comments about the performances. . . . Ideally the reviewer is a trained and fully conscious observer who can point out to us more than we ordinarily see.

But the reviewer's medium does not allow for much in-depth analysis of television programming.[1] Through the decades Harrison has supplemented his program review activities with numerous in-depth reports on the personality conflicts and administrative problems that inevitably plague any creative endeavor which must rely on a team concept. These reports, far from being of the "star-hype" variety, have enabled Harrison's readers to better comprehend the process of making television programs and, more importantly, have helped those readers understand the meaning of what they don't see on their screens. Harrison fits easily into John Wright's concept of the "trained and fully conscious observer."

Because Harrison has been writing regularly about television since 1950, it was necessary to sample his columns. Therefore his reviews, as evaluated in this volume, include those written in 1956-57, 1961-62, 1966-67, 1971-72, and 1976-77. All these columns appeared in either the Washington Evening Star or the Washington Star.

In 1956-57, Harrison wrote a column entitled "On The Air" that ran Monday through Friday in the Washington Evening Star. This column both reviewed television broadcasts and on occasion discussed larger institutional questions including station license renewals and general programming trends. He also wrote a short piece and answered letters from viewers in the Washington Sunday Star's "Tele-Vue" magazine, a weekly listing of television broadcasts.

The 1961-62 period saw a continuation of Harrison's "On The Air" Monday through Friday columns. "On The Air" also ran in the Sunday Star's "TV Magazine," an updated version of "TeleVue." Harrison continued to answer viewer letters in the "TV Mailbag" section of the "TV Magazine."

In 1966-67, "On The Air" appeared Monday through Friday as in the previous periods sampled. During September 1966, Harrison wrote brief reviews of new series episodes in addition to the "On The Air" columns that concurrently provided overviews of programming trends. Harrison also wrote "Sunday Previews" in the "Weekender" magazine that appeared in the Saturday edition of the Evening Star. "On The Air" and "TV Mailbag" continued in Sunday's "TV Magazine."

In 1971-72, Harrison continued his basic 1966-67 format. "On The Air" now also appeared in Saturday's "Weekender" magazine. Clearly, during this entire 1955-1972 period Harrison was a very busy television critic.

By 1976-77, a major shift in format had occurred. The Washington Evening Star had become the Washington Star. Harrison's "On The Air" columns, which frequently explored larger television questions, had been eliminated and replaced with his "TV Tonight" column (Monday through Friday) and "TV Today" column (Saturday and Sunday). These columns contained abbreviated pre-reviews of a number of works that were to be aired the evening or the day the column appeared. Harrison wrote one or two larger pieces of reportage, program review, or personality profile per week. He also wrote an occasional "Comment" on television in the Sunday "Calendar" section. The Sunday magazine "TV This Week" contained the week's television

listings in addition to short pieces of reportage and reviews from the
Star's staff persons writing about television under Harrison's super-
vision.

If Harrison wasn't busy enough prior to the format change in
1974, the new format seemed destined to limit the time he had to do
long pieces on programs and issues even more than previously. When
he spoke to me about the change, I detected at least a bit of remorse:

> As you've undoubtedly noticed, the scope of my activities
> has changed quite a bit. This particular column that I'm
> writing now was conceived by Jim Bellows, who was the
> executive editor of the Star, and is now the executive edi-
> tor of the Star, and is now the executive editor of the Los
> Angeles Herald-Examiner. . . . My column now, since I
> began it, is being carried by the Kansas City Star, and
> Atlanta Journal, and the Chicago Daily News. . . . The
> function of this column is to provide as much useful in-
> formation as someone can who knows the field about what
> is on, actually on television that particular night. . . .
> This is not an essay-type column. I write essays when
> the occasion, the opportunity arises and I have the time.
> But turning out a column of this sort, seven columns a
> week is a major operation.

As one examines a representative sampling of Harrison's columns over the years, three characteristics stand out: first, his attempts to provide, when warranted, economical, balanced opinions
of the programs and personalities he is discussing; second, his occasional unrestricted praise or vehement condemnation of a program
about which he feels very strongly; and third, the dry wit that marks
his style. He writes as one would expect of a person who has "been
around" the scene for a long time. It's almost as if he poses the rhe-
torical question to his readership "So what else is new?" This is not
to say that Harrison doesn't take TV seriously. He does. Rather, his
style is marked with the feeling of the experienced grandfather—there
is that certain knowing chuckle that can be refreshing as well as in-
formative.

Certain examples from Harrison's columns illustrate his stylistic characteristics. Harrison's short reviews clearly point to his
sparing use of descriptive prose. Of the premiere of the now-famous
science fiction series "Star Trek" in 1966, Harrison wrote: " 'Star
Trek' (NBC). Grim, determined, very snappy-looking science-fiction,
but the story leading up to the monster has been done a dozen times,
11 of them on 'Twilight Zone.' Bill Shatner stars."[2] That same 1966
season saw the premiere of the super-hero series "The Green Hor-

net' (Friday, ABC-7). The car is an absolute beauty, the effects were fine, but the opening episode was marred by a dragging story line and poorly staged fights, two major flaws in 'Super Hero' scripts. The 'Hornet' needs more sting. "[3] These reviews, although quite brief, do present balanced evaluations of the programs, noting their major strengths and weaknesses.

In other short reviews Harrison takes a very firm evaluative posture—either positively or negatively—praising or condemning the program under scrutiny without reservation. For example, Harrison had only the highest praise for a 1972 Jacques Cousteau special: "The Jacques Cousteau special Monday (ABC-7), was one of his most irresistible, thanks to his lovable subjects, the gentle, Schmoo-like hyacinth-chomping manatees, imperiled by thoughtless vacationers in Florida's Blue Springs. . . . Reaction should be terrific."[4] On the other hand, Harrison had nothing but complaints about the 1966 premiere of the situation comedy "The Monkees":

> Every now and then a TV series comes along that is so monumentally bad, so palpably derivative, so incredible that it beggars the mind. The last such show was "Gilligan's Island." Last night NBC topped that one with a numbing new half-hour called "The Monkees."
> . . . Everything was borrowed for the opener: slapstick trips and falls, the balloons of dialogue from "Batman" and even the sexy eating scene from "Tom Jones." It played like a pinwheel that refused to stop.[5]

Here one gets a quick, forthright evaluation without frills—the "basic"; at the same time one gets little more than "I liked it" or "I didn't like it," although in the case of "The Monkees," Harrison's wry humor offers clues to that program's ineffectiveness as a poor amalgamation of other television genres.

Harrison's longer reviews of individual programs or series follow the basic pattern of the short reviews—sparing use of descriptive and evaluative prose—but they add elements of plot, action, and description of characterization. An example of this longer review format is Harrison's discussion of the 1966 spy melodrama spin-off "The Girl From UNCLE":

> Last night's new (?) show was a spinoff from "The Man From U.N.C.L.E.," called "The Girl From U.N.C.L.E." The girl is played by Stephanie Powers and she has one of those forgettable stage names, April, Dancer, or Donder, or something like that, and her assignment on the opening show was to hand over a dachshund to the

health authorities on a Greek island that was carrying
fleas that carried an antidote to a deadly new Thrush
drug called apathy.

Viewers who watch "Man From," should like "Girl
From." They'll like Noel Harrison, too, as the man who
accompanies the girl from. Barry Shear directed crisply
and made imaginative use of the sprightly Greek dancing
to give one of the usual fight scenes some sparkle. [6]

While Harrison here seems rather disenchanted with the general characteristics of the spy melodrama formula, he does make an effort to
recognize a directorial effort that in some ways transcends the conventions of that genre. Such special attention given to television directors is unusual. In another context, Harrison, perhaps due to the
rushed qualities of the daily review, overlooked the rather strange
construction "to hand over a dachshund to the health authorities on a
Greek island that was carrying fleas."

Another long review of television serial in a genre closer to
Harrison's aesthetic sensibilities, the drama—or in this case the
docudrama—shows his ability to incorporate discussion of additional
production values such as dramatic pacing and cinematography. The
docudrama received was the 1972 BBC production "The Search for
the Nile":

As chance would have it, the President's message last
night had to be placed by NBC-4 between the two-hour
BBC episodes, and to be fair about it, the leap from Sir
Richard Burton's search for the Nile to the White House
search for peace, and back again, was disconcerting.

I was just beginning to warm to the BBC documentary, after a languidly paced opening that tried to set the
scene and introduce the principals, including the colorful
adventurer, Burton. That part, and it was quite a chunk,
came off badly, proving that the British Broadcasting
Corporation can botch a few, too, like ordinary networks.

But those outdoor location shots in Africa, particularly the sun setting on Lake Tanganyika, were stunning.

Kenneth Haigh, and John Quentin, as Burton and
his associate, Speake, dominated the first two episodes
and communicated their dislike for each other clearly,
and very little else. [7]

Again, Harrison exhibits a desire to be objective in his evaluation,
praising the cinematography and criticizing both the dramatic pacing
and characterization in the production.

On occasion Harrison, given the time, will delve more deeply into the aesthetic design of an individual television work. An example is his review of the televised opera "Queen of Spades," aired in 1972 on PBS. "Queen of Spades" was a television adaptation of Tschaikovsky's opera of the same name, which in turn was taken from Pushkin's story. Kirk Browning, the highly praised director of the "Live From Lincoln Center" telecasts now a regular part of PBS's programming, directed the opera for television. Reviewing the production, Harrison wrote:

> . . . whereas the . . . earlier variations on Pushkin's theme were, each in its way, entities of artistic point, this last version, seen Monday night on Channel 26 and to be repeated Saturday, is a botch.
> The underlying orchestral music is Tschaikovsky's but much of the vocal line is spurious, added merely to accommodate a libretto that bears almost no resemblance to the original. . . . to try to adapt music to dramatic situations for which it was not intended was an attempt as foolish as the result is ridiculous.
> The acting and directing are for the most part so stupid as to be beneath contempt and beyond irony.

Harrison added:

> As I have said about "Tales of Hoffman," television has the opportunity to be our best producer of popular and inexpensive opera. It already has the mechanical techniques available, what it needs now are directors with some slight sense of theater. [8]

While Harrison in this review discusses the complicated aesthetic structures of opera as both music and theater and its relationship to the television aesthetic, one would hope to find even more specific discussion of concepts posed in the review. How specifically was the dramatic structure of the opera changed for its television adaptation? Who imposed the changes and why were they imposed? What specific relationships exist between television technology and "popular" opera that would make television the "best producer" of such operatic works? One may also wonder why Harrison rates Browning so poorly as a television director when critics such as John O'Connor find him to be an "extremely intelligent" director (see Chapter 3). Two possibilities emerge: first, Browning may have been in the early stages of formulating his television aesthetic when Harrison reviewed "Queen of Spades"; second, reasonable critics will differ. Nevertheless, more elaboration by Harrison on these aspects of the production would enable his readership to formulate a more articulate television aesthetic. The concepts raised by Harrison in this column, especially the notion of television as an adapter of existing works of art conceived in other art forms, are important areas for discussion; but that discussion cannot be done justice in a relatively short takeout.

When I asked Harrison if he would agree with my assessment that his best columns were written about music, dance, and drama on television, he answered:

> Well, I've always loved the drama. I think that's possibly because of my background in reviewing the theater and having been around for so long, and my affection for the dramas of the early fifties. . . . This is the way to tackle subjects of the day, not within a sitcom framework where you have to laugh. Where you can be serious, where you can be light, where you can be amusing, where you can be whatever the script, the idea, calls for without being restricted to a series format and trying to fit ideas to particular characters. Although the "Mary Tyler Moore Show" has done a very good job through the years, that was really an exception. [With] "All in the Family" . . . I still have my original doubts about the show. I think Archie is a lot too popular for my taste. He's got to be likeable or you wouldn't watch the damn thing from week to week. You're not going to watch somebody who drives you up the wall. And bigots drive you up the wall. That's the essential contradiction of that kind of show.

I sensed that Harrison had become more cynical in his reviews of standard television programs in recent years. When I asked him if this was so, he replied:

> So much of television is bad now that it seems difficult to work up that sort of anger about individual shows [like "The Monkees"]. I reserve my anger now for the collective programming of the networks, which I think is abysmal. CBS had Silverman in his springtime, ABC had him in his summer, and now NBC has got him in his fall. Popular programs, popular programmers who really operate by gut instinct, what do they like? If it works with them, they say, "O. K. " They have a period of time when they're right up with it, and when things all seem to fall into place for them. And then the fads and the perception changes and they don't change with it, and suddenly they're not the hot

shots any more. . . . I've come to the conclusion that
the only way we're going to get better programming is
through public TV, and I keep hammering away at the
quality shows.

Harrison seems to take special pleasure in discussing programming trends in his columns. His many years of experience as a professional observer of television's shifts in programming direction lend
credibility to his observations. An example of his writing on programming trends is a four-part series he wrote in September 1966 on the
"specials," in which he began his discussion with a definition of the
term:

What makes a special a special? The three men who have
the most say so over what America's millions will watch
in the way of TV entertainment are Michael Dann, of CBS,
Leonard Goldberg, of ABC . . . and Mort Werner, of
NBC, and they are in seeming agreement. A special is a
show that has to have a concept that is distinctive from
normal fare and is staffed by a creative group carefully
assembled to produce something which is truly different. [9]

Harrison divided "entertainment specials" into four general
categories: drama, e. g. , "Hallmark Hall of Fame"; star specials,
e. g. , Bob Hope and Perry Como shows; music, ballet, and variety;
and cultural productions, e. g. , National Geographic documentaries
and the Miss America Beauty Pageants. [10] Not included in these categories were sports and news/public affairs productions.
        In a discussion of why he believed specials were making a come-
back in the mid-1960s, Harrison cited the onset of satellite television,
the growth of educational television, and the UHF boom brought about
by the all-channel receiver bill as factors contributing to what a 1966
Louis Harris poll found to be a boycott of commercial network television series program viewing by the better educated, higher income
families. Sound familiar? Harrison observed:

A few years ago, the networks didn't have to worry. They
could focus on that great mass blob on the bell-curve of
the national I.Q. , buy all the surveys they needed showing the people like TV better than ever, and rake in the
constantly spiraling profits. But now, coming up hard on
the horizon, is an alternative. Network TV is no longer
the only wheel in town. [11]

Harrison's 1966 discussion of alternative programming sources sounds much like the pronouncements of the technocrats of the present day. Equally familiar was Harrison's observation that there existed in 1966 a "schizophrenic split in programming, the series for the masses, the specials for a balance including the leadership element. . . ."[12] Harrison concluded that this balance would not settle for the run-of-the-mill series:

> TV may have been a "vast wasteland" . . . but even within that wasteland, there were fine moments of drama and high purpose—a Shakespearean "Age of Kings" series imported from the B. B. C. . . or the network coverage of astronauts and other news events. The wasteland of weekly comic strips is still with us, but that UHF explosion and the technical developments point to a diversity of programming that hopefully may enhance viewing prospects for the educated or even modestly schooled. Whether "The Year of the Specials" is a flurry of action signifying nothing is up to you to decide. [13]

In retrospect, 1966—"The Year of the Specials"—seemed to signify that undercurrents of viewer dissatisfaction with various series and serial entertainment formulas were surfacing. The Norman Lear revolution and the rapid growth of public broadcasting in this country were yet to occur. The country was beginning to realize it was in throes of a major shift in political and cultural consensus. College students were beginning to organize about such issues as free speech and the war, but TV was still spoon-feeding us "The Beverly Hillbillies," "Green Acres," "The Monkees," and other middle-landscape programs in an attempt to wash our troubles down the drain. A number of critical observers of television programming have indicated that TV seems to lag about five years behind the culture, thus acting as a reinforcing agent for the previous cultural stance. In a sense, in the mid-1960s, TV was carrying forward the age of optimism spawned in the Kennedy years at a time when the New Frontier was rapidly losing its credibility. Did those more educated Americans really want significance? For Harrison, as for many of his "Old Guard" colleagues on the TV beat, hope sprang eternal.

Harrison's commentary on the larger institutional and cultural contexts in which television works are produced can be divided into inside information on the internal activities of broadcast organizations, and comments on local stations' general performance as it relates to perceived community needs.

In his early writings, Harrison often conveyed predictions of industry executives about institutional trends in commercial broadcasting. For example, in 1956 Harrison wrote:

> The word for the oncoming video year—and this is Albert
> McCleery, a veteran video hand and producer of NBC's
> Matinee Theater, speaking—is simply "incredible."
>
> . . . McCleery, one of the first top directors to
> shift westward [to Hollywood] believes this trend is in-
> evitable.
>
> "When the talent holds the upper hand, they prefer
> California. They like to live there and they can pick up a
> quick buck in the movies."[14]

While this prediction may seem mundane in light of subsequent
events, which of course bore out the prediction, when the column was
written, the westward shift was of paramount importance because it
signaled the end of "live" drama produced by the networks in New
York studios and marked the beginning of the Hollywood film production companies' takeover of television entertainment through the creation of a giant telefilm industry in Hollywood. Harrison would come
to view this watershed year with a good deal of remorse; but at the
time the movement did not appear so ominous.

In a more recent column, Harrison explored organizational con-
siderations behind the decline of American broadcast documentary
production:

> Julian Goodman, NBC's president, was in Hollywood re-
> cently imploring production executives to hold the line on
> costs, calling on them to exercise "more self-restraint,
> discipline and efficiency" to seek new ways of making
> shows. It cannot be said that Goodman says one thing in
> Hollywood, and another in New York.
>
> For example, coming up Tuesday . . . are the first
> two sections of the BBC documentary, "The Search for the
> Nile," a six-part series in all which James Mason nar-
> rates. Ten years ago (in October 1962), NBC was pre-
> senting its own documentary on "The River Nile," pro-
> duced by its leading house documentarian, Lou Hazam,
> now in retirement. I don't know what NBC paid BBC for
> its six-part series, but I've a hunch it cost a lot less than
> the production price tag put on Hazam's show ten years
> ago, even with inflation.

Harrison concluded:

> Cutting down on public affairs and documentaries, which
> all the networks are doing, is one way of holding the cost
> line, but I doubt if that way will exhilarate the local talent,

producers, writers, directors and cameramen, many of
whom were riffed long ago from the payroll. [15]

Harrison spoke further of the impact of broadcast executive decision making on the dramatic and documentary creative communities
in our interview. Our discussion centered on NBC's Lou Hazam, for
whom Harrison has the greatest respect:

> . . . many many years ago when [the British] only had
> public television, BBC, before they started commercial
> [television], they were importing our shows, and they
> were embarrassed by some of the things we were doing
> that they weren't doing. But this was the fifties when tel-
> evision hadn't quite settled, when they had cultural docu-
> mentaries on television which they don't have any more.
> NBC retired Lou Hazam who's got a room full of prizes,
> and who lives here in Silver Spring [Maryland]. They re-
> tired him, they had no budget for him any more. The last
> thing he had proposed was to go to King Tut's tomb and do
> a story on the twenty-fifth anniversary of the reopening.
> This was about a year or a year-and-a-half prior to the
> King Tut exhibit coming here. What a marvelous thing
> that would have been for the network. But they claimed
> they had spent too much money covering the McGovern
> campaign in Florida and had nothing left for him, so they
> retired him. . . .

The irony of a television network killing timeless "cultural documentary" because of emphemeral public affairs pressures is not easy to
accept, as evidenced by Harrison's justified bitterness in the Hazam
case.

Harrison has devoted numerous columns to the Washington,
D. C. , local broadcast stations' general performance. One example
of this type of institutional commentary was a column he wrote on the
United Broadcasting Company's operation of WOOK-TV, Channel 14,
and a radio station, both in Washington. Harrison's column appeared
in 1966 as United's broadcast licenses were being challenged at the
FCC by Washington Community Broadcasting Company and Washington Civic Television, Inc. : Harrison commented on the dispute:

> What it reads like is an indictment by the community
> against the operation of the stations.
> . . . Why don't [the challengers] buy a station,
> or possibly, where were they when these UHF alloca-
> tions were up for grabs?

> . . . One's sympathies are undoubtedly with the
> complainants. Channel 14's operation . . . is clearly
> lackluster. But, on the other hand, can't the mass of
> educated Negroes find something to their taste on other
> stations and channels, where Negroes are quietly being
> integrated into the on-and-back-stage operations? If the
> FCC decides to lift WOOK's licenses, look out: The rush
> of applicants filing for other stations should resemble
> nothing that we've seen since the last pony round up at
> Chincoteague. [16]

This column anticipated many of the problems with minority
group broadcast license challenges that were to more clearly emerge
in the late 1960s and continue to the present. However, Harrison's
suggested solutions to the problem of WOOK did not take into account
the complex cultural questions that precipitated the problem in the
first place, questions that include not only access but visible access
to the air waves as well as truly alternative programming that could
meet the needs of minority subgroups within the culture. Fourteen
years after Harrison's column on WOOK appeared in the Washington
Evening Star there are still few minority owned and operated television stations in this country, and but a few minority-owned and -op-
erated radio stations. While it is true that more minority individuals
have been integrated into the dominant broadcasting structure, they
have, with few exceptions, been relegated to positions that do not directly impact on programming decision making. One would hope that
our television critics would take a more activist stance on this social
problem rather than recommending the middle way.

HARRISON ON BEING A TELEVISION CRITIC

We turn now to Harrison's thoughts on role and influence as a
television critic. In the early 1960s Harrison described what he perceived to be the critic's function:

> . . . in part, criticism is an exchange of views with oth-
> er viewers. Also, the more complex our society becomes,
> the more difficult for citizens to express themselves. The
> critic can serve as middleman—between viewers and indus-
> try, [and] government. [17]

Harrison believes he should approach his readership in "a relaxed, conversational style, which is I think the way people themselves refer to television and talk about it. . . . it's as if I were

joining in their conversation and making a few points of my own. " By joining in "their conversation," Harrison tries to provide his readership with useful feedback:

> The feedback function is important. I'm always available on the phone when people call. In fact they often tell me they called the [Washington] Post and had gotten a surly reply, so they call here. I find that it really doesn't take much time, and I usually know the answer. I've been a-round since the year one, so it's no great problem. And I think if they have taken the trouble to call, I should take the trouble to reply. I understand that part of the response to television is emotional; when people get upset about something they're going to call me, and as a reporter, I ought to get interested in what it is that upsets viewers or my readers. There's a story there, and my idea would be to get that story, and to find out if it makes sense, and what's involved. And if I can make points for the people about the nature of the business . . . then I've got their attention. This is the right time to tell them something that's important. They're listening. They've been hit in the head by somebody who's grabbed their attention, who's taken their show off the air or whatever. Now I've got their attention and they're going to be turning to the column especially, and I can tell them something.

In addition to providing information to his readership in response to their inquiries, Harrison also believes he, and all television critics, must function as an educator:

> I feel that part of my function is that while being as entertaining as I can in writing . . . it is also educational. Anybody in the communications field is also an educator. And I want the people to understand why shows go off even though they're good ones, or to understand why they may like a show that's really a bad show, which takes quite a bit of doing. The way I do that is to point out that here's a bad show, but I loved it, and this is why it's bad.

When I asked him whether he felt his writings over the years have had some impact, Harrison replied: "I would say on the whole [my influence] is small. . . . We never changed the theater in any way. We never changed the motion picture. Radio went down the tubes before television did. " However, Harrison did cite some small battles he helped win. For example, in response to a questionnaire printed in the <u>Washington Star</u>, 1,500 readers wrote in their votes for the worst and the best television commercial. Harrison described the results of that survey:

> . . . we got one commercial off the air. It was a Dodge commercial where they used a country music comedian, and his mannerisms and the way he sold Dodge pick-up trucks was really offensive to a lot of people. And the Dodge people realized that <u>here</u> and told their office that they didn't want any more of that in here. There was no use irritating people.

Harrison cited another "victory":

> Jim Hensen's "Muppets" began here in Washington. They did a little three or four minute bit during the news from eleven to eleven-thirty at night, and . . . the local NBC station here was going through its biennial economy wave and it decided to cut them. Well I led the screams. I said to the people in the column, "Call the station . . . and find out why they did it." And they literally could not get through to the station that weekend. There must have been 20,000 people who called, angry over the thing. Monday I called up the fellow who ran the station, Carlton Smith, and he explained to me about the budget cutback. I said, "Carlton, I'll be glad to come over there and go over the budget with you, and I'll tell you what you can cut, but put them back <u>on.</u>" So they put 'em back on, and that response opened the eyes of an advertising man here who realized "The Muppets" might be a good salesman for a product, so he tied 'em in with Wilkens coffee which gave them an advertising base. . . . Then they were being invited up to New York for "The Tonight Show" and now it's the most popular syndicated show in the business.

Since the flow of television programs never ends, and recent years have seen an increased focus on broadcast regulatory controversy, I wondered how Harrison could keep pace with television. I noticed a tendency in his recent "TV Today" and "TV Tonight" columns to capsulize pre-reviews written by <u>Star</u> staffers under his guidance. Harrison described the operation of the <u>Star's</u> television desk:

> There's another important thing that's happened. . . .
> I'm no longer the only person who's writing about televi-

sion. We have other writers here. We do have specialists
on our paper who I love to call on. In the old days I did it
all. I was the fellow who checked into everything, from
ballet to science fiction or whatever.

Harrison elaborated on the process of selecting works for pre-reviewing:

> We don't have a cassette machine here, but all of these
> cassettes are available at all of the stations, and at the
> beginning of the week we are sent a list of the shows, and
> we look at them and determine which would appear to be
> the most noteworthy. And then we look around and decide
> who is going to see it. They may go and see it and say it's
> a bad show, in which case they'll just give me a couple of
> notes on it which I include in my "TV Tonight." If they feel
> that it really came off exceptionally well then they'll do a
> special piece on it, and then I'll refer to it in my column,
> say "Check the preview from Judy Flander." I will see
> shows myself, but with all of the people I have now that's
> not necessary.

When I asked him whether he picked those works he really wanted to
pre-review himself and wrote about them, Harrison replied: "I have
that prerogative. I don't exercise it too much. I like to see it spread
around. I don't want it to be the opinion of one person." While this
approach makes it possible for a greater variety and number of television works to be given critical scrutiny, there remains the problem
of maintaining a consistent evaluative approach that can only be a-
chieved by the single critic discussing the works from a particular
personal perspective.

HARRISON ON HIS READERSHIP

When asked whether he had made some inferences over the
years as to the composition of his readership, Harrison replied:

> I used to think at one time that it was people who watched
> a lot of television, but I've found lately that people who
> don't watch television are reading [my column]. They sim-
> ply want to find out what's on, and they might see some-
> thing that I've highlighted that may interest them. This is
> the discriminating viewer, the person who watches two or
> three shows a week and that's it. So I don't think you can

draw a general pattern any more. Television is of interest to all of us, whether we watch it or not, because we know what it's doing to people's minds.

Harrison has had many opportunities to gauge the general nature of his readership through their responses to questions he has printed in various columns in the Star:

> We've had voluminous mail on a number of occasions. There are certain things we did in the "Television Magazine" where we asked people to vote, and we were stunned, because this is the only place where we said "Please write in." And we had 1,500 people who took time out to list the worst commercial and the best commercial and we also asked them for comments. And it was really fascinating to read what these people from all walks of life had to say about it. Some very articulate, some with not . . . any great command of English, but who had very good points to make, and I found no difficulty going through these 1,500 different things and trying to chalk them up.

CONCLUSIONS

Bernie Harrison, unlike most journalists presently writing about television for daily newspapers, does not need to consult histories of television for insights into the motivations of television's pioneers. He is himself a walking, talking television history book. He has spent the greater part of his professional life as a television critic, growing up with the medium.

Our conversations, highlighted in this chapter, reflect Harrison's extensive knowledge and understanding of television's administrative and creative history, including major trends in programming cycles and the economic imperative that guides the output of television's creative community.

Harrison's vantage point, from which he has for 30 years both praised and condemned the medium and those who have toiled in it, is not Olympus but rather a busy newsroom desk. From that desk have come perhaps as many as 8,000 columns dealing with all facets of the "industry." While a column alone may lack deep analysis of the meaning of television in our culture, the columns taken together chronicle the development of television as an art form and as a mammoth business venture.

Harrison's approach to advocative journalism is grounded in his perception of his role as a conduit for his readers' opinions about television, which, when combined with his own more visible discussion, can occasionally influence broadcasters' and advertisers' programming decisions.

Throughout Harrison's often witty discourse on television programs there runs a human thread; for in the seemingly inhuman, automated world of programming decisions, creative individuals—those people who make programs that are more than simply repetitive formulas—must toil, often without just recognition. In an industry in which so many hours of product are stamped out unendingly and in which the product is so ephemeral, the behind-the-scenes creative individual tends to get lost in the credits. Creators, directors, and writers, upon whom the ultimate artistry of the visible television performer depends, are not given the same respect as their counterparts in theatrical film. Both in his columns and in his discussions with me about television, Harrison has gone out of his way to praise the best of these artists while at the same time bemoaning their plight.

Above all, Bernie Harrison's evaluative approach to television is framed by hope—hope that the creative community will once again, as he believes it did in the 1950s, emerge as the guiding force in TV land.

NOTES

1. John L. Wright, "The Focus of Television Criticism," Journal of Popular Culture 7 (Spring 1974): 888-89.

2. Bernie Harrison, "'That Girl' Looks Good," Washington Evening Star, 9 September 1966, p. D15.

3. Bernie Harrison, "Old Gags and Tricks Still Working for Berle," Washington Evening Star, 12 September 1966, p. D8.

4. Bernie Harrison, "On The Air: Languid History, Fine Photography," Washington Evening Star, 26 January 1972, p. C16.

5. Bernie Harrison, "On The Air: 'The Monkees' Hits New Numbing Low," Washington Evening Star, 13 September 1966, p. A20.

6. Bernie Harrison, "On The Air: A Year of Hope, Susskind Says," Washington Evening Star, 14 September 1966, p. D13.

7. Harrison, "Languid History," p. C16.

8. Bernie Harrison, "On The Air: 'Queen of Spades' Operatic Mishmash," Washington Evening Star, 5 January 1972, p. B13.

9. Bernie Harrison, "On The Air: The Year of the Specials," Washington Evening Star, 6 September 1966, p. A21.

10. Bernie Harrison, "On The Air: Drama Leads the Special Lists," Washington Evening Star, 7 September 1966, p. D15.

11. Harrison, "Year of the Specials," p. A21.

12. Bernie Harrison, "On The Air: The Return of David Susskind," Washington Evening Star, 8 September 1966, p. C18.

13. Bernie Harrison, "On The Air: Should Schools Select TV Shows?" Washington Evening Star, 9 September 1966, p. D15.

14. Bernie Harrison, "90-Minute Era Lies Ahead," Washington Sunday Star, 2 September 1956, p. A30.

15. Bernie Harrison, "On The Air: On Cutting Costs," Washington Sunday Star, 23 January 1972, "TV Magazine," p. 2.

16. Bernie Harrison, "Everybody Wants Eaton's Stations," Washington Evening Star, 2 September 1966, p. A12.

17. Quoted in Julian Burroughts, Jr., "Radio-Television Criticism: Purpose and Effects," Southern Speech Journal 27 (Spring 1962): 216.

5

HORACE NEWCOMB:
GURU OF THE ACADEMIC CRITICS

Until recent years, scholars have chosen to ignore television
as a legitimate art form. Instead they have concentrated their attention on television as a sociological phenomenon—a cultural form that
impacted on viewer behavior in complex and unclear ways. Buzz
words such as "vast vastland," "plug-in drug," "subliminal seduction," "reinforcing agent," and "narcotizing dysfunction" framed research that seemed to start from the unstated premise that television
was guilty of ruining our culture until proven innocent.

As discussed in Chapter 1, little attention was paid to television's claim to be an art form in its own right or what such a claim
signified. Instead, the boob tube, as it was somewhat scornfully called,
was dismissed as popular culture for the masses, low art, or nonart
when compared to music, literature, and the visual arts.

In the early 1970s, however, a group of young scholars, most
of whom had done their graduate work within English departments,
began to take television seriously as an art form with unique aesthetic
properties and cultural meanings. Then, in 1974 a seminal volume
appeared on the shelves of many university book stores around the
country. Written by a 31-year-old scholar named Horace Newcomb,
TV: The Most Popular Art signaled a growing interest in television
programs and the genres or types of programs they represented as
potential cultural signposts. Since that book has appeared, we have
witnessed an increasing volume of literature focusing specifically on
the popular art characteristics of our most pervasive entertainment
and informational medium.

The scholarly academic critics who are exploring television as
a popular art are usually somewhat detached from their subject area
although they are deeply involved in analyzing it—thus they are presumed to exercise a higher degree of objectivity in their evaluations
of television than the journalist critics. The academic critic's writings
are most often detailed and lengthy expositions published in book form

or in scholarly journals, and generally intended for a readership primarily composed of serious students of the art form who bring to the essays at least a general background knowledge of the subject.

Among the academic critics writing about television today, there are four individuals whose explorations of the meaning of television as a cultural form seem to be breaking particularly fertile conceptual ground. These four critics are Raymond Williams, formerly a professor of Political Science at Stanford University and presently University Reader in Drama at Cambridge, England; David Thorburn, formerly an associate professor of English at Yale University who now teaches at the Massachusetts Institute of Technology; Bruce Kurtz, professor of Fine Arts at Hartwick College; and Horace Newcomb, professor of English at the University of Texas at Austin. All of these individuals have published a variety of essays or books that discuss in detail what they believe to be the fundamental aesthetic principles of television and the human meaning of television as one of our culture's significant art forms.

Following a brief description of the work of Williams, Thorburn, and Kurtz, this chapter will take an in-depth look at Newcomb's writings about television, his perception of his role and influence as a critic, and his perception of his readership.

Raymond Williams has written two important books on the relationship of communications technology to culture. [1] In addition to this conceptual work, Williams also wrote a monthly review of television for the British Broadcasting Corporation's weekly journal "The Listener" between 1968 and 1972.

Williams argued at a 1973 conference on "The Future of Communications Studies" that the notion of "mass communications" is disastrous because the term "mass" has become synonymous with a large audience and thereby has prevented analysis of "specific modern communications conventions and forms." [2]

According to Williams, television as a cultural form both borrows from existing cultural forms and creates its own new forms. In Television: Technology and Cultural Form, Williams wrote that the

. . . adaptation of received forms to the new [television]
technology has led in a number of cases to significant
changes and to some real qualitative differences. . . . it
will be necessary also to look at those forms which are
not in an obvious way derivative, and which can usefully
be seen as the innovating forms of television itself. [3]

Among the "received forms," Williams discussed news, argument and discussion, education, drama, cinema, variety, sports, advertising, and pastimes (e.g., parlor games). Williams also discussed "mixed" or "new" television forms, including drama-documentary or "docudrama," education by seeing, the personalized television essay or journal, and short "involuntary sequences" determined in the main by the time segmentation created by commercial interruption.

According to culture theorist James W. Carey, Raymond Williams' "highlighting of conventions, forms, and practices reflects an influence of Marxism—with its emphasis on praxis—and also the influence of literary criticism which emphasizes the forms and conventions of particular works."[4]

David Thorburn, like Williams, has discussed communications forms in the context of their institutional derivation. Thorburn wrote of television that "capitalist greed, the crassest of alliances between commerce and modern technology, may be the enabling conditions of a complex narrative art."[5]

Thorburn related the capitalist system of television program production to the recurrence of images across programs. However, rather than dismissing this sameness of imagery as producing banal programming, Thorburn instead posited a "multiplicity principle" operating in the art form:

> . . . a principle of plotting or organization whereby a
> particular drama will draw not once or twice but many
> times upon the immense store of stories and situations
> created by the genre's brief but crowded history. . . .
> By minimizing the need for long establishing or exposi-
> tory sequences, the multiplicity principle allows the
> story to leave aside the question of how these emotional
> entanglements were arrived at and to concentrate its en-
> ergies on their credible and powerful present enactment. [6]

This repetition of imagery within the genre has produced what Thorburn believes is a sophisticated television audience. He observed that

> . . . television melodrama can rely confidently on one
> resource that is always essential to the vitality of any
> art form: an audience impressive not simply in its num-
> bers but also in its genuine sophistication, its deep fa-
> miliarity with the history and conventions of the genre. [7]

Focusing on other aspects of the medium, Bruce Kurtz has written extensively about artists' video and has recently published a significant work on the television commercial's aesthetic characteristics. [8] Kurtz, like Thorburn and Williams, has defended television as a meaningful cultural form with unique characteristics that must be objectively examined. He has claimed that "Art historical aesthetic hierarchies still tend to discredit popular art forms, erroneously."[9] And he has added specifically about television: "While television has not been conferred the status of a fine art form, as have photography and cinema—once considered only as popular art forms—it is commonly considered a popular art, a first step in aesthetic ascendency."[10]

In his book on TV commercials, entitled Spots, Kurtz examined in-depth what he called "the unique form of the spot as drama." Using a particular television commercial as an example of his contention, Kurtz commented: "Existentialist 'nothingness,' for example, is brilliantly characterized as 'the blahs' by Mike Cuesta's 'The Hill' spot for Alka Seltzer, a 60-second spot as serious as Bergman's Seventh Seal, to which it is intelligently indebted."[11]

Kurtz posited that the significant works of popular art have been able to transcend stereotypes to produce generalizations or archetypes that are then "recycled" to specific experiences:

> The best popular artists work somewhere between stereotypes and generalizations, extending stereotypes to new meanings. . . . It is interesting to note that the language of spots is such that the logic develops from stereotype to generalization to specific experience. . . . Good popular art "recycles" stereotypes to specific experiences.[12]

Kurtz also questioned "fine art's" claim to the status of avant-garde: "To view the avant-garde as the exclusive domain of fine art is clearly ill-considered; for popular art, in its challenge to fine art, may be more avant-garde in that it is not bound by centuries of values and limitations."[13] This idea is strikingly similar to aesthetician Abraham Kaplan's notion that popular art, while it "vulgarizes yesterday's art" may portend the art of the future (see Chapter 1).

Williams, Thorburn, and Kurtz are all attempting to look at television from a new perspective. In tracing the development of particular television genres as texts reflecting the cultural milieu within which they are created, these writers have posited that there is both innovation and complexity of design in popular television works and their genres. Equally significant, they have asserted that the audience for such works has developed a certain sophistication in deciphering the cultural codes inherent in the works—a claim that most sociologists examining the television audience from a class-based perspective have refused to accept or have ignored.

The fourth academic critic to be discussed here is perhaps the most widely read scholar writing about television today—Horace Newcomb, currently a professor of English at the University of Texas. Newcomb's major theoretical treatise, TV: The Most Popular Art, written in 1974, was described by David Littlejohn as "a sound and provocative book . . . on the mythical imagery of various popular TV genres. "[14]

Newcomb was born in 1943 in Jackson, Mississippi, and he was graduated from Mississippi College. He went to the University of Chicago on a Woodrow Wilson Fellowship, received a Master of Arts degree in General Studies in 1966, and completed his Doctor of Philosophy in English in 1969. His doctoral dissertation was guided by noted popular culture theorist John Cawelti. After receiving his Ph. D. , Newcomb taught for a year in the English department at Cornell College, Iowa, and then at Saginaw Valley College in Michigan. He next moved to the University of Maryland–Baltimore County, where he taught popular culture courses in the American Studies department until 1978. That year he moved to the University of Texas, where he currently teaches popular culture in the English department. In addition to academic work on television, Newcomb wrote a column five days a week on television for the Baltimore Sun from March 1973 to May 1974.

Newcomb, like the other three academic critics discussed above, has traced the development of genres in broadcast programming, defending their status as significant cultural texts from which the intelligent viewer can draw inferences about his cultural milieu. [15] Among the genres Newcomb evaluated were situation comedy, domestic comedy with relevancy, Westerns, mysteries, doctors and lawyers melodramas, adventure melodramas, soap opera, news, documentaries, and sports. Beyond these detailed genre evaluations, Newcomb posited a general television aesthetic grounded in the notions of television's intimacy, continuity, and history. Newcomb has also theorized on the relationship between broadcast television genres and artists' video, or what he terms "experimental video. "

In the following I will examine Newcomb's writings about television as they relate to his explication of the fundamental aesthetic principles and cultural significance of television through an examination of individual television programs and genres, as well as the institutional structures within which these works are produced; his theoretical discourse on the historical roots of television as they relate to the development of distinct styles of television programs; his attempts to "fit" television into an established art tradition; and his discussion of the high art/popular art dichotomy as it relates to television.

NEWCOMB ON POPULAR TELEVISION AND CULTURE

Newcomb has moved conceptually beyond the evaluative approach he took in his book TV: The Most Popular Art, in which he interpreted television programs, series, and genres within a framework of their aesthetic design and of the values inherent in the programs themselves when considered apart from the culture in which they are conceived and produced. In his more recent essays, Newcomb has instead begun to evaluate television as a reflection of the cultural symbol systems and myths from which television programs draw their content. While this distinction may seem on the surface to be insignificant, its deeper meaning reveals a significant shift in Newcomb's evaluative approach to television. In the former approach, Newcomb inferred that works of art shown on television had some deep cultural meanings that might be apprehended by examining the values expressed in the works. In the latter approach, Newcomb instead infers that the meanings inherent in the content of the works must be traced to the cultural milieu from which the works emerged. This shift in Newcomb's approach to television is apparent if one compares his writings in TV: The Most Popular Art with his more recent essays on television, culture, and anthropology.

TV: The Most Popular Art is grounded on a central theme that television can be evaluated according to formulas that link programs and series to various genres. According to Newcomb and John Cawelti, from whom Newcomb borrowed the term, formula is a conventional system for structuring cultural products as opposed to "invented structures," which are new ways of organizing works of art. Newcomb wrote of television formulas:

> Clearly, television is essentially a formulaic medium in terms of its entertainment. . . . television repeats its formulas complete with the same characters, the same stars, sometimes for years on end. Even then, it is possible to see a character in a highly formulaic series . . . for years afterward in reruns. Successful television formulas are widely copied. . . . The formulas that survive have wide appeal in a massive audience. Their special appeal is so wide, say the harsher culture critics, that there can be no artistic excellence. But in examining the popular arts, even from the aesthetic point of view, we should keep in mind that discovery of such excellence is not our primary task. [16]

Rather than making snap judgments as to a television program's "artistic excellence" based on the uniqueness of its aesthetic design (a traditional high art approach), Newcomb posited that one must first look at the work's or its genre's formula as a system of values:

> . . . the formula becomes the particular way of ordering
> and defining the world. Much of that ordering in situation
> comedy and other television forms will have a strong sense
> of the "unreal." I suggest, however, that in situation com-
> edy and in all of television there is the creation of a "spe-
> cial" sense of reality. Each has its own systems of values.
> . . . to break with this reality is to create a new formula,
> and in some cases a new form of television art. [17]

Referring specifically to the situation comedy genre, Newcomb
wrote: "This form . . . is a paradigm for what occurs in more complex program types, and its perennial popularity is probably due to
the relatively simple outline it follows."[18] The "simple outline" of
the sitcom to which Newcomb refers often involves nothing more than
some "special funny 'thing'" that happens to a set of characters in an
episode. Week after week, the funny "thing" or situation will change,
but the characters will neither change nor grow. The characters are
not affected by events in the outside world, but rather are affected
only by the confusion that results from their zany interpersonal interactions:

> . . . the most prominent aspect of the central character's
> makeup [is] a lack of any sense of probability. They are,
> in some way, out of touch with our day-to-day sense of
> how things happen, with the set of laws that allow us to
> predict the outcome of our actions. . . . What they lack,
> or what they refuse to recognize, is a knowledge of the
> order of the world. . . . [19]

The sitcoms' aesthetic design refuses to consider the central
characters' motivations. Newcomb cited "The Beverly Hillbillies"
as evidence of this posture:

> No one intends to cause pain in the shows, no one intends
> evil. The problems exist solely at the level of misunder-
> standing. Drysdale may desire the Clampett's money, but
> he is not willing to steal and kill for it. [20]

Beyond this internalized formula, however, Newcomb believes
that sitcom does reflect certain cultural values, albeit on a cursory
level. For example, Newcomb noted that the homes portrayed in situation comedy

> . . . reflect prosperity but not elegance. The standard of
> living is based on comfort; the rule of existence is neatness.

The severity of this middle-class rule is indicated
for us by the upturned world of "The Beverly Hillbillies."
There in the midst of the millionaire's luxury they reflect
the values of rural America—or perhaps it is more accurate to say that they reflect the values of rural America as
conceived by middle-class Americans. [21]

Thus, in Newcomb's early writings on situation comedy, highlighted above, he notes that the genre does not make external references (i. e. , references in the world of "real" experience to which
the audience could relate). However, in his more recent discussions
of television, Newcomb has moved toward the conception that popular
television is a reality in itself, an idea he briefly mentioned in TV:
The Most Popular Art but never developed in any depth.
When I asked Newcomb about the distinction between "fantasy"
and "realism" that must be discussed in a popular television context,
he responded:

> . . . I would probably say now that television is more of
> a mirror than a window, that the mirror involves us with
> fantasies and idealizations, but that those fantasies and
> idealizations may be precisely what we need to develop
> values for living. That is, there's an implied distinction
> there between . . . fantasy and realism. And I suppose
> that was one of the underlying things in the first book [TV:
> The Most Popular Art], that I was saying that that art is
> best on television which is realistic, and now I would not
> necessarily say that. . . . if these things are highly
> charged symbol systems, then they need be no more re-
> alistic than the most extravagant folk tale.

Newcomb recently wrote that "The Beverly Hillbillies" is an
example of this fantastic, idealized popular television reality, and
that this particular situation comedy has major implications in regard to our images of the South in a larger cultural context. Because
this passage is crucial to understanding Newcomb's current thought
about television, it is quoted below at length.

> If we take "The Beverly Hillbillies" as prototypical, as
> one of the most successful television shows of all time,
> we immediately begin to see these [cultural] meanings
> emerge. Two major aspects first become apparent. The
> first is the representation of the hillbilly stereotype. The
> figure is familiar, especially in physical appearance . . .
> from entertainment forms that long preceded television.

The older characters are dressed in overalls, work
shirts, brogans, battered slouch hats, long dresses,
bonnets and so on. The younger ones bear some vague
resemblance to mail order cowboys. Their speech is a
stylized version of rural southern patterns, again developed as much in humorous presentations as in reality.
Malapropisms and ungrammatical constructions are used
to draw laughs. . . .

The fact that the family's wealth is gained by fluke
reinforces the general image of shiftlessness that informs
their appearance and behavior. . . . their continual mis-
apprehension or misinterpretation of what is happening a-
round them speak of massive social isolation. They are
indeed, in this view, strangers in another country, bearers
of a truly distinct cultural code.

. . . Inevitably the plots of the show revolve around
a deep conflict of basic values. . . . Invariably the sim-
pler values of the Clampetts win out over the morally deficient swindlers [of Beverly Hills]. What appeared to be
simple mindedness turns out to be deep wisdom simply
expressed. . . .

This view of the moral superiority of rural wisdom
is as old as those depicting the hillbilly as shiftless, moon-
shine swigging, ignorant and culturally isolated. These
are the representations of the virtues of good heart, simple living, honest values and complex insight into human
nature. In television all of these things are particularly
associated with the Southern mountaineer, but against
contemporary American culture. "We" are the ones with
the deficient value structure. . . .

The final comment on this program and others like
it, however, must recognize that neither attribution is an
accurate picture of the South or of the program. Rather it
is in the complex combination of the two that we find the
appropriate meaning. In this show we must realize that
there are no fully developed adult characters who can be
associated with the positive values I have described. . . .
Things turn out right for these people because they happen
to represent a set of values that must win rather than because they choose to encounter the villains who would
swindle them.

The equation, then, is clear. These Southerners
are children and their goodness is the simple goodness
of children. . . . The real viciousness of these views is
not that hillbillies and Southerners are made fun of. It is

that <u>mountain people and Southerners are not considered</u>
<u>part of the adult population of the country or of the cul-</u>
<u>ture.</u> Programs about the South admit that the virtues
presented there are the important ones, the best ones
for life. But they simultaneously suggest that they are
not available to those of us who live in the "real" world
of adult interaction. Such a perspective is familiar to
anthropologists. The native culture becomes the screen
on which we project our own desires for innocence, for
noble savages, for happy natives and for paradises before the introduction of evil.
    . . . <u>the meanings, the cultural significances, of</u>
<u>rural wisdom, Southernness, and childishness all exist</u>
<u>prior to their combination in these presentations.</u> [22] [Ital-
ics added.]

Newcomb contrasted the Southernness of "The Beverly Hillbillies" with that of "The Waltons," a melodramatic series produced by
Earl Hamner, a "native" of the Southern culture. "The Waltons,"
Newcomb noted, carries many of the same visual images as did "Hillbillies." There is conflict between rural and urban value systems in
both series. Yet there is a significant difference in the two series
created by the cultural contexts in which these images and values are
framed. In "The Waltons,"

    . . . the synthesis of "Southernness" with the meaning of
the Depression offers to American audiences a new cultural object, a new set of meanings. The former meanings
of these two symbolic constructs are changed in the process into something that "speaks," that interprets current
American experience through the lens of fictional Southern
experience. . . . The insider sees in those meanings a far
more potent value. In this view overalls become the mark
of dignified labor. Country food is wholesome, strengthen-
ing, rather than exotic. The slouch hat becomes the indi-
cation of powerful and gentle masculinity, often as the
mark of the patriarch. Elderly wisdom is allied with that
of children as remarkably insightful rather than as arcane
and comic. Most important, however, is the clear demar-
cation between child and adult. "The Waltons" focuses on
the struggle of John Boy to grow out of the child's perspective and to accept the difficult responsibilities of adulthood.
. . . The child, and the audience, must learn the real
meaning of living through hard times in the South. That
meaning suggests that strength, endurance, tolerance,

honor, humility, simplicity, kindness, and mutual support serve as the basis for a successful life and not merely as opportunity for comic encounter or for cynical remarks. [23]

It is generally true that the situation comedy genre, as part of
its formula, tends to exploit character weaknesses for laughs, and
not just those weaknesses that are attributed by some individuals to
"Southernness." In contrast, it is also generally true that the family
melodrama genre tends to exaggerate the strength of the family unit
as an ordering mechanism in our culture, whether that family unity
is manifested in a rural, urban, or suburban context. Thus, a simple
genre-analysis approach to evaluating popular television series is not
sufficient to uncover the deeper cultural structures lurking beneath
the manifest generic formulas. Newcomb astutely recognized this problem, as exemplified by his discussion above of "The Beverly Hillbillies" and "The Waltons." Newcomb summarized his notion of cultural
meanings emerging in the symbol systems appropriated by television
series:

> The television show is . . . a bricolage of symbols, each
> with its embedded significance. Some of that significance
> rises from the field of reference within the formula or type
> of the work. Other significance is rooted in the symbol's
> relation to the world outside popular entertainment forms. [24]

Newcomb added:

> Societies can be constituted around ritual and symbols
> that are equally as repressive as those used in exploita-
> tive messages. . . . The significant difference does not
> lie in the recognition or lack of recognition of symbolic
> content. It lies in the ways in which we see meaning be-
> ing constituted. [25]

In the final analysis, then, symbols are nothing more or less
than organizing ideas by which people develop perspectives about their
relationship with their world. Such a human-centered conception of
television is a far cry from the despair framing much of the social
science tradition of evaluating popular television.

Newcomb's evaluative focus extends beyond the aesthetic designs of television programs since he recognizes that popular television works cannot be considered in isolation from the institutional
context of their production and distribution. Newcomb sees in television "webs of significance" into which are woven both the aesthetic

designs of popular television genres and the television industry's annual imperative to increase profits:

> . . . We can take a significant step in [understanding television] by focusing on Marshall Sahlins' observation that the financial system of capitalist America is the central locus of its symbol system. Buying and selling are means of communication. . . . I would certainly wish to add the television producer to Sahlins' list of "hucksters of the symbol," for it is the successful producer who enables the advertiser to become even more successful. [26]

I asked Newcomb what he perceived to be the meaning of American television in such an institutional-advertising context, to which he answered:

> . . . the question is what does it mean in our culture to sell products? How do you do that? And the way you do it is, it seems to me, at least in television's case is . . . you tap some very deep resonances, you tap some deep cultural meanings. And if we see the programs as commercials for the commercials then they've got to go deeper than the other things.

Newcomb sees these "deep resonances" and "deep cultural meanings" in certain "clearly developed motifs signaling intensified codes to which we should respond as audiences." These motifs emerge in television content, both in the programs and in advertisements. For example, Newcomb wrote "sex is used in television shows as a means of focusing other issues" such as "the validity of conventional marriage" and "the error of judging individuals [e. g. , adolescent boys and girls] by class."[27]

Thus Newcomb has interpreted popular television programs as conforming to what James Carey has termed a "ritual view of communication"—"not the act of imparting information or influence, but the creation, representation, and celebration of shared beliefs."[28] In this sense television is a "text" in which its audience can locate deeper cultural meanings.

Newcomb also approaches television from a distinctive historical perspective that begins by examining popular television's "intensified [cultural] codes." Such an examination, Newcomb wrote, is a significant departure from traditional modes of television analysis:

> Television emerged, almost fully developed, in a form that was familiar to us. Into the old time frames and

broadcast patterns of radio we poured the content of that medium, and of film, popular theater and drama. It flooded into homes with an alarming volume, exciting parents, teachers and researchers. All of it was "brought to us by" the corporate interests of gigantic American business. It was to be expected, then, that our attempts to understand television would follow equally familiar patterns. [29]

Newcomb added that "little commentary on the effects of television takes into account significant differences in programs or the changes in the medium over time."[30]

In order to be able to understand these changes in television over time in a cultural context, Newcomb felt that the television scholar must look at "intensifiers of meaning," such as shifts in basic television formula styles, for clues to cultural change. For example, one might focus on major stylistic shifts such as television's changing focus on the American South from "The Beverly Hillbillies" to "The Waltons," as discussed above, or the extension of the "family" concept from the nuclear family to the work group, as in the newsroom families of "The Mary Tyler Moore Show" and "Lou Grant" or the combat family of "M*A*S*H"; or the extension of comedy styles into the realm of crucial social issues in "All in the Family."

Not only do formula shifts occur in popular television genres, but also, according to Newcomb, the formulas become "self-reflexive," referring back to themselves within historical context:

We can see how new formulas bear the marks of older ones and how, in the process of creating new versions of particular formulas, the audience's knowledge of television's past is used in shaping both the form and the content of the newer shows. We can begin to see, in such a perspective, how even reruns become an essential part of television. . . .

. . . it is when the reruns begin to come to life that we can fully note the historical complexity of television and its dependence on self-reflexivity as a device for the creation of new material with new meanings. "Happy Days" creates a fictional commentary on the world in which we viewed "Father Knows Best." The family members of the fictional Andersons are brought together for a reunion in the fictional frame of a family reunion for "Father Knows Best."

. . . Spin-offs are another example of TV's ability to reflect and reflect upon itself. Apparently the producers are aware that audience loyalty can be developed a-

round single characters without regard to the particular
frame in which they originate. While Rhoda and Phyllis
maintain some of the characteristics they exhibited on
"The Mary Tyler Moore Show," they have developed in
diverging ways as well. . . . Still, our happiest mo-
ments in such shows may occur when the spin-off shows
are related directly to the parent show. We are always
pleased when someone from Mayberry visits Gomer at
the marine base, or when Mary unexpectedly drops in
on Rhoda. [31]

In addition to these general formula shifts, Newcomb also saw
individual series breaking established aesthetic and cultural patterns:

"New" shows break patterns of action, move toward varied value orientations, and refuse to indulge in the pre-
dictability of most television. They sometimes demand a
new understanding of some visual techniques. Some are
edited with a new sense of television narrative, rather
than a standard, cinematic manner. They carry with them
a more sensitive attitude toward character, which in turn
requires a more complex sort of acting. The writing of
new shows is richer in image and tone than that common
to familiar television shows. Ultimately, these factors
prohibit the application of a single set of standards to television. Less dependent on formula and standardized action, these shows move farther along the continuum toward the "fine arts." [32]

Newcomb singled out various "new" shows throughout the period
of television's development that broke established patterns and thereby
modified television history. Sid Caesar's "Your Show of Shows" (1950-
54) asked its audience to participate in its antics; "The Defenders"
(1961-65) asked in the early 1960s that the television audience consider complex moral, social, and cultural problems; "Star Trek"
(1966-69) moved toward questioning our most strongly held human
and national attitudes, and even suggested remedies for many of our
nagging social problems; Rowan and Martin's "Laugh-In" (1968-73)
heralded our increasing concern with family problems by substituting
the "reversed family values" of the swinging singles; "The Prisoner"
(1968-69) explored the late twentieth-century problem of human ano-
nymity in a world that on its surface provides us with most of the
creature comforts needed for physical survival; "Then Came Bronson" (1969-70) explored the development of a character whose interactions with other people were inner-directed and who, through his

wandering, grew in morally subtle ways; and "All in the Family" (1971-79) and "M*A*S*H" (1972-00) demonstrated that in the 1970s comedy could be television's chief vehicle for social criticism. [33] What all these works have in common, Newcomb explained to me, is their ability to help us apprehend "Who we are, and how those images speak to that. "

While Newcomb addresses television as a popular art in much of his writings, he also is continually searching for those specific characteristics that place television in an established art tradition and give it legitimacy in the art world. Newcomb freely admits that television borrows content from other art forms; nevertheless he believes that it can be "art" in its own right:

> . . . television is its own medium. It combines sound
> and picture and writing. In doing so, it brings us ele-
> ments of fiction, poetry, drama, film and radio. But
> it is none of these things. It is television. [34]

Newcomb has also noted that

> . . . we have learned to see television much better and
> to be able to take it on its own terms, seeking formal
> distinctions before assuming that the content is merely
> a simplified and bland version of film or theater or a
> powerful message with no content that transcends polit-
> ical and commercial intent. [35]

According to Newcomb, television's true relationship with other art forms is with the novel rather than with film or radio as is so often established. Television exhibits a "density" similar to that of the novel. This television density occurs over time as patterns of action are repeated throughout the history of genres—a notion strikingly similar to David Thorburn's "multiplicity principle. "

Television's domestic comedy genre bears a distinct relationship to traditional comedic forms. Television's contemporary comedies with relevancy such as "All in the Family," "Maude," and "M*A*S*H" become vehicles for biting social commentary in the best tradition of Aeschylus, Shakespeare, and Charlie Chaplin.

In addition to these aesthetic linkages, Newcomb also believes that television has unique institutional characteristics that tend to separate it from other popular art forms;

> There has always been some question as to whether or
> not we will awaken from our sleep, from the pleasant
> dreams that may be without lasting virtue. It is this fear

that has given rise to serious attacks on television. . . .
It leads to a continuing fear that a nation possessed of a
dreamlike "television mentality" will soon develop. . . .

This point of view indicates an attitude toward television that is distinct from that toward other popular
forms. The popular arts may be condemned as unfulfill-
ing and addictive, but they will not be cited as subversive
or long as it is indicated that the addiction is to mystery
or romantic novels. After all, reading is an activity,
whereas watching TV is, for most people, a highly passive mode of behavior. Similarly, no great alarm will be
raised so long as the popular arts are most strongly represented by the movies, for the movies end and we all
have to go home. Like reading, it is a form of activity
limited in time, demanding some sense of action, and
which interrupts other activities.

These fears are not without foundation. Because of
its association with massive commercial interests, because it serves as the medium for deceptive advertising,
television is obviously different from these other forms,
which have discovered a new respectability since its development. Any student or critic should share the fear.
. . . But none of this should allow us to overlook the a-
esthetic capabilities inherent in the medium itself. [36]

The medium's inherent aesthetic capabilities are manifested in
television programs that transcend mere diversionary entertainment,
thereby becoming works of greater cultural significance. Newcomb
wrote of that significance on television:

The popular arts do not always teach all of us deep lessons about the nature of existence or make life more
richly ambiguous for us. But they can, and for almost
all of us they sometimes do. They also give us great
pleasure. And they help to shape, reflect and reaffirm
prevailing cultural notions. [37]

These "deep lessons about the nature of existence" and "ambig-
uity" are seen by Newcomb as signals for a more significant and complex art:

Human frailty and human valor are the province of all
complex art. Much popular art ignores the specifics
of this task, working instead with veiled and not-so-
veiled cultural assumptions about ways in which human

problems can be eliminated by heroic action, gentle advice, or slapstick resolutions. [38]

As we have seen above, in TV: The Most Popular Art, Newcomb highlighted those specific television series which, he argued, had transcended popular art conventions and produced more complex, meaningful explorations of human experience. His choice of shows tended to employ rather traditional art-critical evaluative standards as a basis for judgment, including the presence of rebellion against the prevailing values of the audience, "human" characters, complexity of the characters' motivations, and narrative continuity. These standards are essentially aesthetic standards.

In our discussion of his work, Newcomb indicated that he is now reconsidering his use of these standards as the only meaningful measure of the distinctions between art and popular art:

> I began dealing with popular culture because . . . I
> wanted to say that the art that was for masses was as
> important as Tolstoy for me. Then I changed that. I be-
> gan to see that some of the stuff was really repressive;
> that some values that were expressed in popular novels
> and popular films and popular television seemed to me
> socially repressive, politically repressive. Bad values
> that I wouldn't agree with. I think that shows up in the
> book [TV: The Most Popular Art]. That is, on the one
> hand I was saying it was all good, and on the other hand
> I was saying, "this is best." Now I think I would have to
> look at it much more closely and read some of the stuff
> that I saw as negative and repressive in a more symbolic
> way. For me criticism is a moral process. I'd much
> rather say something is bad morally than bad aesthetic-
> ally. I think you can enjoy aesthetically the most corrupt
> and repressive art. And I think critics have to make that
> distinction, and critics have to talk in moral terms.

So far I have discussed at length where Newcomb believes television has been and where is is now. But where might it go? I posed that question to him and got this lengthy and guardedly optimistic response:

> I think we've already seen some of the next direction. And
> there are problems with it for me. I think that increasingly
> I see television as a conservative force. I don't necessarily
> mean bad things by that. I see their values of family, love
> of groups, worth of the individual, and laughter as a kind

of healing device. Admittedly that leaves out some social criticism, but it puts it in a context. And I think that all of that occurred because television was a massively popular art. I think what we've begun to see is far more freedom on the part of producers who are making television, and so we're seeing a wider variety of moral, aesthetic, a whole range of attitudes. And we're seeing a fragmentation. That is, the monolith that was television entertainment as briefly as two or three years ago [1975-1976] . . . began [to fragment] with the Lear productions and continues to fragment, so that ultimately three years ago we get "Mary Hartman" which is a parody, not just of television audiences or of television, and in some cases is not always parody, but is a very complex self-reflexive device. And I think television has begun to look at itself. I think that's a mark of maturity, but it's also a mark of social change. . . . even when I say it was at its best in conservative terms, there was always a lot of it I didn't like in moral terms. . . . White upper-middle class kind of things that Gerbner has so carefully documented. Male white upper-middle class. But now I think we're seeing all kinds of variety. We're seeing a lot of change, different points of view. And we're going to have to be much more critically aware to deal with that. I think "Soap" is an attempt at self-parody. . . . So I think we're going to have more shows about television itself. The world of television is coterminus with ours now, and people can make references in it. . . . I think that television offers a special meaning for violence, and it relates to the way in which we talk about violence in our world of experience, but it's not the same thing. . . . we have to see what [violence] means in [the television] world, and then how that meaning relates to the meaning we have in experience. . . . I am saying that we have now come to the end of the first television programming era, and that we're going to begin to see different things.

My conversation with Newcomb took place in February 1978. Two months before that interview a major television movie titled "The Storyteller" was aired on NBC. The film was produced by Richard Levinson and William Link, whom John O'Connor called "two of the more intelligent and most respected toilers in television's strawberry fields forever." "The Storyteller" presented as its central character a television writer who was in the business of grinding out slick melodramas. One of these stories dealt with a young boy who burned down his school. The day following the airing of this fictional episode, a young boy in Seattle burned down his school. Unfortunately the youth was burned to death in the blaze. The writer had to face the possibility that his story had prompted the young boy's fatal imitation. "The Storyteller" was a bold film that questioned the nature of the responsibilities of television's executive and creative communities toward their audience. That the story was telecast at all adds weight to Newcomb's notions that television is beginning to awaken from its complacency and to a degree is willing to publically examine its own motivations. Whether such a trend will continue or whether the audience is really interested in such self-examination remains to be seen, but "The Storyteller" was a positive first step.

NEWCOMB ON BEING A TELEVISION CRITIC

As was mentioned previously, Newcomb has both written books about popular television for the serious student of the art form and has also written a daily newspaper column about television for the Baltimore Sun. Therefore, any discussion of his perception of his role and influence as a television critic must be considered in both forums.

In Television: The Critical View, a book of essays on television that Newcomb edited, he observed that:

> . . . people other than self-styled, self-conscious critics
> are seriously involved with "education in its larger sense."
> . . . Because television has not been given attention by
> those whose professed purpose is the serious concern for
> education in its fullest sense, it has developed no respect-
> ed place in the culture. [39]

By "education in its larger sense" Newcomb was referring to the need for experienced observers to help others less experienced in their ability to analyze television works become "knowledgeable" about what they are viewing. I asked Newcomb how he applied this concept in his classroom teaching, to which he responded:

> When I teach courses in television content, theory, and
> criticism . . . or even when I use a television program
> in a popular culture course, I start with a long harangue
> on "Sit up straight, watch this differently than you do at
> home, watch your posture. If you assume your home view-
> ing style that's going to prohibit you from viewing it anal-
> ytically." . . . I think that being aware of the artistry of

something and the way in which characters and actors and visual sequences are manipulated can <u>enhance</u> the enjoyment of something as well as negate it. So I would like very much to have a critically aware audience who would be able to do things like make a distinction between something that's a copy of a successful formula or a successful program and the program that they liked in the first place.

He added:

We should be educating children to deal critically with television. . . . I think we should have television taught in public schools, K through twelve, not on a year-long basis, but maybe four weeks here or six weeks there. Let's look at some shows, let's look at some ads, here's what's done, this is the kind of thing that's done with the camera . . . and to get the kids involved with [television] . . . as they deal with literature. Be critical about what you see, be knowledgeable, I suppose, is the best word. And then you're not going to be satisfied.

While Newcomb sees his role as an educator of the audience to be important, he believes that his books have had very little impact on practitioners:

I have very little sense of any kind of impact. I know there are people who probably used the books as students who might be working now. I did a phone interview with Earl Hamner once for an abortive piece which was never printed, and he had read the book. Of course I had said such nice things about "The Waltons" that I had Doubleday send him a copy.

Perhaps the most that a scholar can ask of his work is that serious students and other scholars will pay attention to the messages in the book and will build their own work on the foundations of that book. Newcomb's <u>TV: The Most Popular Art</u> has certainly been widely distributed in the university community, and a very large group of media students has been exposed to Newcomb's essentially optimistic ideas about popular television, ideas which address not only what the art form has been and is, but what it has the potential to become.

Turning to Newcomb's thoughts about his role and influence as a television critic writing for a daily newspaper, we find him taking a different tack from O'Connor and Harrison. In <u>Television: The Crit-</u>

ical View, Newcomb discussed the limitations inherent in writing
commentary about television for a daily newspaper:

> The journalist . . . feels the responsibility to form judg-
> ments that will guide the audience to some understanding
> of the issues. The journalist must "keep up" with the lat-
> est problem, whether that means reviewing an important
> show, responding to the latest research report, or writ-
> ing about the most current political or financial restric-
> tions. His subject matter is, in a way, determined by
> what is most important in a journalistic sense, by what
> should go into a daily newspaper designed for a single,
> quick reading. . . .
>
> Frequently, the critic learns that he must develop
> some formula that will allow him to have something to
> say day after day. Some resort to scorn, pouring out col-
> umn after column of satire. Television becomes the whip-
> ping boy, always available and ultimately impervious to
> the blows delivered by the critic. . . . When the critic
> chooses to combine scorn with ready made publicity there
> results the gossip column, devoted more to amusement
> than to commentary on television. . . .
>
> There are, on the other hand, truly responsible
> critics. . . . Superior journalists—Laurent, Jack Gould,
> John Crosby, Robert Lewis Shayon, John O'Connor . . .
> shape television. . . . These critics often see their role
> as one that allows the audience to have its own views cor-
> roborated or challenged. . . . Still, in most cases, there
> is time and space for the expression of only immediate re-
> sponse, and no matter how informed or responsible, such
> immediacy does not tend toward the development of a clear
> overview of television's complex role in culture and soci-
> ety. . . . Ultimately, the journalist gives us small bits
> and pieces of ideas about a great many aspects of televi-
> sion. The business of the journalist is information, and
> we are informed with fragments. [40]

In our interview, Newcomb indicated that he tried to avoid the
pressure of immediacy when he wrote his column for the Baltimore
Sun. He essentially saw the body of his newspaper columns as a continuing, organic lecture:

> I see the role of the newspaper columnist as very much
> like the teacher, and I always defined myself in that way.
> That is, if I had something to say about television, and I

thought I did, which was not drama criticism, then I had
to start at point one and build a set of assumptions and . . .
a set of premises, and demonstrate night after night how
you could say those things about TV . . . This is they
were almost like lectures . . . [with] little illustrations
of those principles. So I could watch fifteen minutes of a
program and legitimately go and write to meet my deadline, because I wasn't talking about the program at all. I
would pick up one little bit out of a show, and that would
illustrate a point about TV. All of my writing for the paper I thought was about television, rarely about the show
that I was reviewing.

Newcomb spoke to me of his perception of the influence of newspaper columnists writing about television:

. . . ultimately I don't think it makes a lot of difference
what critics say in newspapers particularly. I know there
are stories of "The Waltons" staying on because critics
had some say-so, and that they do read the columns . . .
My suspicion is that they read very few of them. They
read O'Connor, and they read a few people from Washington . . . and the coast. But they don't [read] Detroit,
and they don't read Cleveland, they don't read wherever
there's a town big enough to support a newspaper critic.

The "they" to whom Newcomb referred are the industry executives and television's creative community. While Newcomb does not
believe that his newspaper columns had any impact on these individuals, he does feel that viewers read his columns in the Baltimore Sun:

. . . people did read the column and take it seriously. I
heard people talk about it occasionally when they didn't
know who I was. I think people like to talk about TV, so
I think it's important that we have good people doing [tel-
evision criticism], and have a good attitude toward what
they're doing.

NEWCOMB ON HIS READERSHIP

Newcomb sees the readership for his books, articles, and papers as being primarily composed of university students and professors:

. . . I try to write . . . for a popular culture audience,
and that can be English departments, it can be American
studies. Increasingly it's gotten into broadcasting departments, mass comm. programs. . . . In terms of more
prominent kinds of things, I know that Elihu Katz likes
the book [TV: The Most Popular Art] because it feeds into his uses and gratifications thing . . . He's just done a
report for BBC which I've not seen, but David Thorburn
told me the book was cited several times, so . . . it will
get to people in that way. When the book did well enough,
we decided to do an anthology [Television: The Critical
View] and that apparently is being widely used in a number of different kinds of courses. . . . increasingly they're
courses about television.

While Newcomb did not seem certain of the nature of the readership for his newspaper column, he did give me some specific examples of letters he had received while working for the Baltimore
Sun:

The newspaper thing was interesting. I got letters almost every week, three or four, not many, very few
repeats. People would be ticked off about what I said
about Bob Hope. My first letter was from a fourteen-
year-old girl who loved baseball, and I really knocked
baseball on TV, saying that the sport was not really
suitable for a medium like that, but football was, and
she came on with a five-page handwritten letter in this
beautiful schoolgirl hand saying, "Who are you to tell
us? These are just your opinions. Why is your opinion
any better than mine?" And every teacher has heard
that. Some paranoid letters, crazy people. Obscenities.
This one person, one repeat I got two or three letters
from with line after line of closely typed, nonspaced
obscenities, and also racial stuff, associating fornica-
tion and blacks, and social ills, and the world going to
pot, and everything. It closed at one point with a tragic-
ally humorous line saying, "For fourteen years I've suf-
fered from paranoid schizophrenia and colitis."

CONCLUSIONS

In his early writings, including his book TV: The Most Popular
Art, Newcomb tended to evaluate various popular television genres

according to "formula theory." These analyses were both aesthetic-
and value-based. In more recent writings, however, Newcomb has
looked through the works he is evaluating into the deep structures of
the culture's symbol systems that are reflected in television's content and also rooted in the symbols' relation to the world of experience of the audience. To this end, he has noted that television has
become part of the experiential history of the audience to which audience members can make continual reference. Newcomb no longer
views as valid the "fantasy/realism" dichotomy in which "fantasy" is
considered to take the form of diversionary entertainment while "realism" is considered to be an accurate representation of the complex
web of human interactions in the world of experience. To Newcomb,
the world of experience has become a combination of both fantasy and
realism, and both are culturally significant. He thus refuses to take
the traditional "culture elitist" stance that views "serious" drama and
comedic forms as inherently good or healthy and "entertainment" as
inherently bad and escapist. By his objective assessment of entertainment forms as culturally significant and laden with deeper meaning,
Newcomb is able to dispassionately examine the historical roots of
television as an art form.

Newcomb has examined television's historical roots by focusing
on major shifts in style that he terms "intensifiers of meaning." One
such shift occurred when comedy styles changed from the situation
comedy with its internal family development to the domestic comedy
such as "All in the Family" that moved toward exploration of crucial
social issues of the day which impacted on the family unit in the comedy, and by implication on our own families as well. Newcomb has
also highlighted a variety of individual television series that he believes have broken established popular entertainment structural patterns and allowed members of the audience to better apprehend who
they are in a larger cultural context. Newcomb's historical approach
allows the reader to discover a continuity in the development of various styles of television works as they borrow from and modify previous television styles.

Newcomb has not been caught in the trap of trying to distinguish
popular art and so-called high art according to the nature of the television audience. Rather, he has continued to focus his search for television art on programs and series that seem to transcend the limitations of formula and exhibit characteristics he has established for a
more complex art.

Newcomb views his role as a television critic to be that of an
educator who should help viewers become knowledgeable about the
ways in which images and sounds are manipulated to produce works
of art in television, and he believes that such knowledge can enhance
the viewer's enjoyment of television programs. The outcome of this

knowledge, claims Newcomb, should produce better viewer understanding of their dissatisfaction with particular television works.

Newcomb believes his writings about television have made an
impact on some students of television and popular culture and perhaps on some of his newspaper column's readers. However, he does
not feel his writings have impacted directly on either television industry executives or most of the creative community engaged in making television programs. The latter groups, Newcomb believes, restrict their reading of critical commentary to those individuals writing about television for major daily newspapers in New York, Washington, D. C. , and on the West coast.

One of Newcomb's major strengths as a television critic is his
ability to express complex ideas in a manner that is both meaningful
and understandable. Unlike many other academicians who are presently writing art criticism, Newcomb is writing for an expanded readership that includes students and other interested individuals with
many different levels of understanding of television. He is not engaged
in the game of obtuse discourse comprehensible to a select few with
knowledge of some complicated analytical lexicon (as seems to be the
case, for example, with contemporary semiological film criticism).
Newcomb's is a sophisticated audience-oriented criticism.

Newcomb's genre analysis and discussion of symbol systems
as they relate to television will likely continue to bear critical fruit
as other serious observers of television draw from and expand on his
ideas. One also eagerly awaits an update of his book TV: The Most
Popular Art, which left us in the early 1970s of the television art.

NOTES

1. See Raymond Williams, Communications, rev. ed. , (London: Barnes & Noble, 1967), a treatise primarily concerned with the
cultural institution of print; and especially Television: Technology
and Cultural Form (New York: Schocken Books, 1975), which discusses television as a "text" from which one can draw references to
the cultural makeup of a people by examining programs' sequencing
and flow.

2. James W. Carey, "Communication and Culture," Communication Research 2 (April 1975): 175.

3. Williams, Television, p. 44.

4. Carey, "Communication and Culture," p. 176.

5. David Thorburn, "The Evolution of the Television Detective"
(Paper presented at the American Studies Association Convention,
Boston, Mass. , October 1977).

6. David Thorburn, "Television Melodrama," in Television as a Cultural Force, eds. Richard Adler and Douglass Cater (New York: Praeger, 1976), p. 85.

7. Ibid., p. 86.

8. Bruce Kurtz, Spots: The Popular Art of American Television Commercials (New York: Arts Communications, 1977).

9. Ibid., p. 5.

10. Ibid., p. 8.

11. Ibid., p. 11.

12. Ibid., pp. 31-32.

13. Ibid., p. 37.

14. Littlejohn, "Thoughts on Television Criticism," p. 169.

15. See Horace Newcomb, TV: The Most Popular Art (Garden City, N.Y.: Doubleday, Anchor Press, 1974).

16. Ibid., pp. 22-23.

17. Ibid., p. 28.

18. Ibid., p. 27.

19. Ibid., p. 36.

20. Ibid., p. 41.

21. Ibid., pp. 29-30.

22. Horace Newcomb, "Fiction as Anthropology: Images of the South in Popular Television Series" (Paper presented at the University of South Carolina Conference on Visual Anthropology and the American South, Columbia, S.C., October 1977), pp. 9-14.

23. Ibid., pp. 14-16.

24. Horace Newcomb, "Television and Cultural Theory" (Paper presented at the Conference on Postindustrial Culture: Technology and the Public Sphere, Center for Twentieth Century Studies, University of Wisconsin, Milwaukee, February 1977), p. 15.

25. Ibid., p. 10.

26. Newcomb, "Television and Cultural Theory," pp. 13-15.

27. Ibid., pp. 16-17.

28. Carey, "Communication and Culture," p. 177.

29. Newcomb, "Television and Cultural Theory," p. 8.

30. Horace Newcomb, "Toward Television History: The Growth of Styles" (Paper presented at the American Studies Association Convention, Boston, Mass., October 1977), pp. 1-2.

31. Ibid., pp. 6-8.

32. Newcomb, TV: The Most Popular Art, p. 211.

33. Ibid., pp. 212, 216, 226, 229, 231-32.

34. Horace Newcomb, "The Audience Is Crucial as Television Begins to Grow Up," Baltimore Sun, 31 May 1974, p. B5.

35. Newcomb, "Television and Cultural Theory," pp. 11-12.

36. Newcomb, TV: The Most Popular Art, pp. 20-21.

37. Horace Newcomb, "Television Big and Unwieldy, but It's Changed Our Lives," Baltimore Sun, 26 March 1973, p. B5.

38. Newcomb, TV: The Most Popular Art, p. 181.

39. Horace Newcomb, ed. , Television: The Critical View (New York: Oxford University Press, 1976), p. xxi.

40. Newcomb, The Critical View, pp. xvi-xvii.

6

DAVID ROSS:
A SPOKESPEPRSON FOR
ARTISTS' VIDEO

The acceptance of new styles of making art in any given art form is nurtured by the writings of "radical" critics who, according to art critic Richard Kostelanetz, "prefer works that are formally unlike anything they have seen before" (see Chapter 2). Among those critics one might classify as radicals are artists, agents, anthologists, and gallery and museum curators. According to Kostelanetz, these critics frequently write polemical critiques of avant-garde art works and they tend to be more closely involved than other critics with the actual creation of avant-garde works, works which while important may not find their way into the dominant (i. e. , traditional) cultural marketplace.

In the dominant cultural world of television art, those works that are created and distributed on the outer fringes of television's mass distribution network are usually given the title "video art" or, more appropriately "artists' video" to separate them from traditional formulaic television products.

When one talks of television in its broadest sense, it is necessary to first distinguish what are "traditional" works and what are "innovative" works. Generally, the distinction as applied to television leads to the presupposition that popular television programs or series are traditional in that they draw upon and essentially translate works from other art forms such as theater, film, literature, dance, and music, and, further, have achieved a certain acceptance in our dominant cultural scheme. On the other hand, the innovative works are presumed to be those works of artists' video that are distinguishable from mainstream television productions. Such innovative works are characterized as being more personalized than their television counterparts (often being intrapsychic explorations); frequently, but certainly not always, being nonnarrative in structure; and often being interactive tools allowing the audience to interact with the content of the works on a one-to-one basis in "real time."

114

Since these works of artists' video are clearly more esoteric than standard television fare, broadcasters have been extremely reluctant to open their massive distribution mechanisms to such exploratory efforts. The artists therefore have gotten little play for their works and consequently have had to seek alternative distribution mechanisms. Enter the radical video critics.

The radical critics who take upon themselves the challenge of defending artists' video in a world predominated by television fall into two general groups: artists themselves who both create and write about video works, and video curators and anthologists who work closely with artists to ensure that the artists' efforts reach the public in a variety of forums.

Video curators and anthologists are a relatively new breed of "critic" on the contemporary art front, for video as a tool for individualized artists' statements did not arrive on the art scene in America until the mid-1960s with Nam June Paik's use of the Sony portapak in New York City. As the number of artists employing video in their work grew in the late 1960s and early 1970s, a corresponding need to publicize and distribute this new work developed, and a number of radical critics came to the aid of those artists working with video. These critics were acting as public relations persons, promoting novel styles of making video. They began to formulate well-defined plausible criteria by which to evaluate video works and developed a well-conceived, if somewhat polemical, defense of video as a legitimate art form. This often meant controverting traditional standards of artistic significance by convincing their readerships that these standards, while perhaps reasonable in themselves, should be applied to video in new configurations.

The radical video critics are members of the inner circle of artists working with video; they function as mediators between artist "clients" and a cultural public limited in number but involved with artistic attitudes on the cutting edge of the art form.

Among the most prominent radical critics writing about video in the United States today are John Hanhardt, Russell Connor, and David Ross. We will take a brief look at the activities and writings of Hanhardt and Connor below and then examine Ross's activities and writings at greater length.

John Hanhardt, presently Curator of Film and Video at the Whitney Museum of American Art in New York City, has, during the past five years, established himself as one of the most powerful voices in defense of artists' video as a significant art medium. His curatorial activities include scheduling exhibitions of independent artists' video works at the Whitney, one of this country's most respected museums. He has done this with characteristic élan, keeping artists' video works in the public spotlight when they might have otherwise been ignored or

accorded a status less than their due. Hanhardt has also written significant tracts on the meaning of artists' video and the nature of the
video experience that have been included in print anthologies on artists' video and journals such as TV Magazine. He also writes notes
for the video exhibitions appearing at the Whitney. His prose is marked by a clean, concise style that renders difficult, complex concepts
understandable.

One of Hanhardt's more interesting pieces discusses the significance of the multi- and single-monitor installation genre in the
context of the cultural and social experience of television viewing:

> . . . the television screen is a part of a piece of furni-
> ture which the viewer takes in from a variety of per-
> spectives and levels. . . . program design and narra-
> tive structures do not require close attention or any
> concentration.
> All these factors come into play when the artist
> approaches video and the audience perceives it. Much as
> the independent film artist is in a continual process of
> discovering new forms of narrative structures, or new
> forms of expression to make his work independent of
> those structures . . . the video artist is in the position
> . . . of working against the conventions of a medium
> which is so associated with the forms of commercial
> television. . . . it does propose that we appreciate the
> associations and tensions that the viewer brings to video
> art. By this is meant the content and form of the image
> and the contradictions of the television monitor in gallery
> and museum contexts. [1]

One of those contradictions, Hanhardt argues, is the fact that
the viewer, in the traditional television-viewing experience, is least
familiar with the television screen, which is perceived as but one focus in a home-viewing environment that contains a variety of additional simultaneous inputs.

Another internal contradiction evident in the growth of broadcast television over the years is its desertion of the live telecast in
favor of prerecorded, standardized product. Asserting the need to
recapture the qualities of live TV, Hanhardt turns to the potential of
cable television:

> . . . Cable television is based on the myth of the "Golden
> Age" of television, the era before its qualities were lost
> to slick packaging. . . . The non-professional (read non-
> standardized) look of most cable shows has given cable the

look and feel of live broadcast even though it is also largely pretaped. The future of cable lies in its potential, largely unrealized, for restoring to live television what it never realized: an awareness of itself as a medium of infinite possibilities and risks. [2]

Hanhardt has shown a desire to locate nexuses between the video experience and the television experience. Such an endeavor is sorely needed in the critical dialogue, and it will come from critics like Hanhardt with an expansive cultural perspective.

Russell Connor began his career as a painter. In 1963 he came to public station WGBH-TV in Boston to produce a weekly series called "Museum Open House," which dealt with the ongoing activities of the Boston Museum of Fine Arts. Connor surveyed the museum's collections and did a few experiments in television as part of the broadcasts. In 1970, he organized the "Vision and Television" exhibition of video works at the Rose Art Museum at Brandeis University, the first exhibition to incorporate video in a museum context. Connor also joined the staff of the New York State Council on the Arts that year, and between 1970 and 1973 he was in charge of granting funds through the council to both independent video artists and local broadcast stations throughout the state. One of the significant outgrowths of the council's funding efforts was the creation of WNET-TV's TV Lab in New York City. The TV Lab is a video research and experimentation center that has provided production facilities and technical production assistance for numerous artists working with video. In 1975 Connor wrote and hosted a broadcast series on artists' video for WNET-TV. The series, called "VTR: Video and Television Review," consisted of 22 installments show late at night in New York City and Boston. In his introduction to the series, Connor told the audience:

> Happily, there were people out there, like Nam June Paik, Stan Vanderbeek, and others whom you'll meet in this series, who were actually doing something in this medium, and using it for personal and artistic expression. In the mid-60s a prototype of this relatively inexpensive, portable VTR appeared on the scene, and a new generation of artists and social activists who had literally grown up with television seized on it as both an artistic tool and a cybernetic means of circumventing the network's control of media information.
>
> It became possible for one person to record his or her view of the world and play it back immediately. Artists grappled with the technology and developed video synthesizers which allowed for electronic paintings of infinite subtlety and variety. [3]

Connor thus distinguished between artists' "personal" expression through video and television networks' impersonal "control of media information." To counteract this network control, Connor argued that the optimum wedding of artists' video and "television" should come through the use of cable channels as transmission conduits for low-cost artists' videotapes. However, Connor did not limit his interest in cablecasting art to artists' videotapes. Also of interest to him was finding a public forum for film, dance, poetry, painting, sculpture, music, architecture, and crafts. Connor wrote of cable television's potential association with the arts:

> Cable television will eventually allow for the most scholarly, didactic, and elitist presentations of the arts as well as more popular entertainment-oriented ones. We'd like to test response to a lively co-existence of traditional and advance-guard directions in the arts and to bring art sharply up against life now and then to hear what the people have to say.
>   . . . It is vital, no matter how often we get the feeling that we are projecting slides on the other side of the moon, that a foothold for the arts be created now amidst the diversity of minority interest programming which cable promises. [4]

Connor has focused his energies on bringing art, including artists' video, to the public through the use of broadcast television as a link between the museum and the television audience. He has also explored the use of cable television's public access channels as a means of transmitting works in a variety of art forms to small groups of viewers within a time structure that allows for the frequent repetition of individual works and thus enables the cable audience to reexamine those works.

While Connor's activities as a polemicist for artists' video have placed greater emphasis on the actual production of video anthologies than on written critical evaluations of artists' video, David Ross has taken a somewhat more integrated approach to his involvement with video. Ross has combined his activities as a promoter of artists' video through his work as a museum video curator, with numerous essays on video appearing in art magazines, museum exhibition catalogues, and print anthologies on video.

Ross was born in 1949 in New York City. He received a Bachelor's degree in Art and Communications from Syracuse University in 1971, and from November 1971 to June 1974 was Curator of Video Arts at the Everson Museum of Art in Syracuse. Ross found funds for and established this country's first museum video department at the Everson Museum in 1971.

In June 1974, Ross left the Everson to become the Deputy Director for Program Development and Television at the Long Beach Museum of Art in Long Beach, California. While at the Long Beach Museum, Ross acted as its head curator with responsibility for organizing all the artists' exhibitions at the museum. One of his significant contributions during this period was the organization and exhibition of the video works of over 100 Southern California artists working in video. Titled "Southland Video Anthology," the exhibition was staged in four parts during 1976 and 1977. While at the Long Beach Museum, Ross also attempted to involve the museum in cablecasting through his efforts to revitalize KVST-TV viewer-supported television in the Los Angeles area.

In November 1977, Ross took a position as Assistant Director for Exhibitions and Programs at the University of California Art Museum in Berkeley, California. Although he is now heavily involved in a variety of museum administration activities, Ross has maintained his interest in artists' video.

Ross's entry into the world of artists' video was a bit unusual, but in a rapidly evolving youthful art form such as video was in 1971, often anything goes. Ross described his video beginnings in our interview:

> I was doing video [at Syracuse University] after having done printmaking and photography. Video seemed like a logical step to me. It didn't have any, at that point, what I considered base in an object or production of a material thing, but in the production of information. After that I started graduate school at Syracuse, and I was going to develop a video program as part of my graduate degree. But it was during that period that I met James Harithas, who was the Director of the Everson. . . . I was employed to take a photograph of him as he'd just been brought to the museum there . . . as the Director. He had a reputation of being somewhat radical at that time in 1971. The air in general was fairly radical, and I felt that museums, especially the Everson, had become fairly irrelevant in the ways in which they were prepared to deal with communities in general, and the ways that they were ignoring contemporary art forms that challenged their own structure. So when I met him I thought I had nothing to lose by insulting him and trying to at least get him to react—I thought I could maybe get a good photograph out of him. But also I thought this was a reasonable opportunity to tell this new museum director how I felt about the museum he was taking over, and I told him I thought the museum was really

a piece of shit and that he was getting into a situation that was completely irrelevant in relationship to the real community and Syracuse, and that the museum would be obsolete in five years if it didn't become a television station. And I said this with a kind of sarcastic attitude through it all, and thought that he would say something to me about it. He turned around and said, "Why don't you be Assistant Director of the Museum?" So I left graduate school that day and started working in the museum as assistant to Jim, and he taught me the museum business. After about a year of that I managed to fund and establish the first museum video department, because that's what I ultimately felt the museum had to do in order to start to work its way back toward being somehow a relevant institution in relationship to the majority of the culture that saw museums as somehow outside of their lives, their life-styles or their life interests. And although they were paying in part for museums through taxes, and could benefit by visiting the museum, I thought the museum had a responsibility at that point to start to support the kind of art that would be . . . brought into their homes, and that the museum actually could become a television channel by investing in the support of the development of cable and in the support of the development of artists' use of television or video.

Thereafter Ross became heavily involved in the video movement as a museum video curator, a new area he helped carve in the museum structure. He also began to write about artists' video in a variety of forums. He has written articles on artists' video for Arts Magazine. His essays on video and interviews with artists working with video are included in Video Art: An Anthology (1976), and The New Television: A Public/Private Art (1977). The majority of his writings about video have appeared in museum exhibition catalogues and focus on such notable artists working in video as Douglas Davis, Nam June Paik, Peter Campus, and Frank Gillette; and on group exhibitions such as "Art Now '74, A Celebration of the American Arts," in Washington, D.C.; "Project '74 in Koln," in Cologne, West Germany; and the artists' videotapes produced by Art/Tapes/22 in Florence, Italy. He also compiled and wrote the introduction for the catalogue that documented the Long Beach Museum's "Southland Video Anthology."

ROSS ON ARTISTS' VIDEO

Ross has discussed in various essays what he considers to be video's "first principles"—well-defined plausible criteria by which one can adequately evaluate both the aesthetic designs and subjects internal to video works, as well as video's place in our culture. According to Ross, these first principles of video include: video's inherent spatial and temporal illusions that become surrogate realities; the ability of real-time or unedited video to bridge the gap between these illusions and the realism of life experiences; video's inherent two-way communicative capability; video's intimacy or personalness; cable television's potentially unlimited channel capacity, which offers a forum for individuals' unrestricted personal statements; and video's capacity, when linked to cablecasting, to bring the art museum into the home. Each of these hypothesized first principles of video are examined below.

Ross has often focused his writing on video's ambiguous relationship to both "realism" and "illusion":

> It seems odd that although nearly everyone is all too aware of the incredible lack of fidelity and resolution inherent in the television picture, the video image has become an unquestioned and unquestionably surrogate reality. It is, for many, as natural to see the world on television as it is to look at it out of a more conventional window. For some, television watching has totally replaced direct experience of the world. The problem that arises from this phenomenon is not that a "phoney" experience has attained "real" status, but rather than the structure of mass communication systems makes it difficult to see both experiences as real.
>
> The notion of "phoniness" stems, of course, from the odd way in which voices sounded via telephonic connections; that tinny somewhat lo-fi representation of direct speech was, after all, a real connection to the consciousness of another person no matter how awful it sounded. The mistrust connoted by "phoney," however, reveals not only the lo-fi bias, but the initial uneasiness with which a society greeted electronic extensions of sensory capacity, logic and consciousness. In time, the universally experienced telephonic reality imparted to even the evanescent radio message a similarly credible experience. . . . Electronic communication is no longer phoney per se, though the content of any particular call may be completely phoney.

But the eye is quicker than the ear, in the case of
television, and while we can imagine (with eyes closed)
that a telephone connection is in reality a direct link of
one consciousness with another, it is all too clear that
even the sharpest Sony Trinitron image of a moon walk,
a presidential address, or an artist's work is a gross al-
teration—and in some cases, reduction—of what we experience by simply looking at a corresponding corporeal
reality. In order to justify a television image as reality,
then, the viewer must impart to that image a measure of
significance arising from recognition and understanding
of surrogate, disembodied co-existing realities formerly
ascribed to divine experience. (In other words, an acceptance of a phoney reality taken on faith.)[5]

Ross pointed to Peter Campus's museum video installations as
examples of how the artist could effectively deal with video's spatial
illusions by in essence forcing the viewer to examine his or her relationship to the illusory characteristics of the medium:

Peter Campus creates complex sculptural systems using
television cameras, video projectors and picture monitors
as primary structural elements while relying heavily upon
light-defined fields and viewer interaction for the framework.
. . . In his own words, Campus is dealing with the
medium as a "function of reality." In other words, the
artist has constructed an equation in which there is a real
and knowable relationship between what one might call directly perceived reality and the seemingly altered reality
evidenced by the video image, the reflection, or even the
shadow.
. . . The works deal with the mediation between op-
posing or at least dissimilar aspects of image and the viewer's perception of image. The fact that each piece essentially exists when the viewer is in the field prescribed by
the work serves as a reinforcement of the primary emphasis upon individual exploration and perception of the nature
of the differences at play. One is tempted to view the works
as a series of oracles waiting silent until approached by the
inquiring mind.[6]

Not only did Ross see video as creating spatial illusions taken
by viewers as surrogate realities, but he also recognized the temporal illusions created by videotape: "When we play back a videotape,

even one made in real time, it acts as an overlay on another time, thus becoming a temporal illusion. "[7]

Ross described the video installation works of Frank Gillette as effective attempts to deal with the temporally illusory characteristics of video. One such installation piece, "Track/Trace," was a complex time-based work that attempted to draw the viewer into the temporal illusion of video. Ross described the work:

> In Track/Trace . . . fifteen monitors are stacked in a pyramid with an eight foot apex and eight foot base. . . . Three cameras and a sequential switching device provide an alternating scan of the viewer's space while a five-point delay loop brings the changing images through the apex (in real time) to the base (12 seconds removed from the origination of the image). The cameras are switched every eight seconds. Track/Trace . . . [centers] on the relationship of consciously manipulated time to the sum of information exchange. [8]

The net effect of "Track/Trace" is that the viewer sees himself in present time standing before the piece. He also sees himself as he was approaching the piece 12 seconds earlier.

While Campus's and Gillette's works refer to video's inherent illusory characteristics, they both do so in the context of sculpture locked into the museum confines. It was left to other artists working in video to expand on this notion of temporal and spatial illusion in the context of the broadcast or cablecast structure itself. Ross noted how the notions of video's spatial and temporal illusions were effectively explored in a broadcast context by video performance artist Eleanor Antin:

> Eleanor Antin's performance works have always employed a great deal of artifice in the creation of her alter-ego characters. Video, for Antin, is perhaps the most effective way of framing her work and directing her audience. In The Adventures of a Nurse (1976), Antin presents a series of fantasies set within the overall fantasy/character of nurse Eleanor. In the live version of the performance, nurse Eleanor sits on her bed and acts through several socially and sexually loaded situations using a set of paper dolls as players and another set of hand drawn dolls as audience observing from a shelf. In the taped version of the work, we see more than a document of the performance, as the soap opera quality of the piece suddenly attains a curious sort of credibility through the imposition

of the structured language of camera shots and cuts that
we have come to know as television reality. In the act of
taping the performance, and in fact removing the story
and storytelling from reality by one layer, Antin manages
to set the performance and the content of the performance
inside a context that we read, as a result of our experience with "real" soap opera, as somehow more "believ-
able. "[9]

Antin's subtle references to the aesthetic text of the traditional
television soap opera genre may be viewed on one level as parody and
on a deeper level as both a formal exploration of television's time signature and a conceptual exploration of television's "intimate" qualities.
In both cases, television tradition is stretched and thereby questioned.
In this sense, Antin's work represents a direction of the new video
narrative—that of exploiting, while at the same time heightening, what
Newcomb referred to as the audience's highly evolved television liter-
acy.

Another of Ross's principal focuses is that of real-time or unedited video. Unedited video, according to Ross, offers the viewer an
opportunity to bridge the perceptual gap between video's spatial and
temporal illusions and the realism of life experience outside the art
context:

The use of real-time video coverage of . . . various ecol-
ogies provides more than a documentation of ongoing processes, and once again suggests an evaluation of the way
we perceive life processes. The video level confronts the
viewer with the split between two realities (the visceral
and the electronic re-construction) and forces a reconcil-
iation between the way we perceive and the particular orientation within which we perceive. [10]

According to Ross, artists working in real-time video are also
moving toward the integration of the audience into the creative process itself. Ross cited Douglas Davis's video works as examples of
the meaningful use of real-time video:

[Davis's] closest juxtaposition of art time and real time,
as well as the finest psychic edge, is reached in Studies
in Myself II (1973). Davis is seen seated at the keyboard
of a television typewriter called a character generator.
The camera pans around him, from side to side, as he
begins to type at the keyboard. Within a few minutes, he
is typing at full speed, allowing his thoughts to flow as

freely as possible. What takes place is a gradual realization that the viewer is being synchronized with the
artist's creative process.

In a way, we are observing the artist coming to
grips with a piece of foreign technology and with the notion that he is quite publicly externalizing his private
thoughts and fantasies. [11]

By eliminating the artifice of editing from the video work, the artist
can thus exploit the real-time or "live" characteristics of the medium—immediacy and unpredictability—even though the piece in real
time may have been taped and overlaid on another time. The immediacy and unpredictability of real-time video is both self-reflexive
in its reference to the so-called Golden Age of live television drama
in the 1950s and a direct assault on today's highly segmented dominant television structures. Intimate real-time video, according to
Ross, offers a direct challenge to those dominant structures:

Video allows the artist the opportunity to address a number of vital concerns in relation to the viewer. First of
all, an essentially personal statement can be related (in
a very direct way) in a mode that is as singular and personal (in scale and intensity) as face to face communication. Further, the time-based nature of the statement
adds a captivating element to the message which the artist can either exploit (by extension over a long period of
time, creating a resultant boredom/tension/release cycle) or bypass (by creating work that is immediately grat-
ifying). In other words, the real-time consciousness of
the viewer becomes the blank canvas, which can obviously
be dealt with in a variety of ways. On a socio-political level, video is an effective and nonprecious activity aimed,
primarily, at extending the range and breadth of the artists' commitment to, and relations with the audience. The
notions of a dematerialized art that united a highly diverse
group of sculptors, dancers, poets, painters, and docu-
mentarians in eclectic multi-media investigations into the
nature of art, seem to have jelled into a set of activities
called (fairly effectively) video art. . . . As co-equals,
working with a medium that has little traditional grounding, video artists (a term some consider derisive) find
themselves involved in a generalized exploration of the
nature of communication rather than the nature of the medium itself. [12]

Ross saw another of video's first principles as its inherent two-way communicative capability, a capability that he asserted had not been realized in broadcasting and was just beginning to be explored within the context of developing cable television technology:

It has become obvious to artists and other students of communication that the major problem facing those interested in re-structuring the information network is its de facto one-way nature. The growing awareness of up-stream-downstream potential (brought about in part by the advent of CATV technology) angered and frustrated many who realized just what the implications of two-way communication were. In 1929, [Bertolt] Brecht had written his Theory of Radio in which he stated that it was the two-way capacity of electromagnetic communication that gave the radio medium its potential importance. The same theory holds for television. The essays of Walter Benjamin, influenced by Brecht, defined the growing portability of art. But it is only now that these concepts are taking flesh and form. [13]

Video's two-way potential can produce a context in which the viewer can interact directly with the artist and/or the images the artist produces. Ross again cited Davis as one of the pioneers exploring video's two-way interactive capability:

Douglas Davis is prime among that group of contemporary artists whose concern and unique vision have been changing the very fabric of mass communication. His grounding in conceptual events and performances during the late sixties, leading up to his now historic Electronic Hokkadim (1971) placed him at the vanguard of those artists who are concerned with the new information aesthetic. Electronic Hokkadim, in which thousands of callers participated in a telephone to television direct access experiment, and Talk Out!, Davis' open input dialogue, are telecasts in which the artist both sends and receives messages from the public. [14]

As will be discussed at length in Chapter 7, Davis and others have continued their experiments with two-way interactive video. For example, in August 1979, Davis gained access to Warner Communications' "Qube" two-way interactive cable system in Columbus, Ohio, where he did a talk format/performance piece called "How to Make Love To Your Television Set." Viewers were asked to both call-in and ask Davis and the show's host to do a variety of activities in which viewers could also participate at home, and to register their "votes" on such questions as "Did you embrace your TV screen either in fact or in your imagination? 1. yes 2. no."

As interesting as the Qube experiment was, a serious question remains as to artists' ability to gain <u>unrestricted</u> access to channels. Ross addressed this specific problem:

> Nam June Paik, the Korean-born composer and video pioneer, summed up the basis for this kind of thinking in a 1972 collage "Do You Know" (dedicated to Ray Johnson, one of the first correspondence artists). Paik added a few lines to an early forties magazine ad which queried "how soon after the war will television be available for the average home?" His response becomes a leading question for the seventies, "how soon will artists have their own TV channels?"[15]

The answer to Paik's question, according to Ross, ultimately lies in the potential of the unlimited channel capacity of cable television. However, it is at this point that artists' video and the dominant broadcast structure collide in a struggle for control of air time and audience. Much of Ross's writing about video and his nonwritten activities promoting artists' video have focused on this notion of unrestricted access to communication channels:

> . . . broadcasters had little use for the majority of this esoteric work, which they judged inadequate by their prevailing technical and programming standards. . . . The artist, working alone, is never allowed direct access to the viewer. His work is always interpreted. Broadcasters continue to see their role as that of central translator for the entire society. . . . The Western concept of television viewing . . . has always been connected to the politics of the individual controlled in privacy. . . . For many, this fact confirmed a growing feeling of futility in terms of political efforts to introduce the personal attitude directly into the macro-television system.[16]

Ross elaborated on this perceived artist sense futility in dealing with broadcasters:

> The video artists' role, in relation to television, has always been, and will probably remain, a posteriori. The fact that the artist now possesses the tools of television

production has given him the illusion that he is an active participant in the process. The smoke screen produced by the quasi-admission of the artist to the television process has totally obscured the fact that there will never be any but the most limited tolerance of the individual artist within television's broadcast structure. It remains that the artist's responsibility lies not in producing programs, but in dealing with notions of art and artistic responsibility made evident by the state of television in its grossest sense. [17]

However, by 1977 Ross had come to believe in the potential of cable television as a significant avenue through which individual artists could gain unrestricted access to a small, but interested audience:

CATV offers the rare opportunity to create a neutral yet intimate space for the artist to commune directly with the public. Much of the best video art that has been produced to date shows a real understanding and respect for the nature of this relationship, as it questions the nature of art rather than the nature of any one medium. It marks the return to the individual of a primary visual art experience, while at the same time it creates a real public art. Unlike the dancer, musician or poet, the visual artist has been denied direct access to a home audience through television. Even in the most enlightened ETV programming, the artist is presented in a packaged and somehow contained format. The message is indirect. [18]

Ross does not believe that artists' video should or could eventually overthrow traditional broadcast programming. Artists' video's appeal is obviously limited. However, both should be allowed to co-exist with equal presence in relation to the entire system. He discussed this concept of peaceful video/television coexistence in our interview:

The key is in looking at the structure and not in the nature of the programming. And the structure is one in which repressive tolerance is the key notion in the system. The notion of "Fairness" is used to prohibit the expression of unfiltered ideas. . . . all ideas are filtered and weighed against each other and then put out in a mix that's supposed to be neutral. Now it's clear that it's not a neutral system, that it has monetary profit gain involved, that it has clear political and ideological biases. . . . But the notion of

"Fairness" . . . is still held in front of us like some kind
of a carrot to keep everybody following in line—"This is
the best we can do, this is what we're stuck with. We're
just going to try and make it fair."... And people understood that when the decisions were made to give 90 percent of available frequencies to commercial licensees . . .
we were essentially providing a certain ideological basis
for the broadcast system . . . So the only way to fight a-
gainst that is to establish . . . alternate structures which
don't inherit any of the biases and problems of the original
structures. And the only way to do that . . . is to work towards . . . multiple or hundred-channel . . . or thousand-
channel . . . or unlimited number channel systems in which
the need for information is the determining factor, for the
need to produce information is all that's really critical. . . .
NBC will still exist, and the Republican Party and General
Motors will still be able to put [on] bigger, more packaged
. . . advertising or more polished material than Socialist
Alliance or than a single artist, but their presence won't
have any more structural strength then the other. In other
words, it will be possible for a single artist who works in
his own studio and wants his own channel because that's his
work . . . [to] have channel 825 and General Motors Corporation will have their "Masterpiece Theater" channel with
which they want to attract a class of buyer for the Cadillac
on channel 89, and for their Corvettes they may have a vio-
lent program. . . . It will be a product- and idea-related
use of the media. Ideas are products in our culture. . . .
I wouldn't want to put anybody in a position of eliminating
broadcast type of programming. . . . It's not of interest
to me to eliminate anything. It's much more in my interest to be inclusive and to . . . tolerate to the extent that
we're going to expand the entire system.
    . . . artists' video . . . [is] surely not going to re-
place television. Hopefully it will find its own niche. That's
all any independent use of television can hope for and can
work towards.

While serving as Deputy Director of Program Development and
Television at the Long Beach Museum of Art, Ross himself began to
work toward opening up the dominant broadcasting system to individual artists working in video such as those Southern California artists
whose works formed "Southland Video Anthology." Ross was a member of a four-person steering committee that tried to revitalize KVST-
TV, channel 68, in Los Angeles. KVST was a viewer-supported tele-

vision outlet that tried to find an audience for minority programming
in the Los Angeles area, In essence, KVST was functioning in a manner similar to a public access cable channel. Internal management
problems ultimately forced the station off the air. Ross's group was
attempting to set up a situation in which the channel would be reacti-
vated and artists and other groups with specialized interests would
have access to KVST's studio production equipment and postproduction facilities. I asked Ross to elaborate on the KVST experience:

> KVST was a very sad situation. Securing a channel and
> funding a basic plant is the most difficult part of estab-
> lishing a channel. . . . KVST viewer-supported televi-
> sion in L. A. was a great idea that became so overly po-
> liticized that it killed itself and turned upon itself in the
> struggle to survive. It was very poorly managed and nev-
> er really figured out a way of securing any real audience
> support because where they did do a number of radical
> political shows, they weren't able to provide the kind of
> diverse level of quality programming that . . . listener-
> supported radio can provide, and weren't able to provide
> it with a consistency that kept people watching . . . since
> one of the projects of the developing Long Beach [Museum]
> situation was to develop a cable head end for the museum
> . . . we had worked towards that end and had secured a
> number of agreements if the building got built with the ca-
> ble system to produce one day's worth of broadcast pro-
> gramming and of finding six other groups that wanted to
> produce a single day's [programming each] . . . that
> could contextualize itself rather than having to exist in
> some kind of a mix determined by a group of outside pro-
> fessionals. . . . There could be very directed promotion
> of the material, directed toward the small sub-groups that
> were interested in it, and it was a way of breaking down
> one of the central difficulties of [broadcasting] which is the
> notion that it has to serve everybody all the time, and [in-
> stead of] serving select audiences who are addressed se-
> lectly for select reasons—user-demand television. In oth-
> er words, the art world would then be called upon to sup-
> port the art channel, and . . . the Young Socialists Alli-
> ance, if they wanted a channel or a day, they could sup-
> port their day. . . . It's the same notion of expanding the
> capacity of the system that applies to cable applied to a
> broadcast situation where scarcity is still the key—scar-
> city of licensing and scarcity of hardware and technical fa-
> cilities—so that the station would become a common car-

rier and would serve with no programming decision making at all. The programming responsibility in relationship
to the community needs and FCC regulations would be . . .
[vested in] a board representing all the different people
with no one having more power than anyone else.

. . . The museum [would be] acting as one of the
participants and a producer for art programming and a
conduit for grants and a conduit for artists' projects in
the same way as it does for other kinds of artists' projects.

The KVST reactivation plan was never brought to fruition—a very interesting concept unrealized. Ross explained why:

The problem was that . . . one of the radical groups that
made up the station was intimidating others, and intimidating board members, and people were just dropping out
and didn't want to deal with this kind of bullshit any longer.
. . . It had just gone too far. They could have . . . made
some decisions about turning it around because the community college district had vowed some support, and the
museum was ready to participate. I thought that I could
find some other kinds of foundation support. . . . As far
as I know it's completely dead. I think they've had their
construction permit revoked.

While KVST was an attempt to create "alternative structures that do
not inherit any of the biases and problems" of the original dominant
broadcast television structures, the new structure as developed created a new bias and problem of its own—namely, the problem of plu-
ralism in the programming decision-making process. Shared channel
use, especially for minority subcultural groups, may in the long run
prove unsuccessful precisely because of these groups' fervor for
sharply divergent causes. Ross's "one channel-one voice" idea regarding expanding cable systems would seem the more practical of
the two alternative systems.

The KVST-TV experience examplified Ross's concern with finding new ways of linking the activities of the art community with the
television system. Ross told me he is "basically interested in . . .
how interaction with the art world can produce new models for the use
of television." One such model, to which Ross alluded above, is the
use of the museum as a producer of art programming that is subsequently cablecast or broadcast throughout the community served by
the museum. Ross described the potential of the museum as cable-
caster:

> As CATV grows . . . the museum will be in a position to
> use television channel time in the same way it utilizes gal-
> lery space within the museum's building. Hours, weeks,
> or even months may be offered to the artist in addition to,
> or instead of, the physical spaces that would traditionally
> be used in the presentation of an artist's work. It actually
> will not matter whether or not an artist wants merely to
> repeat a short work over a long period of time in order to
> gain maximum exposure for his or her ideas, whether the
> artist wishes to present a wide variety of works over a pe-
> riod of time, or to present empty air-time as a frame for
> a short statement; the museum will have, in each case,
> forged a new forum for artistic interchange.

In addition to artists' programming, Ross noted, the museum has a
responsibility to transmit purely informational programming to viewers:

> . . . the development of open channels of communication
> between the museum and the public at home will also pro-
> vide for the transmission of purely informational program-
> ming not produced by an outside agency, but by the muse-
> um's curators, and scholars themselves. As surely as it
> is the responsibility of the curator and scholar to publish,
> it is equally contingent upon them to develop a capacity to
> produce television statements about their particular areas
> of interest and expertise.

Finally, Ross noted, the museum's cablecasting activities would extend the "museum without walls" concept even further into the community:

> . . . the museum (by establishing itself as a television
> channel on a cable system) finally offers a real alterna-
> tive for the viewer at home. The alternative is simply
> that a specific activity is being transmitted directly to
> the public, completely unfettered. In all other forms of
> television, whether commercial or educational, the tele-
> vision station serves as a central translating operation,
> essentially taking many aspects of the culture and trans-
> forming them into a language that it feels will not extend
> beyond the mean educational level of its audience. . . .
> this method of programming . . . has a destructive effect
> on the information it processes, continually extracting its
> nutritive value. . . . All parties to the television inter-

change deserve better. The notion of museum interaction with television is primarily based upon a societal model which requires that institutions dealing with information have the responsibility and should have the capacity to make the results of their activity accessible to their entire community. For the artist, the relationship is inevitable: for the museum it is imperative. [19]

ROSS ON HIS ROLE IN THE VIDEO COMMUNITY

In our interview, Ross said he perceives his role as a video curator and writer about video to be that of a participant in and commentator on the larger cultural systems that contain art and video as integral elements of the systems:

> I've had to reconcile the fact that I didn't continue to become an artist or that I've stopped for the last seven years being an artist, and I've been able to direct the energy I was putting into that into museums and into larger systems that contain art or that work with art or that serve art and support it. Analogous to that is how I see my own role.

Regarding his perception of the extent of his influence as a writer about video, Ross told me:

> There's no way of measuring. To the extent that you've called me and are involving my writing in your book, that's the kind of feedback; the extent that . . . you see yourself quoted, that's a kind of feedback, but who ever knows?

When I asked Ross whether he got much feedback from artists working with video, Ross replied:

> Oh sure, mostly telephone calls, and personal visits and letters. Anyone who puts anything out gets some kind of feedback. Nothing is feedback also. . . . you learn very fast not to wait for the phone to ring when you write art criticism or art theory . . . because you don't get the same kind of feedback you get when you're writing editorials. . . . What I'm saying doesn't really challenge people, I don't think. I think it might present a different point of view and it might challenge their conceptions of how me-

dia work, but I don't think they challenge them on any significant level.

ROSS ON HIS READERSHIP

One of the defining characteristics of the radical critic is his
or her role as a "middle-person" between the artist and the nonartist
member of a cultural public who generally is quite interested in artistic attitudes on the cutting edge of the arts. In our interview, Ross
described his readership as being composed of such individuals. When
I asked him who he felt generally read his writings about video, Ross
replied:

> I would assume that artists who are interested in it or
> students who are interested in it or people who are inter-
> ested in the areas that I've been interested in. I would
> like to hope that broadcast people have gotten interested
> in [video] but I don't think so. I've never met a broadcast
> person yet, I've only met a few people in the whole broad-
> cast or film industries that had any awareness that video
> art exists. They're rare, and it doesn't relate to their use
> or need for media. So, if they read the art magazines they
> might have come across it in an article, but rarely.

CONCLUSIONS

Ross's writings about video and his curatorial activities throughout the 1970s promoting both alternative video statements and alternative video/television communications systems have significantly aided
the development of video as a legitimate art form. In that sense, he
represents well that group of cultural observers we call radical critics.

His discussion of individual artists' work in video have helped
define many of the diverse directions in which video has moved since
its birth in the mid-1960s. While he seems to especially favor the video performance genre in his writings, Ross has not neglected other
important video movements such as gallery installations. Beyond his
defense of video as an art form worthy of serious consideration, Ross
has also tackled the tough institutional issues that involve the nature,
processing, and control of information in our culture.

In a sense all radical critics are dreamers; but they are dreamers who work hard to actualize their dreams. Ross's attempts to link
the art museum to both broadcast and cablecast technologies, while
commendable, have yet to bear much fruit. It is a sad fact of life in

our society that a new art such as video that directly challenges a dominant cultural institution such as broadcasting must confront and deal in its own way with both the fear and scorn of its threatened big brother. The fear in this instance is not so much a fear of sharing control of information dissemination as it is a fear of offending segments of the television audience by in essence challenging their strongly held value systems (which are in large measure reinforced by popular television itself); and possible loss of audience translates as potential loss of revenues, whether they be derived from advertisers, viewer contributions, foundation grants, or direct government support. That is fear not easily overcome in the glorious name of "art."

Like all critics writing in defense of an emerging art form, Ross must sometimes wonder whether he is shouting in a vacuum or talking to himself. One detects an ambivalence on his part about the impact of his work. While there is a certain satisfaction that his writings are being read and quoted by the video community and thereby are contributing to video's continual definitional refinement, Ross seems upset that the broadcasting community, which he feels desperately needs video education, has all but ignored the efforts of both artists working with video and critics such as himself writing about video. Yet video is alive and growing, no doubt due in part to the efforts of radical critics such as David Ross.

NOTES

1. John Hanhardt, "Video/Television Space," in Video Art: An Anthology, eds. Ira Schneider and Beryl Korot (New York: Harcourt Brace Jovanovich, 1976), pp. 220-21.

2. John Hanhardt, "Douglas Davis: Video," exhibition notes from the Whitney Museum of American Art, New York, February 1977, n.p.

3. Russell Connor, "Video Gets a One," in Video Art: An Anthology, eds. Ira Schneider and Beryl Korot (New York: Harcourt Brace Jovanovich, 1976), p. 164.

4. Russell Connor, "A Is for Art, C Is for Cable," in The New Television: A Public/Private Art, eds. Douglas Davis and Allison Simmons (Cambridge, Mass.: MIT Press, 1977), pp. 171-72.

5. David A. Ross, "Introduction to Part 1," Southland Video Anthology 1976 (Long Beach, Calif.: Long Beach Museum of Art, 1976), p. 2.

6. David A. Ross, "Peter Campus: Closed Circuit Video," Peter Campus (Syracuse, N.Y.: Everson Museum of Art, 1974), n.p.

7. David Ross, "Interview with Douglas Davis," in Video Art: An Anthology, eds. Ira Schneider and Beryl Korot (New York: Harcourt Brace Jovanovich, 1976), p. 32.

8. David A. Ross, "Frank Gillette: Development and Recent Works," Frank Gillette Video: Process and Meta-Process (Syracuse, N. Y.: Everson Museum of Art, 1973), p. 27.

9. Ross, "Part 1," Southland Video Anthology, p. 3.

10. Ross, "Frank Gillette," p. 28.

11. David Ross, "Douglas Davis: Video Against Video," Arts Magazine, December 1974, p. 62.

12. David A. Ross, "Americans in Florence: Europeans in Florence: Notes on the Exhibition," Americans in Florence: Europeans in Florence. Videotapes Produced by Art/Tapes/22 (Florence: Centro Di, 1974), n. p.

13. David A. Ross, "Time As Form," Douglas Davis: events drawings objects videotapes (Syracuse, N. Y.: Everson Museum of Art, 1972), n. p.

14. Ibid.

15. Ross, "Americans in Florence," n. p.

16. David Ross, "The Personal Attitude," in Video Art: An Anthology, eds. Ira Schneider and Beryl Korot (New York: Harcourt Brace Jovanovich, 1976), p. 246.

17. Ibid., p. 245.

18. David Ross, "Video and the Future of the Museum," in The New Television: A Public/Private Art, eds. Douglas Davis and Allison Simmons (Cambridge, Mass.: MIT Press, 1977), p. 115.

19. Ibid., pp. 115-17.

7

DOUGLAS DAVIS:
THE VIDEO ARTIST AS CRITIC

Many people naively presuppose that artists are either incapable of or unwilling to discuss their art in print. The notion that great artists make inferior critics or aestheticians has been slow to pass despite much recent evidence to the contrary. One need only look to T. S. Eliot, Sergei Eisenstein or John Cage, to name but a few, to dispel this unfounded generalization. Artists can and do write about their work, often very successfully.

There are some special traits of the artist-critic that bear close examination. While these traits do not apply universally to the group, they are nevertheless indicative of approaches taken by many artists who write about art. Artist-critics usually defend those styles of art making with which their own personal styles are closely affiliated. They generally have a keen intuitive sense of the correctness of "design" of individual works and genres. These critics write in response to contemporary art movements evolving around them and affecting their own work at the time of their writing. Therefore, the articulate artist-critic is a sensitive barometer of the shifting movements of art over time.

The artist-critic's admittedly polemical opinions are frequently published as essays in print anthologies or as manifestoes. These writings are likely to seem somewhat dogmatic to the objective reader because they tend to indiscriminately praise the style of art making with which the artist-critic is directly and personally involved while at the same time taking lightly or even dismissing contradictory styles.

Noted art critic Lawrence Alloway has provided a detailed inventory of the manner in which contemporary artists have merged their art works with their discourse about those works and about art in general:

The idea that two systems of signs, one visual and one literary, are antithetical is not generally shared . . . to judge from the copious writings by artists that actually exist. To consider the genre, it is useful to assume a principle of coexpressibility, in which verbal and visual forms can be translated into one another with at least a partial fit. [1]

The "verbal forms" to which Alloway referred include artists' statements or manifestoes, interviews granted by artists, and museum or gallery exhibition catalogues, all of which Alloway viewed as personal expressions of the artists. Of the artist's statement, Alloway observed:

> In America the artist's statement has developed into a specific mode. In this usage a statement is not an article, which is longer and more formally structured. A statement is taken to be a projection of the artist writing in the first person. We read a statement not because of its literary interest or intellectual argument, but because an artist has written it to indicate something. The authority of a statement derives from who is making it. With the contraction of the role of the writer as general intellectual, the artist, to a large extent, has taken the role of commentator on current values. . . . The statement is a means of extending the studio into the world and making art a model of behavior. [2]

According to Alloway, the interview granted by an artist is another meaningful form of personal statement:

> . . . the use of the interview . . . developed to a considerable level between the wars . . . since the interview form is journalistic in origin, it has expanded the sources of first-person statement beyond conventional art resources. . . . Any study of artists as writers must allow for artists as respondents in a wide range of interviews. [3]

In the 1960s, according to Alloway, artists moved away from the personal statement and toward more formal discourse that was primarily of an art-critical nature:

> . . . increasing distribution of the [artists'] work was solidly bound in with artist-originated information concerning it. The art of definition was not separated from the act of appreciation. The artists' statements did not

take the form of manifestoes, which are frequently geared
to future realization, but of articles that were focused on
current issues and problems. This no doubt owes to the
fact that this generation of artists . . . was college educated . . . Thus, neither the exhortatory nor the sibylline
held much interest for them, though the process of thinking, the conduct of argument, did. [4]

Alloway's discussion of the artist as critic focused on the traditional artist working alone and distributing his work and information
about it through traditional art world channels such as museums, galleries, and art magazines and journals. However, when we consider
the artist-critic writing about television or video, we must expand
that focus somewhat. Artist-critics writing about television and video generally fall into two categories: the artist-critic working within
the dominant broadcast television structure; and the artist-critic
working independently in artists' video, which employs alternative
distribution bases such as the museum, gallery, video theater, or
local-origination cable facility (although occasionally the artist working in video will gain limited access to PBS production and distribution mechanisms).

Among the artist-critics who fit the first category are teleplay
writers David Rintels and Reginald Rose. While creating television
works within the dominant broadcast structure, these individuals have
not hesitated to lash out against that structure when they feel that their
creative freedom has been compromised. Rintels and Rose both exhibit in their writings about television a pessimism regarding the ability
to broadcast television networks to transcend their never-ending battles for increased profits and move toward what each man in his own
way defines as "serious" television art. I will briefly examine each
of these artist-critic's writings below.

David Rintels is a teleplay writer and past president of the
Writers Guild of America, West. In 1971 he won the Guild's award
for the best dramatic television script for an episode of "The Senator."
He was cowriter of the 1977 miniseries "Washington: Behind Closed
Doors." In an essay he wrote for Performance in 1972, Rintels an-
grily noted that television writers were being prohibited from having
their scripts produced when those scripts dealt with such "sensitive"
subject areas as venereal disease, possible amnesty for draft evaders,
the United States Army's storage of nerve gas near urban areas, anything in the field of antitrust, or the manufacture by drug companies
of drugs intended for the illegal drug market. [5] Rintels added:

TV censorship has a second face to it. It is not only what
we cannot write about; what is equally troubling is what

we <u>must</u> write about. Requirements of Teaser and four Acts, each twelve minutes long and with a melodramatic climax, mandatory car chases and fist fights, simplistic steel-jawed super heroes, no sex or politics or religion, required happy ending, etc. , so limit the form that quality seems to be forbidden. [6]

Rintels has written similar "exposes" for such notable publications as the <u>New York Times.</u> He also coordinated the 1975 campaign, led by the Writers Guild and Norman Lear, against the FCC's concept of "Family Viewing Hour": Claiming that Family Viewing Hour would kill whatever creative freedom the writers and producers still had in television, Rintels was successful in getting the courts to overturn the FCC rule.

Reginald Rose, a prolific and much-honored writer of teleplays, has also written about the proscriptions of broadcast television. Rose worked for an advertising agency before breaking into dramatic writing for television during the "Golden Age." He sold his first teleplay to director Sidney Lumet in December 1951 for $650. The script—"The Bus to Nowhere"—was produced for the CBS-TV series "Danger." In 1954 Rose had six original one-hour dramas produced for "Studio One." He wrote "a dozen or so" episodes for the acclaimed dramatic series "The Defenders" in 1960. But from 1960 until 1967, when he wrote "Dear Friends" for "CBS Playhouse," Rose did not write a single original drama for television. In a 1967 <u>New York Times</u> essay, Rose discussed the problems that existed then for teleplay writers:

> Sixteen years ago . . . my experience in writing television scripts was absolutely nil, my name unknown, my talent questionable. ["The Bus to Nowhere"] script was read immediately and bought because Sidney Lumet and his producer Charles Russell liked it and needed it.
>
> Today such an event is highly improbable, if not altogether impossible. It is enormously difficult for a new young writer even to avail himself of the services of an agent . . .

Rose continued:

> One wonders: what went away? Probably a naiveté, an innocence, a lack of cynicism (if such a thing as a lack can be said to disappear). Then the rating services were still unsophisticated, no one grieved over vast wastelands. . . . It was all a joy.

Instead of "serious writers," Rose asserted that broadcast television had, by the 1960s, produced

> . . . a kind of computerized writer . . . writing to for-
> mula, the kind of formula which excludes character de-
> velopment, complex relationships and everything but the
> most perfunctory allusions to the interrelationships be-
> tween human behavior and story line which is the essen-
> tial ingredient of good serious drama. [7]

"It was all a joy!" One would be hard-pressed to find a member of television's contemporary creative community making such a state-ment about today's "industry." Rose was shut out of television in part because he tried to deal seriously and subtly in his teleplays with hu-man concerns. Viewers, the networks seem to believe, desire above all to have their value systems reinforced rather than challenged. So, exit Rose, Paddy Chayefsky, and others, stage left to the cinema.

Individuals working independently in artists' video comprise the second category of artist-critics. These artist-critics generally hold opinions about the overall "quality" of broadcast television program-ming similar to those of Rintels and Rose. However, independent art-ist-critics tend to take an optimistic stance with regard to the state of artists' video as an alternative to the creative constraints of tele-vision. The two most prominent members of this group writing about video today are Nam June Paik and Douglas Davis. The writings of Paik and Davis are quite divergent in style though similar in focus. We will briefly examine Paik's writings below, and then discuss in depth both Davis's writings about video and his video works.

Nam June Paik is acknowledged by most observers to be the "father of video." Born in Korea in 1932, he studied piano, composi-tion, art history, and philosophy at the University of Tokyo where he graduated with a degree in aesthetics in 1952. In 1958 he went from Japan to West Germany to work at the electronic music studio in Co-logne where he met and worked with the American avant-garde com-poser John Cage. Paik began working with video in the early 1960s, focusing his attention on distorting broadcast images. In 1968 Paik, with Japanese engineer Shuya Abe, made a major breakthrough in video by developing a workable electronic machine that "synthesized" video images. Characteristically using what Alloway termed the "per-sonal statement," Paik discussed his revolutionary creation:

> The video synthesizer is the accumulation of my nine
> years' TV shit (if this holy allusion is allowed), turned
> into a real-time video piano by the Golden Finger of
> Shuya Abe, my great mentor. Big TV studios always

scare me. Many layers of "machine time" running paral-
lel engulf my identity. It always brings me the anxiety of
Norbert Wiener, seeing the delicate yet formidable dichotomy of human time and machine time, a particular contin-
gency of the so-called cybernated age. (I use technology
in order to hate it more properly.). . . .
. . . Travel is one method of communication but not
vice versa. Therefore if people could find a new and cheap-
er and more efficient way to communicate, the necessity to
travel, drive or fly would naturally decrease. Here various broad-band telecommunications methods will come into play. . . . New forms of video, which are being pioneer-
ed by video art, will stimulate the whole society to find a
more imaginative way of telecommunication, which leads
directly to energy savings. Where will so-called pleasure
driving go? Much of its function will be absorbed by the
video synthesizer. Pleasure driving is a form of communicating with oneself. . . . This psychological ontology is
exactly the same as playing with the video synthesizer,
which modulates itself . . . some day a video synthesizer
in every home will substitute for much of today's frustrated pleasure driving—a kind of electronic Nirvana, without
the consumption of energy and without the hazard of taking
drugs. [8]

Perhaps the federal government should enlist Paik in its efforts to
solve our nation's energy problems. Certainly Paik's conception
probes much more deeply into the relationship between people and
"energy." Paik's statement presaged the development of somewhat
more pedestrian video applications such as video games, the self-
contained home video computer terminal, and "video wallpaper," all
of which in various ways promote social decentralization as the individual viewer becomes an active information processor.

Paik's use of aphorism in describing the potential positive sociocultural impact of the video synthesizer while summarily dismissing "big TV studios" as dehumanizing may be tongue in cheek, but
with very serious intentions.

DAVIS ON HIS VIDEO WORKS AND HIS WRITINGS
ABOUT VIDEO AND ART

Douglas Davis, like Nam June Paik, has produced many personal
statements about his video works. He has also expressed his verbal
ideas in a more formal literary vein through numerous essays pub-

lished in art journals and "mass circulation" magazines, and in books he has authored and edited. Before we begin our discussion of Davis's writings and video works, however, some background information will help situate Davis in the artists' video movement.

Davis was born in 1933 in Washington, D. C. , and presently lives in New York City. He received a Bachelor of Arts degree with a major in English from American University in 1956 and a Master of Arts degree from Rutgers-The State University, New Jersey, in 1958.

As an artist, Davis poineered the use of video as a two-way participative instrument linking together the artist and viewers in "live time." As a writer, Davis has published two books—Art and the Future (1973) and Artculture: Essays on the Post-Modern (1977)—and coedited an anthology of writings about video with Allison Simmons entitled The New Television: A Public/Private Art (1977). Davis was art critic for the National Observer in the 1960s, a former contributing editor for Art in America, and is presently senior writer in the arts for Newsweek, with special emphasis on photography, architecture, and contemporary ideas. He has also written essays on the arts and ideas for The American Scholar, Artforum, Arts Magazine, the New York Times, Radical Software, American Film Institute Journal, Arts in Society, Village Voice, and New York Arts Journal. In addition to this more formal discourse on art and video, Davis has produced "statements" on his works in the tradition defined by Alloway— and responded informally to questions and interviews.

Davis is currently combining his roles as artist, teacher, and video theorist as the Artistic Director of the International Network for the Arts, a video consortium of university art schools. The project, partly funded by the Rockefeller Foundation, involves Davis, other artists working with video, and video critics. These artists and critics work with specially selected groups of students in advanced video workshops at universities in this country and abroad. The outgrowth of the workshops is the production of a videotape or a "live" performance by each student to be distributed on a local cable channel or PBS outlet. In addition to the production of tapes or live performances, the program is designed to raise the level of the general audiences', video critics', and educators' understanding of alternative video.

Unlike many artists and critics, Davis's art and his writings attempt to grapple with a broad range of ideas as well as mediums. This methodological diversity is both fascinating and, in some cases, confounding. In an attempt to understand it I asked Davis about his early involvement with art and its impact on his thinking about art. He responded at length:

All during my adolescence there was a war between painting, writing, and acting—the theater—those were the three things that interested me the most. And I didn't know which one I was really going to go after in college. I remember that spring we were taken by the various universities in [Washington, D. C.] on tours of the campus, and I remember when I went to American University I passed by the painting studio and I saw them painting a nude, saw several of them painting this very beautiful nude, and I said to myself, "That's it! That's what I want to do. I want to be a painting major and I want to do that, I want to come here." So finally I did go to American University and I did have that in mind. But the more I got involved in the University and the more I knew about the Art Department and I knew about the artists, the less friendly I became toward them, and I wound up being an English major basically because the professors were good, much nicer, and I was much more interested in that than I was in the artists who were teaching at the University. That was really the time that Clement Greenberg was in the process of taking over the city, and there was a very strong anti-intellectual trend in the art theory of that period and in the mind of the artist. I just couldn't be a part of that. I really felt alienated from the painters, and so I got away from it. But then, when I went to Rutgers for a Master's degree I came right into the midst of a lot of artistic ferment and activity. That was the late fifties . . . and there was just a lot going on there at that time. It's never been written about or catalogued. There's never been an exhibition about it, but obviously there will be at some point, because it's a very important part of contemporary art history. The first Happening occurred when I was on the campus. Pop Art had a lot of its beginnings there. Roy Lichtenstein was teaching at Douglass College, and George Segal was working on a farm just outside the city, and everybody knew about him. . . . And George Brecht, for me the most important person was George Brecht. Allan Kaprow of course was on the faculty, and I knew him and talked with him. . . ? But George Brecht was the most important person for me because . . . I didn't know him at that time, I just read things that he had written. Do you know anything about George Brecht? Americans don't. It's ridiculous. George Brecht was maybe the first conceptual artist—maybe. He was, I thought, the most interesting and the most radical person in that whole Fluxus, Pop Art, Neo-Dada group. He was at that time . . . working for Johnson &

Johnson in New Brunswich, New Jersey, which is where Rutgers was. He was a chemist, and he was working on Tampax—he got some patents for Johnson & Johnson in connection with Tampax. He was also very much involved ed with the whole Rutgers scene and he was not an artist— he had not done any art at that point, but he was kind of interested in it, and he took some classes at night at the University and he also travelled to New York and took a class with John Cage. He began to write really incredible papers about art and chance, and art and metaphysics, and art and ideas. I have some of them here. Dick Higgins later reprinted them for the Something Else Press. They are in print. I read them and I really just couldn't believe them. Also he did things like he sent out little cards in the mail to you and there's one I remember getting . . . called "Drip Music." And the score was, "Go to the kitchen. Turn on the water faucet. But not too hard. And just listen" or something like that. He was doing pieces like 1957, 1958, and he kept doing it for five or six years after that. And I was on his mailing list. Then somewhere around the mid-sixties he left and went to Europe, and he's been living there ever since. He's a hero in Europe. He has many collectors. He makes objects—conceptual-type objects, and does some photography. He had one show—the only major exhibition in the United States was at the Los Angeles County Museum in the late sixties—of chairs. He just repainted chairs. Take old chairs and repaint them. So, anyway, when I went to Rutgers and I fell into all of this, it made art seem like a viable enterprise again, because all that stuff was about the mind. It didn't deny the mind. That's what really got me back in. . . .

With this grounding in conceptual art, Davis could easily move toward integrating the "mind" into his work. He became preoccupied with bringing art, through video, into the context of everyday life events. To this end he has, among other things, explored in his work the process of direct video interaction with his audience. As Davis noted in our interview, he was profoundly influenced by George Brecht's writings on art and chance.[9] One of Brecht's central ideas that Davis has applied to his own video work and writings about video is that the artist could create situations in which the images and/or sounds being produced in a work were ultimately not under the artist's control but rather the spectator/participant's control.

Davis was also influenced by the Happening/event movement in art that evolved in the 1960s. A central characteristic of the Happening movement was a combination of living, artists workshop, and theater. Davis, however, felt the need to stretch the context of the Happening with its inherent elements of chance from the artist's loft/museum/gallery space to the entire community normally outside art confines. Video offered the ideal vehicle for the expansion.

The most important of Davis's early community events was a work titled "Look Out," which was performed and engineered by Davis and Fred Pitts in Washington, D.C., in June 1970. Telephones were set up at the Corcoran Gallery in Washington so that people could call in comments. The Corcoran was opened to all the people of Washington one evening. Davis had distributed messages throughout the city (à la Brecht) asking anyone to bring in found objects, written statements, and drawings. People responded, and as these items were delivered to the Corcoran they were put on a 20-foot by 30-foot photosensitive canvas, and exposed to strong arc lamps producing a "heliographic print."[10] "Look Out" also marked Davis's initial use of video technology. He described to me how this came about:

> I moved to New York in the fall of 1969, and by a variety
> of means I met a guy who's now forgotten in television history named Don West, who was a vice president of CBS television network at that time. And he had somehow or other
> got turned on to underground video. He requested a leave
> of absence from the president of CBS to try to get together
> some of this work into a series that would appear on the
> network. He wound up working with the Video Freex, of
> all groups. By a couple of accidents I got to know Don
> West. I came to some of the meetings. I began to meet
> people who had video systems. . . . I began to work on
> tapes. All of this was the fall of 1969. Then, in the spring
> of 1970, by which time Don West had been fired from CBS,
> I did a performance at the Corcoran called "Look Out."
> Don, who was still a friend of mine at that time, and who
> had a portable video system, offered to come along and
> document the performance. So I worked with him in documenting it. And after it was over, that summer, the summer of 1970, we sat down and looked at the tapes, and that
> was the point at which it really became important to me because it was looking at those tapes and realizing a lot of
> things about videotape and about video—its kind of weird
> relationship to time, its kind of strange reality, the fact
> that in some ways the tape was more real than the performance itself. A lot of things like that happened to me. Another thing you should know about is that "Look Out" ended
> with the creation of a large canvas, and the following day,

as part of it all, we were installing it in the Corcoran, in the museum, and while we were installing it, it occurred to me that it was wrong that the videotape should not be hanging in front of the canvas. So I insisted that it be done. There is a photograph of this canvas in the Corcoran, this huge canvas, and four video tapes are hanging in front of it. And I thought, as I was doing it, that this may be the first work of art that ever had the capacity to depict its own making, because in effect that was what they could do. But that was it. It was beginning the fall of 1969 and then the creation of the tape that supposedly documented the event. In fact it [the tape] was a thing itself. The relationship with the event was quite tangential.

Davis next extended the context of the event to the television audience participating in the event at home in the intimate television space. Davis's first "television event" was a work called "Electronic Hokkadim" performed in 1971 at the Corcoran Gallery. "Electronic Hokkadim" was a live 30-minute telecast carried over WTOP-TV in Washington, D. C. , and was intended as an alternative to Tricia Nixon's wedding. Viewers throughout the city phoned in sounds they wished to make which in turn modulated the video images generated at the Corcoran and at the television studio. Davis later wrote of "Electronic Hokkadim":

. . . video is better than life. The small screen focuses and intensifies real time experience. The first step I wanted to take with video was to contact the viewer in such a moment, and share it with him. This was achieved . . . in Washington, D. C. , through the Corcoran Gallery and WTOP-TV, in Electronic Hokkadim I. We allowed an entire city to sing and chant to itself, through the means of sets scattered about the videosphere. Their chanting modulated the electronic images they saw, while the images were forming. Film lacks this potential; it is edited and then rendered public. . . . The kind of immediacy I am discussing has to do with a malleable future. The sense that the next minute is open to every option, your or the artist's. . . . The videosphere is both linear and moving onward toward a future. 11

"Electronic Hokkadim" was a tentative first step in opening up television channels to the audience. At the same time, the video piece marked the end of Davis's preoccupation with the large-scale event, a written correspondence, Davis described this crucial turning point in his reconceptualization of the meaning of video:

. . . the Hokkadim was a turning point in my life. I turned away from those ["global village"] ideas, thereafter, and marched off in a completely different direction—toward personal, not choral structures, toward the glory of private perception, and the de-centralization inherent in CATV.

A Davis manifesto printed in the 1972 Everson Museum of Art catalogue supplementing the exhibition of his art addressed this conception of the sanctity of the individual viewer/participant's private perception and the resultant decentralized, pluralistic communication structure:

for mind

TO

against physical

    FORGET

against physical

    VIDEO

against physical

      IS

against against art

        TO

against keeping minds down

          MAKE

against counting measuring calculating edit burn the manuals.

           VIDEO

for living

            MIND AND BODY

for ascending thin subtle awful mysteri

              DISCARDING NAMES

looking fresh immediate

direct to mind to direct

STOP THE NAMES

the camera is a pencil.   a hand. hold here. [12]

In his next interactive video work Davis began to refine his notion of "direct to mind to direct" communication to allow participative audience discourse with him. In 1972 Davis created a work titled "Talk-Out!" which took place at WCNY-TV in Syracuse, New York as an adjunct to an exhibition of Davis's work at the Everson Museum. Davis set up video cameras around the city so that people could visually link with him on the air. He asked viewers how they felt about talking to their television sets and getting on the air live. Using a character generator, Davis typed messages on the television screen from callers throughout the city. His friends, including Nam June Paik, phoned in thoughts. There were also preplanned telephone conversations discussing aesthetics. Davis's image on the screen was replaced at various times with film clips of other scenes. The entire event evoked the feeling of unpredictability, but unpredictability within a conceptual framework. Davis wrote of "Talk-Out!":

> TV time corrupts life, politics, and art by speeding it up, brutalizing issues and minds, and, paradoxically, castrating the sense of actual time passing. . . . "Talk-Out!:. . . took place at WCNY-TV in Syracuse . . . late in 1972. Our aim was to "broadcast" a museum exhibition in live time to its wider public, and to have a dialogue with that public, responding to what it saw, on the air. From the start we knew we needed duration—time for conversation to unfold in depth, time for the viewer to think and respond. . . . "Talk-Out!" was broadcast for three and one-half hours, an eon in TV time, comparable only to baseball games, moon walks, and assassinations. [13]

Following "Talk-Out!" Davis moved toward a more personal or intimate style of video making without sacrificing his link with his audience in video/television space. For example, in "The Austrian Tapes" (1974) telecast over the Austrian Television Network (ORF), Davis asked the viewer to place his or her hands against Davis's hands, which were extended toward the camera lens giving the appearance of his touching the television screen from inside the set. Davis next asked the viewer to link his or her fingertips with Davis's fingertips, to "touch" Davis's cheek, to "touch" Davis's lips, to take off his or her clothes as Davis had done and press against Davis's chest, and finally to turn around and press against his back. In the end Davis asked the viewer to "think about what this means. What is the end of this?" "The Austrian Tapes" can be viewed as a step in Davis's aesthetic toward greater mind-to-mind intimacy with the viewer—a step all but impossible on American broadcast television.

Davis wrote of his experience with "The Austrian Tapes":
The making of art may begin in the mind—like literature—
but it never ends in easy abstraction, words typed on paper. It ends in a physical act, and in an object, in the face
of intense resistance from the medium, or from the politics that surround the medium. I had to travel three thou-
sand miles (to Austria) to put my hands on your television
screen. But the work exists now, apart from me, a presence in the world beyond the self where it began. It is a
Utopia in itself. [14]

Davis viewed "The Austrian Tapes" as an attempt to break through
dual barriers—resistance by broadcasters to allow exploration of intimate interpersonal interaction on television, and resistance from
the television set itself, which sets up a glass barricade between
sender and receiver.

Davis discussed viewer reaction to "The Austrian Tapes":

It is always interesting to see what people say when they
touch my hands on the TV screen in The Austrian Tapes.
Here it is often understood as a good joke, or as an exploration of the box, or of the flat (gently rounded) screen.
In Poland, a TV director looked at a photograph of the image and shook his head, refusing to speak. A lady from
the Midwest wrote and said that it warmed her hands on
a cold winter night and for that she was grateful. In Austria, there was a debate among European TV producers
about it. Pierre Schaeffer, the director of experimental
TV in France, was against it—we should be touching each
other's hands, not the TV, he said—but thought it a legitimate investigation. [15]

He added:

Late one night in Boston we telecast The Austrian Tapes
. . . on a commercial station. The viewers were invited
to phone in their responses to the several acts involved.
. . . Finally a man called in and said: "I've enjoyed this
very much but now I'd like you to play a game with me,
on my TV screen. Please get up and come over to the
camera." I did what he asked, while the cameramen and
producers held their heads in horror; I saw myself in the
monitor with my hand right over the top of the screen.
"No," said the viewer at home, "over to the right—further—further. Now down, lower, to the right hand corner

of the screen. Now press your thumb against it, hard."
I did all these things. When I pressed hard, he let out a
loud "Ahhhhhhhhh. Thank you very much." To this day,
no one knows what he was doing there at home, in the
privacy of his room. [16]

In February 1976 Davis performed "Three Silent and Secret
Acts," the first live performance cable television work emanating
from Manhattan Cable's access channels C and D in New York City.
The work was performed simultaneously at The Kitchen Center for
Video and Music and Manhattan Cable's public access studio by various performers and was ultimately transmitted live to a home audience on the public access channel. "Three Silent and Secret Acts"
was a technologically and aesthetically complex work. Davis videotaped a "private" performance (encountering and physically crashing
through a piece of plexiglass [television screen?]) at The Kitchen—a
conceptual extension of the "barrier" concept explored earlier in "The
Austrian Tapes." The following day the tape was cablecast over channel D into The Kitchen where it was shown on a large Advent video
screen to a live performance audience as Davis reperformed the acts.
At the same time channel C was cablecasting a performer in its studio
who was performing the three acts by mirroring the cablecast over
channel D. This performer's acts were transmitted back to The Kitch-
en and shown on a monitor there. Near the end of the half-hour performance, live video from channel C and audio from The Kitchen merged with the cablecast on channel D that was being transmitted throughout the Manhattan Cable system. The work's technological complexity
focused a theme central to Davis's developing aesthetic. Davis spoke
to Ingrid Wiegand, artist and video critic for the Soho Weekly News,
about the piece:

> I've always dreamed of making work that originates si-
> multaneously in several places and reaches both a live
> audience and the one at home. . . .
>   . . . I want to make it very clear that the participa-
> tory aspect of the program is solely for the private, indi-
> vidual viewer, and not for the live audience. You see, tel-
> evision is really a private medium by definition, a private
> space with only one or two people watching. The reaction
> at home is private. You just can't predict what a given
> viewer is going to do. And that single, private person in
> front of his screen is the person for whom I make tapes.
>   And that's why I'm enthusiastic about cable—it is
> potentially the most personal TV form. [17]

In February 1977 Davis performed a work titled "Four Places Two Figures One Ghost" at the Whitney Museum of American Art in New York City. The performance was cablecast over Manhattan Cable as it occurred "live" at the Whitney. The 30-minute performance began with the ticking sound of a clock accompanied by character generator titles moving across the screen telling the audience at home that as the performance began the ticking would cease and asking the viewers to supply their own sound source for the work. This simple act of viewer participation fixed the performance in both a temporal and an interactive context. In front of the performance audience at the Whitney, Davis mirrored the actions of a "private" performance he had earlier videotaped. While the two images (Davis live and Davis taped) shadow boxed, wrestled, hugged, reached for, and touched each other, a series of words was typed on the screen. Of the many words that appeared, certain words seemed to define the work itself, for example "chance," "simple," "attitude," "death," "egotism/vanity," and "single/double/triple." The performance inside the Whitney with Davis's "selves" interacting was juxtaposed with an image of Davis outside the Whitney typing on a character generator, ostensibly recounting a dream from his youth in which his various personalities battled until one personality emerged victorious (the painter/writer/actor Davis spoke of in recounting his early years in art—or perhaps the ghost of Davis future/content overcoming the ghost of Davis past/technique?). Central to the work is the notion of time, past and present, prerecorded and live, past events and their meaning now.

From his earliest interactive video works such as "Electronic Hokkadim" to the more recent "Four Places Two Figures One Ghost," Davis has concentrated on drawing the viewer into the video work and at the same time developing visual metaphors for what he terms direct "mind-to-mind" communication between the work's creator and the viewer. While the artist has a plan from which the basic work takes shape, as in traditional broadcast television, the viewer is urged to participate in that plan and to modify it, within eatablished parameters, according to his or her desires at home in front of the family TV set. Even such limited viewer control of information is incomprehensible to the great majority of the broadcast community. Davis is using the technology of television in a more personalized manner, following the dictates of both Bertolt Brecht and George Brecht.

While Davis has accessed both cable and, to a lesser extent, over-the-air broadcasting for his performance works, his urge to use increasingly more sophisticated telecommunications technologies and to thereby expose their misuse by the broadcast institutions has led him into an exploration of both satellite transmission and Warner QUBE's two-way interactive cablecasting.

On December 29, 1976, at 9:41 P.M., Davis performed "Seven

Thoughts" from the floor of the Houston Astrodome, in which he sent
audio messages up to a global communications satellite to be transmitted to receiving stations around the world. The content of the messages was "secret." Only Davis and those at the ground stations receiving the satellite transmission would know the communication. The
piece, although documented by a videotape, was ephemeral, the communication in real time, on a one-to-one level—the antithesis of the
"public" transmission characteristics of the satellite as traditionally
used. Davis later wrote of the Astrodome experience:

> When I went to speak to the president of the Astrodome
> in Texas about sending a voice signal to the global sat-
> ellite from the floor of the stadium . . . he wanted to
> know what I would say. "I can't tell you that," I said,
> worried that he would not understand. "I want to know
> what it means," he insisted. "If I told you," I replied,
> nervous about saying too much, "you wouldn't know. If
> I don't tell you . . . " I hesitated, but went on. ". . .
> you will." He never replied to this point, but he let me
> use his stadium, which means that he agreed. [18]

Using a highly sophisticated, "expensive" technology for expansive personal ends opens the traditional broadcasting system to fascinating alternatives and removes the layers of mystique surrounding
the technology. The following year, 1977, Davis again used the communications satellite; this time the message was sent up to the bird
(to be received by more than 30 countries) from the Documenta 6
exhibition in West Germany, which highlighted artists' work from a-
round the world. In such a global context, the transmission took on
heightened significance. Davis later wrote of the Documenta transmission:

> What seems intriguing to me about satellite transmission,
> across the nation, or the world, is its privacy: vast space
> are traversed and compressed into a tiny circumference,
> a glowing tube housed in a small room, in front of Mom,
> Pop, or Fido. . . . at Documenta in 1977, I tried to make
> a pact with Mom in Moscow, Pop in Caracas, and beyond:
> let us destroy this screen between us, I whispered. [19]

In June 1980 Davis again tapped communications satellite technology in a performance. This time, in a piece titled "The Shadow
Shadowed," Davis accessed the National Public Radio (NPR) satellite
service at a cost, he told me, of $31. 10. The piece was performed
live at The Kitchen in New York (with the performance audience see-

ing) and satel-cast to seven NPR stations around the country (New York, Madison, Berkeley, Santa Monica, Miami, Albuquerque, and Louisville). The stations in New York City, Madison, and Berkeley participated in the drama via live local interaction with Davis. This may have been the first use of the NPR satellite by an independent artist. With this "low-cost access" available, the possibilities for use by independent artists increase exponentially.

Why radio? References to the classic radio mystery "The Shadow" and the very use of this "old" electronic medium many consider passé are significant in light of Davis's recent reassessments of art and culture. In 1979 Davis wrote: ". . . we are giving up the urge to break through on physical grounds, to test the new tool. . . . Even the new tools—which of course remain—will be used to antique ends. I have an unquenchable desire . . . to transmit by satellite, across the world, a transcendent, blurred image, thousands of years old."[20]

The "blurred image" may be that of art once feared lost, or worse yet, dead—an art with its significance grounded in content/ message. Davis observed:

> Now we are beset by images grounded not in mediums but in meanings; it is the voice, the content, that speaks to us in the new decade.
> A vast network of pipes. For some reason that phrase is on my mind. It's from Bertolt Brecht's 1932 essay "Theory of Radio," in which he calls for a new radio, with the listeners speaking as well as listening, exchanging thoughts, not greetings. Networking.[21]

Davis's "antique ends," then, include such basic ideas as interpersonal communication with the radio and TV set assuming the role of communal campfire. His satellite performances address these antique ends. So also did his live performance at Warner QUBE, the two-way interactive cable system in Columbus, Ohio. In the summer of 1979, Davis appeared on a QUBE channel in the context of a talk-show format. As part of the show, he discussed and demonstrated his performance work entitled "How To Make Love To Your Television Set." QUBE viewers were requested to answer questions posed by Davis about their relationship to TV. They also called in instructions to Davis and his studio hostess. The instructions asked the two "performers" to do various acts before the viewing audience sitting in front of their TV screens. One of my students who went with me to the Columbus studios to view the performance called in a rather difficult request from off-studio. Davis, very comfortable in the interactive situation, complied. But the hostess, jerked from the security of her traditional one-way communication pattern, was visibly non-

plussed; for the first time in her professional TV career she was being asked by a viewer to <u>respond</u> to him in a human way. Her self-
assurance shattered, it was up to Davis to save her from her audience. He did so gracefully, but the message was clear and in a sense
profound.

In 1980 Davis extended these antique ends even further by returning to the silent film in a performance context. The film, entitled
"Silver Screen," was shown at the Ronald Feldman Gallery in New
York before an audience seated in old theater seats. In the film Davis
was dressed in a white shirt and bow tie, further emphasizing the for-
mality and entertainment context of cinema. The short silent film used
self-reflexive devices such as title frames, piano accompaniment,
chase scenes in double time, and wild gesticulations. Davis played
himself, haunted by "the ghost of Davis past" and "the ghost of Davis
future." "Old radio" was used tongue-in-cheek as the answer to the
star's "mid-career crisis" (really as an extension of Davis's Post
Post-Art philosophy of returning art to content). Voices emerged
from a "live" radio in the back of the "theater." On the screen, Davis
pretends to hide in "old radio," but finally pops out of the screen image and declares "I never left flatland."

Davis told me, in a conversation about the piece, that "radio is
visually powerful because it removes a sense [that of sight] and thereby invites high audience participation." He added that "Post-Modern-
ism is really an openness toward the past." Davis highlights this openness by exploring the artistic context of both radio and silent film in
"Silver Screen." Perhaps there is some truth to McLuhan's notion that
each new medium makes the previous medium into an art form. Davis
neatly summarized these "new/old" possibilities: "Everything now is
'plural,' grounded in the specifics of decentralized personal choice."[22]
He added "Regions separate. Voices multiply. Art, architecture, and
photography are invaded. . . . The spider web, the network, the decentralization, the anarchy that is eclecticism, that is choice. Now
it's your turn."[23]

Thus, Davis answers my question about his wide ranging aesthetic strategy, raised earlier in this chapter. Art, like the eclecticism of experience itself, is open-ended for both the artist and the
spectator.

> . . . you will find many lines spraying out from the cen-
> ter of the web we began to weave . . . narration, the lin-
> guistics of meaning, performance, CATV (the decentral-
> ized network), artifice, decoration, left, right, center.
> But let us not dismiss these parallel lines as "eclectic-
> ism." . . . Eclecticism means freedom. Freedom means
> choosing, among all styles, one style, yours. Choice

means conflict. The reverse is tyranny, however be-
nevolent. . . .[24]

We turn now to Davis's more formal writings about video as an
art form. A close examination of these writings reveals a shift in
Davis's evaluation of artists' video genres that in many ways paral-
lels the progression of his own video works as outlined above.

In one of his initial theoretical essays about the nature of video,
Davis wrote of the medium's effect on time:

> Most of us now send and receive messages along channels
> that grow progressively more condensed. It is no accident
> that the art on commercial television is compacted to 30
> seconds, down from 60 seconds a decade ago. . . .
> . . . The media are low-energy exposure, compar-
> ed to the high-energy implicit in museums and galleries,
> but the channel is wider at the other end, and more egali-
> tarian by its nature. Very, very few people have even be-
> gun to think about structuring work suited to that channel,
> but they soon will. Contrary to common belief, this work
> can be highly esoteric and private, as well as the reverse.
> The only formal restriction is condensation. Be swift,
> don't be simple. [25]

That statement was written in 1971. By 1972 Davis began to break out
of the "formal restriction" of condensation of television time in his
own work:

> I experimented in run-on recording during most of 1971.
> . . . But the first sustained work was accomplished late
> that year and early in 1972. . . .
> . . . "Studies in Color II" unfolds—in television
> time—with agonizing slowness, that is, thirty minutes.
> Yet in human time, thirty minutes is a second. . . . I
> wanted to bridge the gap between television time and hu-
> man time. [26]

Davis carried this notion of live time further in a later essay in which
he rejected condensation of time in favor of lengthy visual development
of an idea as it unfolds, without editing:

> What we have come to call "live" video links with "life"
> in a highly concentrated form; when we are watching "live"
> phenomena on the screen we participate in a subtle exist-
> entialism. Often it is so subtle that it nears boredom. Yet

we stay, participating. The endless moon walk, the endless convention, the endless, in another way, American
Family. In all these cases, the "live" dimension kept its
audience there, before the small screen, alone, at home,
watching. [27]

Davis's strongest statement about the relationship of personal time
to contemporary art and to broadcast television came in a 1978 essay
on "Post-Modern Form." In the essay Davis urges the artist to work
to recapture human, experiential time from the grip of mechanized
public time:

> Why is time so important now, in so many bodies and
> genres of contemporary work? Clearly it is an organic,
> even formal, element in film, in performance, in video,
> in narration, or story, in many kinds of ecologically ori-
> ented art. Here are a few thoughts: The recognition of
> time keeps the work of art placed in and responsible for
> its own present tense—no pretense that the work is be-
> yond time and therefore neutral, in the manner of mod-
> ern arthitecture, which builds against the past and along-
> side—not for—the present. "Our time" is the only time
> we live in. Private time is the most immediate and pal-
> pable experience we have. It is also the most personal.
> Finally, its nature is irrational, beyond the powers of
> logic to define. . . . Public time is not only arbitrary:
> the counting of time by objective standards of measure-
> ment is impersonal and unreal. Useful as a means of
> keeping records and placing events, it is useless as a
> means of keeping or evaluating human time. The moment
> that you and I experience is nothing like the last; each
> moves at a different beat or cadence. The great lie—per-
> petuated by television—is that time moves at a regular,
> predictable beat, that everything is under control, includ-
> ing our clocks. Lulled into that cadence, we can sleep a
> life away, thinking that the next minute will be like the
> last. Each moment is a precious and subjective material,
> not an objective presence. [28]

Another example of Davis's shift in emphasis in his more formal writings about video concerns the idea of form versus content in video
works. In his early writings about movements occurring in artists'
video, Davis frequently discussed the formal aspects of the art form.
He noted that the artist working in video could have command over a
total field of color, color change, field density, layering, and kinetics,

which he felt was more flexible than was possible with film. He wrote in 1972:

> . . . the video picture cannot accommodate environmen-
> tal scale, but it can encompass a broad complexity of ab-
> stract forms and activity. The work executed by Paik,
> Vanderbeek, Seawright, Reilly, Richard Felciano, Rich-
> ard Lowenberg, Hamid Naficy, and others is saturated
> with these forms. . . . In all of this work, from Reilly
> to Paik, the evanescence of the image is the central fact.
> No form is static. [29]

Since 1972, Davis has shifted from a concern with form to a preoccupation with content which, as previously discussed in this chapter, centers on notions of both mind-to-mind communication between artist and viewer in a "private" video space created by telecast/cablecast and the unpredictability of events telecast/cablecast in live or real time. After six years of working with interactive video, Davis noted that we must move past any preoccupation with abstract video imagery (i. e. , form) for its own sake, and toward an understanding of video in its message/transmission/reception/perception context (i. e. , content), which is both aesthetic and political:

> Form is incidental of the quality of the message. Which
> is to say that it serves content, not that it dictates form.
> Form distinguishes between levels of excellence—in this
> I thoroughly agree with the Greenbergians. But the dis-
> tinctions operate on ascending levels of subject matter,
> levels that are indeed structured by content. The organi-
> zation of a work in which both content and form are equal
> partners is thus always a mystery: we cannot separate one
> from the other. Nor is "style" the proper answer. A post-
> modern art must rid itself of the very notion of style, or
> trademark, because it implies that the organization . . .
> can be controlled by issues beyond content. Style is furth-
> ermore a betrayal of the meaning in a work of art, and the
> meaning inside us. . . . style makes no allowance for
> time—the recognition of the fluidity and instaneity [sic] of
> our perceptions, thoughts, and feelings. What we perceive
> in one moment is of necessity different from that in anoth-
> er, though of course there is a connection. . . . what I am
> saying implies a hierarchy of content—that some subjects
> are inherently more important and demanding (and there-
> fore deserve larger, less self-contained forms) than oth-
> ers. I could list the hierarchy right now, but I would sim-
> ply duplicate what you already know. [30]

These are but a few of many examples of Davis's shifts in his evaluations of video as an art form. Yet they serve to demonstrate both the timeliness and flexibility of the artist-critic's approach to discussing art.

As noted earlier, the artist-critic writing about video tends to praise the style of making works with which he is directly and personally involved while tending to either regard lightly or to dismiss contradictory styles. Nowhere is this distinction more apparent than in Davis's discussions of artists' video and broadcast television programming.

Davis provided an overview of the differences between artists' video and broadcast television in an essay tracing the development of artists' video since the mid-1960s:

> From its inception, television aesthetics has been in the hands of the corporate and bureaucratic few, not the many, yet these few have insisted on defining its nature as thoroughly mindless and populist. With a few exceptions—early live telecasts, athletic events, sly popular entertainers—television . . . from its first day . . . was middle-aged, dedicated to bland, soothing effects. It is not surprising—considering who "owned" television in the beginning (governments and corporations)—that this should be so. What is surprising is that so many intellectuals have accepted this fact, cheered on by McLuhan and the preachers of Papal-Global-Village ethic.
>
> It is into this context that Video Art has come—at first through the form of works of sculpture containing TV monitors and playback self-images, then through brightly colored special-effects wizardry, recorded on tape—and is now operating. But it was inevitable that Video Art would not stay anchored in this retrograde base. The moment the first Sony videotape recorders were being marketed in the United States and Europe was a moment when the avant-garde in the West was moving toward a greater concern with patterns of thought and politics than with halcyon imagery: the videotapes that began to appear in art galleries and museums (and occasionally broadcast on adventurous television stations) between 1968 and 1972 were anything but "pretty." They dealt in ideas and in positions. . . . These rough, badly thought-out videotapes may have been the first attempt to use "television"—either in closed-circuit or in broadcast form—for anything like the intense communication (mind to mind) that is the very substance of print. [31]

Davis takes a clear-cut position in his writings that all of broadcast television is today "thoroughly mindless and populist," appealing to the sleepwalkers among us. However, in our interview, Davis did cite one broadcast television production that had made an impact on his thinking and in his own video work:

> The only thing that I can think of in my entire life other than the presence of TV in my home and my thinking about television . . . other than the structural presence of TV in my home, the only significant work I can think of that really influenced me was a series on PBS . . . called "An American Family." That's the only one. . . . The thing that interested me about "An American Family" was that it rather openly indulged in boredom, the passing of real time in conversation. There were long stretches of conversation that seemed absolutely meaningless, and I found that interesting and fascinating . . . It made me think a lot about why it was fascinating on television and it was not fascinating in real life. That's the only work I can really think of that's ever really influenced me or forced me to think in some way productively in terms of my own work. Everything else I have done has been against what I have seen on television.

Davis noted that many artists working in video who had received grants to produce works at experimental public broadcasting facilities such as WGBH-TV in Boston, WNET-TV in New York, and KQED-TV in San Francisco had tailored their works to reach a "mass" audience:

> Most of the work now being produced at experimental television centers is impressive chiefly on physical grounds. It is pleasantly abstract, radiant in color, and accompanied by crackling, synthesized sound. It is also dedicated in the main to the entertainment ethic—on a higher level than commercial TV but similarly motivated. It responds to a weakened and democratized definition of public art: that the work must seek first to serve a large and middle-level audience, rather than the vision of the maker. . . .[32]

Davis has continually asserted that the artist working in video must approach the viewer as an individual, not as a member of some anonymous "mass." To do this, Davis believes, artists must reject the mind-numbing premise of broadcast television and instead begin to utilize cable channels to reach "specialized" audiences with the kind of works that draw viewers into the works as active participants:

I have no doubt that we will yet use cable effectively to buy and sell goods. But the real challenge to us is deeper. We now have in our hands the means to change irrevocably the mind-numbing course of television, as we write a new communications act. We can insist that the owners and operators of CATV systems across the country keep channels open to the public and to specialized audiences, both high and low. We can discard the primitive notion of an electronic global village for a more pluralistic, individuated model. [33]

This passage appeared in Newsweek in November 1977. There was hope in the air that Congress would rewrite the Federal Communications Act of 1934 to provide for a greater diversity of programming sources and for more secure funding for independent producers. In late 1977 public access cable channels, mandated by the FCC, were expanding their operations throughout the country. Two years later, however, there was no new Communications Act, and the United States Supreme Court had held that the FCC could not require cable system owners to provide access channels in their communities. Now access would be a local jurisdictional decision rather than a national mandate. In 1980 the future of public access is a very clouded one. Yet compared to the level of artists' access to television in the late 1960s, today's environment for access is healthy: more artists than ever before have had their video works shown on cable television.

Ultimately one must question whether television is as bad as Davis believes it to be. Davis perceives a clear split between video works he calls "art" and broadcast television programming (including artists' video tailored for broadcast television), which he views as "bland," "soothing," "mind-numbing" nonart. To the objective observer this dichotomy must seem to be an oversimplification. Indeed counterarguments taking a more balanced approach to the evaluation of the art form, especially those works that are the standard fare of broadcast television, are presently being made by various writers about television. For comparative purposes, note Horace Newcomb's discussions of popular television in Chapter 5.

It should be remembered, however, that the artist-critic, like his compatriot the radical critic, will tend to use polemic for a purpose: to promote one particular style of art making that has not gained acceptance in the "cultural mainstream." With video there are two mainstreams that the artist-critic must challenge: first, the traditional art world of the museum and gallery exhibition, and second, the "most popular art" of our time—television. In the following section, Davis assesses his own role and influence as a challenger of this dual mainstream.

DAVIS ON HIS ROLE AS AN ARTIST-CRITIC

In an early essay, Davis described the fusion of the functions of the critic and the artist: "The task of the critic is to become art, as that of art is to become life."[34] In another essay Davis noted that "The critic must . . . transform his traditional concern for craft into a concern for ideas, a concern for concept rather than product."[35]

As has been discussed previously in this chapter, Davis perceives his role as an artist-critic to be that of providing ideological contexts within which the viewer or reader can better understand art and video. I asked Davis to elaborate on his perception of this role. He replied:

> . . . when you start thinking about the act of putting your hands on the screen [in "The Austrian Tapes"], which appears to be very simple, you really go a long way. You can't really stop thinking about the meaning of that. Not only do I keep thinking about it, keep having new conclusions about it, but viewers do that too. I get letters all the the time from people who have touched the screen who've thought about that, and they come up with new thoughts and ideas. One such thought that it implies is that the TV screen is not a window. Think about the meaning of that for a moment. That's really a very basic, penetrating idea on all kinds of levels—political, metaphysical, social. If we are aware that the TV screen is not a window, there is no way in which it can lie to us, there's no way it can dominate us. If you think of TV as partly a threat to civilization as I do and as most people do . . . that's a shattering idea.

Davis himself believes it is impossible to separate the ideas contained in his video works and in his writings about video, although the contexts in which his ideas are presented may differ widely. I asked him if he had any difficulty reconciling his performance works and his conceptual writings about art and video. He responded:

> The ideas that they express—that is the writings and the manifestoes on the one hand and the performances and the . . . videotapes on the other—the ideas they express are the same, but since each one . . . deals with a different situation, a different context, and a different audience, I never try to reconcile one with the other in any obvious formal way. The reason this position I'm expressing is often difficult for us to understand . . . is that in

general . . . in the twentieth century particularly in this
country we have adopted a very romantic view of the artistic process, and we have lost the sense that people had
in the eighteenth century of the importance of genre. We
think of the artistic creation as being very pure and simple, basic and fundamental at its height or at its optimum
and when it comes out, when it's expressed, it can only be
expressed in one way. And we've lost all sense of genre,
of differentiation, which I maintain is wrong. Just think
for a minute of your conversation. When you converse with
people it's always different. It depends on who you're talking to, when, and where. Now in terms of writing and of
art, the same thing pertains. They are acts, they take
place at specific times, and imply specific contexts. So
. . . although the ideas are—I would maintain in everything I do you'd see a deadly similarity in ideas—the way
in which I express those ideas hugely varies. It has to do
with a sense of context, always with a sense of context.

Davis has tried to place his ideas in a wide variety of these
"contexts." In doing so, he believes he has defined his own role as
an artist-critic in a way that differs from a great many other artist-
critics. He spoke with me about this perceived difference:

I'm perfectly willing to write for Newsweek, to appear on
NBC as well as to appear on Cable Soho or to exhibit at
the Ronald Feldman Gallery. And every time I do that, I
do that with a certain trust that somebody's out there who
shares the same concerns that I have. It's very basic and
simple, but it isn't, because I'm obviously in vast disa-
greement with many, many, many, many, very, very
powerful and intelligent people. This is one of the continuing fights, continuing struggles that I have with the
editors of various journals and with TV producers. I've
done a lot of very difficult things on television and in various mass circulation journals, and I can't recall ever
once having my trust violated.

Davis's perception of his role as an artist-critic is closely tied to his
perception of the audience for his video works and of the readership
for his writings about video, which are discussed in the following section.

DAVIS ON HIS AUDIENCE AND READERSHIP

Davis perceives that both the audience for his video works and the readership for his writings about art and video extend far beyond the limits of an inner circle of artist friends and devoted gallery goers. Davis spoke with me at length about his perceptions of his audience and readership:

> I always think of the viewer as . . . existential. I have no idea who he is going to be or she is going to be. I also think of the viewer as somebody I can trust. I think that's so in everything I do. I think that's true with the writing as well. . . . This obviously sets me apart from lots of people running our society and many other artists and many editors. . . . I don't know why there is this difference, but there certainly is. The one thing that impresses me most about editors, for example, not all editors but most editors, and most television producers, is their scorn for and fear of the person who's on the other end. I don't know why that's so, why people have that inbred scorn and fear. I don't. I don't have it. . . . I've had a lot of critics, and I've had a lot of letters from people who violently disagree with me or misunderstand me. But nearly always when that happens, one is aware of a certain bias or a certain premise from which your critic is coming that explains why he saw what he did or read what he did in a certain way. My trust has never been violated by this existential person who I'm trying to talk to you about, with the vast majority of the people that I deal with, that I communicate with in all of these areas. When I hear from them, I hear that they're getting it straight. The viewer to me is existential. I trust in his or her equality with me. By equality I mean not only equality of intellect but equality of interest, and if I have a burning interest in a certain issue that he or she will have it too, simply because we are members of the human family. I think that democracy is inherent in such a position, which is the reverse of what is often claimed. That is to say, often the commercial TV producers and the editors of mass magazines will say to us, the artists, that we are elitists and they are the true democrats . . . they do not trust the viewer or the reader. This is obviously wrong. Once one thinks about it, one realizes that the real democracy is resident in the position of trust, that is the trust in the existential equality of the viewer and/or the reader. In years of ex-

posure to millions of people, a very large audience, both
through video and through writing and through performance and through art of various kinds, I have yet to find
the moron, I've yet to find the person who is a staple of
the media theories on the other side, who is absolutely
required by those media theories.

    . . . I wouldn't want to leave the impression that
there is any lack of humanity in the position that I take.
In other words, because I can't think of a specific person or a specific set of persons in the way that the producer of a television program who has statistics supplied
to him on the ages and the preferences of his viewers, it
doesn't mean that I'm inhuman and that the guy who has
the statistics and who has the very specific nature of the
audience in mind is. . . . the . . . assumption which requires quantifying: sixteen percent of my viewers have
graduated from college, thirty-five percent have graduated from high school, which is what the TV producer
can _tell_ you and I can't, is absolutely a dehumanizing
view of the viewer.

Davis, however, did qualify the notion that he had no idea of the
nature of his audience other than its existential equality with him. He
spoke with me about the difference in his perception of the "live" audience at his performances and the viewers watching the performance
at home on their television screens:

In the pieces that I have done here on the Soho cable, I
have not presupposed in the TV viewer at home any special sophistication. I have presupposed in the performance audience a special sophistication. That's why I'm so
interested in doing that kind of piece now, because I'm really intrigued by being able to present a certain idea or a
certain thought to two audiences at once, and give them the
same thought, but at the same time delight and glory in the
differences. That is to say the difference not only of the
audience, of the two audiences, but also the difference in the
way they perceive the _same_ thought, and that is what has happened
in these pieces so far. They have presumed in the performance audience sitting there in The Kitchen or in the Whitney or in Anthology [Film Archives] a certain sophistication that _is_ higher than the national average. That same
presumption has not been made of the viewer at home. . . .
    . . . I don't make any hierarchical distinction be-
tween the value of the two audiences. People who come
and sit there and see the performance are as important

to me as the guy on the other end of the TV screen. As I
said before, everything you do has a certain context and
a certain place. So I have, up until now, taken into account the sophistication of the performance in New York.
. . . I have taken that into account, and it has permitted
me a certain freedom and elusiveness in the performance
part of those pieces that I probably would not extend to
other audiences though it would depend a great deal on
the situation. . . . Right now I'm having some discussion
with "The Today Show," and they're thinking about putting
me on the air at some point, and we're having this argument right now. And I'm saying, "All right, if you put me
on the air I want to do a totally nude piece, live, in front
of the camera. I want to ask the viewer to do this, that,
and the other thing." They're saying, "Wait! Wait! Wait!
We're talking about Mr. and Mrs. America here. We're
not talking about some artie Soho audience." And I'm saying, "No, you're not! You can't tell me what these people
like, because I know they're not like what you think."
There's no compromise on this issue as far as I'm concerned. Either they're going to let me do what I want or
I'm not going to do it. . . . It's a matter of really believ-
ing in the existential equality of the TV viewer. I absolutely believe in that. Nothing will change my mind about
that.

Davis described the "specialized" performance audience who
comes to the performance space to view his work:

Now the performance audience . . . is the audience that's
right there watching, right there in front of me. . . . The
audience for the Whitney piece were 125 people. Most of
them were artists, half of them were my friends. I knew
I could do anything with them. I could put seventeen monitors in that place and they would be just quite relaxed about
it, they'd be able to pick out the major point of emphasis
which was me, the live person. They wouldn't be freaked
out by the appearance of that big Advent video screen.

Finally, Davis told me that he never made the assumption that
the audience for his video works and his readership were composed
of the same individuals:

I have no idea whether the person who sees my tapes or
sees my performances has read anything I've written at

all. So I always approach this person as an unknown. And
I always try to orient him from point zero. I never assume anything in this person. I try to orient him as though
he knew nothing [about my work].

CONCLUSIONS

Of all the artist-critics working with and writing about video today, Douglas Davis is certainly the most expansive both in terms of
his coverage of a broad range of ideas and his use of a great variety
of artistic mediums. He looks into, through, and around video for
clues to our larger culture and our use of contemporary art mediums
for specific ends. Framing his thoughts about art and its relationship
to life is the central notion that art is above all a human endeavor, directed toward and to be used by the spectator in highly personalized,
individual ways.

One of Davis's most alluring constructs is his view of the "existential equality" existing between the writer/artist and the reader/
viewer. Davis has put the egalitarian principle to work by writing for
a variety of publications with highly divergent readerships, ranging
from the populist Newsweek to the esoteric Artforum and New York
Arts Journal—the same ideas presented in different ways in different
forums for different readers. His video works range from live performances before the "art community" in spaces like The Kitchen, the
Ronald Feldman Gallery, and the Whitney Museum of American Art
to television talk shows incorporating video performance elements
aired on public television stations, commercial broadcast networks,
and cable-access channels. By reaching out to his "public" in these
ways, Davis overturns elitist art community notions of art as a pre-
cious commodity available to the privileged few. Thus Davis serves
notice that artists need not be co-opted by popular mediums such as
television, film, and radio; rather artists can explore the traditional
contexts in which these mediums operate by accessing a medium and
then using the medium for statements both about and against itself.
For example, the notion of who controls content shifts from a one-way
domination of the communication process (us to them) to a two-way
interactive communication process (me to you to me).

To achieve his conceptual goal of spectator participation in his
work, Davis has employed such diverse mediums as the art event,
video performance with cablecasting and viewer feedback, and radio
performance. The answer to the question "What is the end of this?"
that Davis once raised in his "Austrian Tapes" may well be found in
two-way, upstream-downstream, mind-to-mind communication between equals. Part of that answer lies in the technological potential

of electronic communication with its built-in biases of immediacy and
intimacy; but, more importantly, part of the answer rests in the artist's ability to both access the technology and have something to communicate to his public once he has secured access.

Davis has ably demonstrated his ability to accomplish the latter.
No other artist working with video has been able to gain access to such
a wide variety of telecommunications mediums for purposes of dis-
seminating his individual statements; and Davis stands on the cutting
edge of the art-critical dialogue evolving from and in many ways guiding contemporary art movements, not the least significant of which is
artists' video.

Much of Davis's writings and his video works are highly charged
political statements about both television and the contemporary artist's relationship to this pervasive medium. His message is clear:
link the artist and the viewer together in "live" time in "mind-to-
mind" communication and thereby bring art out of the temple/muse-
um/gallery context and into the "lived world" of human experience
(the individual's intimate, private space). One hopes that the manipu-
lators of television's dominant structural mechanisms will heed his
word and begin to operate with the same "trust" Davis accords his
television audiences. After all, what is there to fear about the individual viewer sitting at home, alone, in front of the TV set?

NOTES

1. Lawrence Alloway, "Artists as Writers, Part One: Inside
Information," Artforum 12 (March 1974): 30.
2. Ibid. , p. 33.
3. Ibid. , p. 34.
4. Lawrence Alloway, "Artists as Writers, Part Two: The
Realm of Language," Artforum 12 (April 1974): 31.
5. David W. Rintels, "Not for Bread Alone," Performance 3
(July/August 1972): 53.
6. Ibid. , p. 55.
7. Reginald Rose, "TV's Age of Innocence—What Became of
It?" New York Times, December 3, 1967, sec. 2, p. 21.
8. Nam June Paik, "The Video Synthesizer and Beyond," in
The New Television, eds. Douglas Davis and Allison Simmons (Cambridge, Mass. : MIT Press, 1977), pp. 44-46. See also Nam June
Paik and Paul Schimmel, "Abstract Time," Arts Magazine, December 1974, pp. 52-53, and Paik's interview with Douglas Davis in
Douglas Davis, Art and the Future (New York: Praeger, 1973), pp.
147-50.

9. George Brecht, Chance-Imagery (New York: Something Else Press, 1966).

10. Jonathan Price, Video Visions: A Medium Discovers Itself (New York: New American Library, 1977), p. 201.

11. Douglas Davis, "Video Obscura," Artforum 10 (April 1972): 71.

12. Published in "Douglas Davis: events drawings objects videotapes 1967-1972," exhibition catalogue, Everson Museum of Art, 1972. The manifesto is reproduced here with changes in typescript.

13. Douglas Davis, "Time! Time! Time! The Context of Immediacy," in The New Television, eds. Douglas Davis and Allison Simmons (Cambridge, Mass.: The MIT Press, 1977), p. 78.

14. Douglas Davis, Artculture: Essays on the Post-Modern (New York: Harper & Row, 1977), p. 145.

15. Ibid., p. 155.

16. Ibid., p. 157.

17. Ingrid Wiegand, "Three Silent and Secret Acts," Soho Weekly News, February 19, 1976, p. 36.

18. Davis, Artculture, p. 159.

19. Douglas Davis, "Post Post-Art II: Symbolismo, Come Home," Village Voice, August 13, 1979, p. 41.

20. Douglas Davis, "Post Post-Art: Where Do We Go from Here?" Village Voice, June 25, 1979, p. 41.

21. Ibid., p. 38.

22. Davis, "Post Post-Art II," p. 41.

23. Ibid., p. 43.

24. Douglas Davis, "Symbolismo Meets the Faerie Queene," Village Voice, December 17, 1979, p. 47.

25. Douglas Davis, "Media/Art/Media," Arts Magazine, September-October 1971, pp. 44-45.

26. Davis, "Time! Time! Time!," pp. 77-78.

27. Douglas Davis, "Video in the Mid-70's: Prelude to an End/ Future," in Video Art: An Anthology, eds. Ira Schneider and Beryl Korot (New York: Harcourt Brace Jovanovich, 1976), p. 198.

28. Douglas Davis, "Post-Modern Form: Stories Real & Imagined/Toward A Theory," New York Arts Journal (February/March 1978): 12.

29. Davis, "Video Obscura," p. 71.

30. Davis, Artculture, pp. 159-60.

31. Davis, "Video in the Mid-70's," p. 197.

32. Douglas Davis, "Public Art: The Taming of the Vision," Art in America, May-June 1974, p. 84.

33. Douglas Davis, Let's Hear It for the Cable," Newsweek, November 21, 1977, p. 29.

34. Douglas M. Davis, "The Critic Now," Arts in Society 5 (1968): 358.

35. Douglas M. Davis, "Art & Technology—Toward Play," Art in America, January-February 1968, p. 47.

8

REDEFINING
TELEVISION CRITICISM

We have explored a variety of distinctive approaches to television and video criticism in the preceding chapters using selected critics themselves as our guides. One thing should be immediately apparent: the subject of this criticism is much broader and runs conceptually much deeper than we might have initially suspected.

Broadcast television remains with us today as the dominant link to the 99 percent of American households who participate daily in a polycentric electronic community. Prior to entering elementary school, a child may spend as many as 3,500 hours before a TV screen. It is becoming increasingly apparent to those of us in the education community that today's "TV child" is quite "visually literate." As these TV children grow to adolescence and adulthood, they are coming to expect something significant from the pens of professional television critics. Television critics, who spend a good portion of their professional lives discussing this pervasive entertainment and informational medium, are increasingly recognizing their important responsibility to those of us who watch the box but may not always have the time or the finely tuned critical skills to fully comprehend the meaning of this powerful cultural force.

But broadcast television is no longer the sole focus of this criticism. The expansive television critic must also contend with movements toward an "alternative" television: artists' video and independent community video documentary. These forms of alternative television art, which were born in the mid–1960s and have continually expanded the scope of their activities, do not now and are not ever likely to challenge broadcast television for huge numbers of viewers; yet they do offer a distinctive challenge to broadcast television in terms of content (idea or message).

The most significant television criticism is now occurring and will undoubtedly continue to occur precisely at the nexus of the deeper cultural meanings of broadcast television and "alternative television."

One cannot be understood outside the context of the other, and neither can be understood without acknowledging the entanglement of art in the web of predominant cultural and social systems. While artists' video may not owe a debt of gratitude to broadcasting, these video works cannot avoid reflecting back on broadcast television, its programs and its dominant programming control mechanisms, even though in many cases that may not be the primary intent of such works. Likewise, broadcast television may deny access to independent artists working in the documentary form or in alternative fictional narrative, performance, installations, or formalist imaging; but it cannot escape the deeper meaning of its exclusion of these works from the cultural mainstream—a deeply imbedded and unarticulated fear, guided by a pecuniary philosophy, that a multiplicity of voices, some challenging rather than reinforcing conventional value systems, will offer choices to its slumbering but restless audience.

The five television and video critics whose writings and ruminations on the art form examined in this book all have the same goal in mind—to help their readers recognize the need for an expansion of the choices available to them. Each critic has his own personal perspective as to what those choices should be and how the expansion of the telecommunications system should be accomplished.

John O'Connor sees a distinct need for improved quality in dramatic works presented on television that he believes can be accomplished by bringing new indigenous creative talent into the television mainstream and allowing them the flexibility to stretch existing dramatic conventions as they explore new dramatic forms. This notion harks back to the early 1950s "Golden Age" of commercial television when then unknown writers such as Reginald Rose, Rod Serling, Paddy Chayefsky, and Robert Alan Arthur were given carte blanche by producers desperately in need of material to fill air time. O'Connor feels that today's most practical outlet for these dramatic explorations is public television, but he bemoans the fact that public TV in the United States has been shirking its mandate by not sufficiently nurturing these new creative talent.

Bernie Harrison sees television as this culture's most potentially significant educator. Two of television's principal educational forms, the documentary and the personal essay or journal, have received lip service but little support recently from the commercial networks after flourishing in the 1950s and early 1960s. Harrison, like O'Connor, believes public television can serve as the conduit for an expansion of this educational function.

Horace Newcomb, peering beneath the surface structures of popular television, finds that TV is our principal educator today. The message embedded in the episodes, series, and serials speak to us about what we are and might become. To Newcomb, the stories on television

both mirror our larger culture and feed back into that culture, reinforcing dominant value systems. Newcomb urges the viewer to sharp-
en individual critical skills and take notice of what the programs are
telling us about ourselves; above all, Newcomb believes, we must
understand and question popular television values and demand programs with "positive" values.

David Ross, as a defender of artists' video, is concerned about
independent artists' exclusion from the distribution mechanisms of
the dominant broadcast television institutions. It is not enough, he
notes, for artists pursuing alternative video explorations to have the
distribution of their work confined to the traditional art community
contexts of the art gallery or museum; rather, the artist, with the
help of the museum curator, must work toward acquiring a multitude
of cable channels to present this work to a larger public within a temporal context determined by the artist rather than the cable operator.
Cable television, Ross believes, can become the ultimate manifestation of the "museum without walls" concept.

Douglas Davis, an artist working with and writing about video,
believes that the dominant culture's television distribution mechanisms
can be accessed by independent artists and can be used to highlight the
personal, one-to-one human communication potential inherent in existing telecommunications technology. Achieving that access, Davis as-
serts, will demonstrate the deception of broadcasters who claim they
give the public what it wants while they misuse the technology to promote one-way communication and thereby stifle true audience feedback. Much of Davis's two-way interactive video performance work
is conceptually grounded in securing that needed access and then using
the channels he has opened for personal, interactive communication
ends, drawing his viewing audience into his performances by allowing
them to complete his ideas as they choose, but within the work's structural parameters.

A common thread running through all five critics' writings is
that television as we perceive it today has not begun to approach its
potential as a communications medium, that it could do so much more
for its audience then it presently does. The message is the same,
whether it is focused on television as a purveyor of quality drama,
documentary, or personal essay to a huge audience; television as a
teacher of "positive" values; television as a transmission device for
controversial ideas; or television as an intimate two-way communications medium.

QUESTIONING THE CRITICS

As the critics question television, so too must we question the
critics. Have they contributed significantly to our understanding of

television? Could they be doing more then they are presently doing? The answer to both questions is "yes." Based on this book's evaluations of the critics' work, one could say with assurance that television critics are making significant contributions to help untangle the web of meanings that is television. But there is much more yet to be done.

To date, television critics writing for daily newspapers or general circulation magazines have on the whole failed to consolidate their essays into integrated book-length examinations of the medium, although there are exceptions. Michael Arlen, television critic for The New Yorker, has written two books that are compilations of his essays about television, Living Room War and The View From Highway 1. Many of the essays in the former deal with television's treatment of the Vietnam War, while the essays in the latter cover a broader spectrum of television programs and cultural issues. John Leonard, former television critic for the New York Times, included essays about television in his book This Pen For Hire, a compilation of Leonard's thoughts on a variety of art forms. Robert Lewis Shayon compiled many of his more significant essays about television, written originally for Saturday Review, in an important book entitled Open To Criticism. In that book Shayon ingeniously tied his work as a television critic to the exploits of the wise but weary traveler of Coleridge's poem "The Rime of the Ancient Mariner." But the list does not extend much farther.

Many more such compilations of the essays of our major journalists writing about television are needed. True, these journalists (as exemplified by O'Connor and Harrison) see a large part of their function as providing timely pre-reviews of upcoming programs; and true, the pressures of the daily deadline do not allow much time for prolonged reflection on the deeper meanings of television in our culture. But the time must be found to allow these writers, who are on the "front lines" day after day, the opportunity to write about the deeper insights they have gained during their day-to-day reporting. This is a problem that should be addressed by the critics' managing editors.

Such books could give both the general reader and the serious student of television sorely needed insights into the real world pressures of conceiving, producing, and distributing television programs. One can forsee such a book by John O'Connor focusing on the history and importance of the battle over access now raging between the commercial and public broadcasting networks on the one hand and the independent television producers on the other, and on the implications of that battle for quality television. In another vein, one can forsee a book by Bernie Harrison on the history of television's programming trend changes and the personalities working behind the scenes—a personal look at the relationship of programming realities to "the dreams and the dreamers."

The academic critics, as represented by Horace Newcomb, David Thorburn, Raymond Williams, and others, have made significant strides since 1974 toward decoding the deeper meanings of popular television programs. Their examinations of popular television formulas, program structures, and operational myths and value systems have opened new critical vistas for the serious student of television. They have demonstrated above all that television should be taken seriously and that it can be approached in much the same manner as such previously developed popular art forms as popular literature and film. They have carefully documented the fact that while television frequently operates as a translator of "received forms" from other popular arts, it has also developed innovative forms of its own. More explication is needed from these critics. An immediate need is an update of Newcomb's seminal 1974 book <u>TV: The Most Popular Art</u> that incorporates his refined anthropological approach to television, which focuses on popular television genres' tendencies to reinforce widely held misconceptions of certain social groups' character traits.

There is little doubt that artists' video and independent community video documentary have today secured legitimate status as ideological alternatives to popular television, yet the access to the dominant communications apparatus they so desperately need has been slow in coming. The efforts of radical critics such as David Ross, John Hanhardt, and Russell Connor in promoting this work and providing distribution mechanisms for its airing should not be underestimated. Yet the battle for access is just beginning. Ross's attempts to open a museum channel via KVST-TV in Los Angeles, while ultimately unsuccessful, provided a needed impetus in this direction. Such efforts must be continued until artists' cable channels are a reality, not just in urban centers on the coasts but in all areas throughout the country that are capable of supporting such independent work. The next step, of course, is museum program interchange via communications satellite. The radical critic as activist has a greater responsibility than simply writing about new, challenging work that has not made its way into the cultural mainstream—he or she must, it seems, actively push it into that mainstream by playing the roles of local civic leader, politician, and programmer. Anything less will not adequately serve the cause of alternative video.

Artists working with video are challenging our traditional notions of what television is and are thereby stretching the boundaries of television as an art form. An important adjunct to this video activity is the process of <u>writing</u> about the new video work. The artist as critic is in a unique position to be able to examine the creative process from the "inside" out. The combination of creating video works and writing about the motivations guiding that creative process can go far toward conceptually redefining the nature of the medium. Douglas Davis stands out as an artist who also possesses the requisite critical skills to be able to provide clear directions in the ongoing drive to redefine television. While his is not a single voice in the flatland wilderness, more of his kind of carefully reasoned critical essays are needed from the many artists presently working with video. Those essays must address a more general readership in addition to the members of the traditional art community; to accomplish this, these artist-critics will need to seek print distribution mechanisms such as general interest magazines and daily newspapers. Davis has led the way with his Newsweek columns. Other artists should follow that lead.

Equally important is the need for the creative community working in broadcast television to speak out on the proscriptions inherent in this dominant cultural form. Essays such as those by teleplay writers David Rintels and Reginald Rose are worthy examples of this approach. These artist-critics could make a significant impact on readers, for they possess a legitimacy by virtue of their acceptance into the dominant communications structure. If readers thus recognize the fact that some highly intelligent members of television's creative community are dissatisfied with television's control mechanisms and will not allow themselves to be co-opted by television's imperative for formatized programs, much will have been accomplished.

There is no question but that serious television criticism is being written in a variety of forums serving a multiplicity of functions. Yet a certain doubt lingers about the impact of this criticism. That doubt is expressed by all the television and video critics examined in this book. Are their messages getting through? If so, are they reaching the "proper" people? The consensus is that while the general viewer, the television scholar, and the art community are reading this criticism and to varying degrees are benefiting from it according to their individualized needs, there is a deep concern, expressed by the critics themselves, that those with the greatest need for substantive criticism—the leaders of the broadcast television community—have turned a deaf ear to the words of the television critic. There is a growing sense of frustration on the part of concerned television critics as they begin to realize that while they may win an occasional battle to keep a program on the air or to secure access for an alternative video vision, they are not making much headway toward winning the war—toward opening up broadcast television both to consistent quality of production values and to the presentation of controversial ideas.

Perhaps the responsibility for redefining television in the long run rests less squarely on the shoulders of its professional critics than it does on the masses of viewers who daily participate in the electronic ritual. As Horace Newcomb eloquently noted in the introduction to his anthology of television criticism, Television: The Critical View:

A true climate of criticism . . . will involve not only those who consider themselves to be professional critics, researchers, journalists. It will also involve most of the population, for most people do care in their own way about the general education of the culture. Such caring is at the heart of the critical enterprise. . . .

. . . Until the audience understands what it sees in larger contexts, until it develops its own critical facilities we will live in a world dominated by one-eyed monsters. When all of us participate in the critical climate we will live in a world more thoroughly humane than any other. [1]

Yet the general audience cannot adequately comprehend television's webs of significance without guidance from those who represent us before the powerful broadcast tribunal—our television critics.

There is some truth to the notion that in the past television has not been taken seriously by many of its critics. Newcomb elaborated on this:

. . . television . . . is denied qualities and properties of its own and is only judged comparatively. Usually the comparisons are invidious ones in which television is condemned for what it is not rather than for what it is. . . . Excellence in television is taken to be the exception with continual surprise, as if this were not also the case in literature and film. Television, then, has no heritage of its own, no place in the culture except as an intruder. And while it should be clear that more comprehensive critical approaches would not see television exclusively in virtuous terms, it should also be clear that an assumed negativism can effectively prevent thorough analysis. [2]

Interestingly, this same negativism has been applied to television criticism by many who evaluate the critics' performance. Hopefully this book has countered that widespread negativism. But let us not linger long to revel in the virtues of television criticism, for the there is much of significance about television and video that is yet to be written.

NOTES

1. Horace Newcomb, ed. , "Introduction," <u>Television: The Critical View</u>, 2d ed.   (New York: Oxford University Press, 1979), pp. xxi-xxii.

2. Ibid. , p. xv.

BIBLIOGRAPHY

BOOKS

Antin, David. "Video: The Distinctive Features of the Medium." Video Art. Philadelphia: University of Pennsylvania, Institute of Contemporary Art, 1975.

Arlen, Michael J. Living Room War. New York: Viking, 1969.

____. The View from Highway 1. New York: Farrar, Straus & Giroux, 1976.

Arnheim, Rudolph. Art and Visual Perception: The Psychology of the Creative Eye. Berkeley, Calif.: University of California Press, 1954.

____. Film as Art. Berkeley, Calif.: University of California Press, 1957.

Battcock, Gregory, ed. New Artists Video: A Critical Anthology. New York: E. P. Dutton, 1978.

Bazin, Andre. What is Cinema? Vol. 1. Berkeley, Calif.: University of California Press, 1967.

____. What is Cinema? Vol. 2. Berkeley, Calif.: University of California Press, 1971.

Benjamin, Walter. Illuminations. New York: Harcourt Brace Jovanovich, 1968.

Berlyne, D. E. Aesthetics and Psychobiology. New York: Appleton-Century-Crofts, 1971.

____, ed. Studies in the New Experimental Aesthetics: Steps Toward an Objective Psychology of Aesthetic Appreciation. New York: Halsted Press, 1974.

Bluem, A. William. Documentary in American Television. New York: Hastings House, 1965.

Brecht, George. Chance-Imagery. New York: Something Else Press, 1966.

Carey, James W., and Albert L. Kreiling. "Popular Culture and Uses and Gratifications: Notes Toward an Accommodation." In The Uses of Mass Communications: Current Perspectives on Gratifications Research, edited by Jay G. Blumler and Elihu Katz, pp. 225-48. Beverly Hills, Calif.: Sage Publications, 1974.

Cashill, John R. "Packaging Pop Mythology." In The New Languages, edited by Thomas H. Ohlgren and Lynn M. Berk, pp. 79-90. Englewood Cliffs, N.J.: Prentice-Hall, 1977.

Cater, Douglass, and Richard Adler, eds. Television as a Cultural Force. New York: Praeger, 1976.

____. Television as a Social Force: New Approaches to TV Criticism. New York: Praeger, 1975.

Cavell, Stanley. The World View. New York: Viking Press, 1971.

Connor, Russell. "A Is for Art, C Is for Cable." In The New Television: A Public/Private Art, edited by Douglas Davis and Allison Simmons, pp. 170-74. Cambridge, Mass.: MIT Press, 1977.

____. "Video Gets a One." In Video Art: An Anthology, edited by Ira Schneider and Beryl Korot, pp. 164-71. New York: Harcourt Brace Jovanovich, 1976.

Davis, Douglas. Art and the Future. New York: Praeger, 1973.

____. Artculture: Essays on the Post-Modern. New York: Harper & Row, 1977.

____. "Video in the Mid-70's: Prelude to an End/Future." In Video Art: An Anthology, edited by Ira Schneider and Beryl Korot, pp. 196-99. New York: Harcourt Brace Jovanovich, 1976.

Davis, Douglas, and Allison Simmons, eds. The New Television: A Public/Private Art. Cambridge, Mass.: MIT Press, 1977.

Dufrenne, Mikel. The Phenomenology of Aesthetic Experience. Evanston, Ill.: Northwestern University Press, 1973.

Eisenstein, Sergei. Film Form. New York: Harcourt, Brace & World, 1949.

Ellul, Jacques. The Technological Society. New York: Alfred A. Knopf, 1964.

Friendly, Fred. Due to Circumstances Beyond Our Control. New York: Random House, 1967.

Hall, Stuart, and Paddy Whannel. The Popular Arts. Boston: Beacon Press, 1964.

Hanhardt, John. "Video/Television Space." In Video Art: An Anthology, edited by Ira Schneider and Beryl Korot, pp. 220-24. New York: Harcourt Brace Jovanovich, 1976.

Henry, Jules. Culture Against Man. New York: Random House, 1963.

Hoggart, Richard. Speaking To Each Other. Vol. 1: About Society. London: Chatto & Windus, 1970.

_____. Speaking To Each Other. Vol. 2: About Literature. London: Chatto & Windus, 1970.

Innis, Harold A. The Bias of Communication. Toronto: University of Toronto Press, 1951.

_____. Empire and Communications. Toronto: University of Toronto Press, 1972.

Institute of Contemporary Art, University of Pennsylvania. Video Art. Philadelphia: Institute of Contemporary Art, 1975.

Kostelanetz, Richard, ed. Esthetics Contemporary. Buffalo, N.Y.: Prometheus Books, 1978.

Kurtz, Bruce. "The Present Tense." In Video Art: An Anthology, edited by Ira Schneider and Beryl Korot, pp. 234-43. New York: Harcourt Brace Jovanovich, 1976.

_____. Spots: The Popular Art of American Television Commercials. New York: Arts Communications, 1977.

_____. "Video in America." In The New Television: A Public/Private Art, edited by Douglas Davis and Allison Simmons, pp. 178-83. Cambridge, Mass.: MIT Press, 1977.

Laurent, Lawrence. "Wanted: The Complete Television Critic." In The Eighth Art, Robert Lewis Shayon et al., pp. 153-71. New York: Holt, Rinehart and Winston, 1962.

Leonard, John. This Pen For Hire. New York: Doubleday & Company, 1973.

Littlejohn, David. "Thoughts on Television Criticism." Television as a Cultural Force, edited by Douglass Cater and Richard Adler, pp. 147-73. New York: Praeger, 1976.

Macdonald, Dwight. Against the American Grain. New York: Random House, 1962.

_____. "A Theory of Mass Culture." Mass Culture: The Popular Arts in America, edited by Bernard Rosenberg and David Manning White, pp. 59-73. Glencoe, Ill.: Free Press, 1957.

Margolis, Joseph. The Language of Art and Art Criticism. Detroit: Wayne State University Press, 1965.

McLuhan, Marshall. The Guttenberg Galaxy. Toronto: University of Toronto Press, 1962.

_____. Understanding Media: The Extensions of Man. New York: McGraw-Hill, 1964.

Mendelsohn, Harold. Mass Entertainment. New Haven, Conn.: College and University Press, 1966.

Mills, C. Wright. The Power Elite. New York: Oxford University Press, 1956.

Newcomb, Horace. TV: The Most Popular Art. Garden City, N.Y.: Doubleday, Anchor Press, 1974.

_____, ed. Television: The Critical View. 2d ed. New York: Oxford University Press, 1979.

Nye, Russel. The Unembarrassed Muse. New York: Dial Press, 1970.

Osborne, Harold. Aesthetics and Art Theory. New York: E. P. Dutton, 1970.

Oxford English Dictionary, Oxford: The Clarendon Press, 1933.

Paik, Nam June. "The Video Synthesizer and Beyond." In The New Television: A Public/Private Art, edited by Douglas Davis and Allison Simmons, pp. 38-47. Cambridge, Mass.: MIT Press, 1977.

Price, Jonathan. Video Visions: A Medium Discovers Itself. New York: New American Library, 1977.

Revel, Jean F. Without Marx or Jesus: The New American Revolution Has Begun. New York: Doubleday, 1970.

Rosenberg, Bernard, and David Manning White, eds. Mass Culture: The Popular Arts in America. Glencoe, Ill.: Free Press, 1957.

_____. Mass Culture Revisited. New York: Van Nostrand, 1971.

Ross, David. "Interview with Douglas Davis." In Video Art: An Anthology, edited by Ira Schneider and Beryl Korot, pp. 32-33. New York: Harcourt Brace Jovanovich, 1976.

_____. "The Personal Attitude." In Video Art: An Anthology, edited by Ira Schneider and Beryl Korot, pp. 244-50. New York: Harcourt Brace Jovanovich, 1976.

_____. "A Provisional Overview of Artists' Television in the U. S. " In New Artists Video, edited by Gregory Battcock, pp. 138-65. New York: E. P. Dutton, 1978.

_____. "Video and the Future of the Museum." In The New Television: A Public/Private Art, edited by Douglas Davis and Allison Simmons, pp. 112-17. Cambridge, Mass.: MIT Press, 1977.

Sahlins, Marshall. Culture and Practical Reason. Chicago: University of Chicago Press, 1976.

Sarris, Andrew. Confessions of a Cultist. New York: Simon and Schuster, 1973.

_____. The Primal Screen. New York: Simon and Schuster, 1973.

Schneider, Ira, and Beryl Korot, eds. Video Art: An Anthology. New York: Harcourt Brace Jovanovich, 1976.

Seldes, Gilbert. The Public Arts. New York: Simon and Schuster, 1956.

Shayon, Robert Lewis. The Crowd-Catchers: Introducing Television. New York: Saturday Review Press, 1973.

____. Open to Criticism. Boston: Beacon Press, 1971.

Simon, John. Acid Test. New York: Stein and Day, 1963.

____. Private Screenings. New York: Macmillan, 1967.

Sitney, P. Adams. Visionary Film. New York: Oxford University Press, 1974.

Sontag, Susan. On Photography. New York: Farrar, Straus & Giroux, 1977.

Thorburn, David. "Television Melodrama." In Television as a Cultural Force, edited by Douglass Cater and Richard Adler, pp. 77-94. New York: Praeger, 1976.

Tillman, Frank A. , and Steven M. Cahn, eds. Philosophy of Art and Aesthetics. New York: Harper and Row, 1969.

Tyler, Parker. The Three Faces of the Film. 2d ed. New York: A. S. Barnes, 1967.

____. Underground Film: A Critical History. New York: Grove Press, 1969.

Weber, Max. The Theory of Social and Economic Organization. New York: Oxford University Press, 1947.

Whitehead, Alfred North. Modes of Thought. New York: Macmillan, 1938.

Williams, Raymond. Communications. Rev. ed. London: Barnes & Noble, 1967.

____. Television: Technology and Cultural Form. New York: Schocken Books, 1975.

Wollen, Peter. Signs and Meaning in the Cinema. 3d ed. Bloomington, Ind. : Indiana University Press, 1972.

Wood, Peter H. "Television as Dream." In Television as a Cultural Force, edited by Douglass Cater and Richard Adler, pp. 17-35. New York: Praeger, 1976.

Youngblood, Gene. Expanded Cinema. New York: E. P. Dutton, 1970.

Zettl, Herbert. Sight, Sound, Motion: Applied Media Aesthetics. Belmont, Calif.: Wadsworth, 1973.

EXHIBITION CATALOGUES

Hanhardt, John. "Douglas Davis: Video." Exhibition notes from The Whitney Museum of American Art. New York, February 1977.

Ross, David A. "Americans in Florence: Europeans in Florence: Notes on the Exhibition." In Americans in Florence: Europeans in Florence. Videotapes Produced by Art/Tapes/22, n.p. Florence: Centro Di, 1974.

____. "Frank Gillette: Development and Recent Works." In Frank Gillette Video: Process and Meta-Process, pp. 24-29. Syracuse, N.Y.: Everson Museum of Art, 1973.

____. "Introduction to Part 1." In Southland Video Anthology, pp. 2-3. Long Beach, Calif.: Long Beach Museum of Art, 1977.

____. "Peter Campus: Closed Circuit Video." In Peter Campus, n.p. Syracuse, N.Y.: Everson Museum of Art, 1974.

____. "Time as Form." In Douglas Davis: events drawings objects videotapes, n.p. Syracuse, N.Y.: Everson Museum of Art, 1972.

JOURNAL AND MAGAZINE ARTICLES

Alloway, Lawrence. "Artists as Writers, Part One: Inside Information." Artforum 12 (March 1974): 30-35.

____. "Artists as Writers, Part Two: The Realm of Language." Artforum 12 (April 1974): 30-35.

Brakhage, Stan. "Metaphors on Vision by Stan Brakhage." Film Culture, no. 30 (1963): n.p.

____. "The Silent Sound Sense." Film Culture, no. 21 (Summer 1960): 65-67.

Burgheim, Richard. "Television Reviewing." Harper's Magazine, August 1969, pp. 98-101.

Burroughs, Julian, Jr. "Radio-Television Criticism: Purpose and Effects." Southern Speech Journal 27 (Spring 1962): 213-19.

Carey, James W. "Communication and Culture." Communication Research 2 (April 1975): 173-91.

Cawelti, John G. "Notes Toward An Aesthetic of Popular Culture." Journal of Popular Culture 5 (Fall 1971): 255-68.

Champlin, Charles. "TV: The End of the Beginning." American Film, October 1975, pp. 60-65.

Condon, George. "Critics' Choice." Television Quarterly 1 (November 1962): 24-31.

Connors, Bruton. "Criticism Pure or Applied?" Twentieth Century, no. 1032 (1967): 10-11.

Davis, Douglas. "Art and Technology—Toward Play," Art in America. January-February 1968, pp. 46-47.

____. "The Critic Now." Arts in Society 5 (1968): 357-59.

____. "Let's Hear It for the Cable." Newsweek, November 21, 1977, p. 29.

____. "Media/Art/Media." Arts Magazine, September-October 1971, pp. 43-45.

____. "Post-Modern Form: Stories Real and Imagined/Toward a Theory." New York Arts Journal (February-March 1978): 9-12.

____. "Post Post-Art: Where Do We Go From Here?" Village Voice, June 25, 1979, pp. 37-41.

____. "Post Post-Art II: Symbolismo, Come Home." Village Voice, August 13, 1979, pp. 40-43.

____. "Public Art: The Taming of the Vision." Art in America, May-June 1974, pp. 84-85.

____. "Symbolismo Meets the Faerie Queene." Village Voice, December 17, 1979, pp. 42, 45-47.

____. "Television's Avant-Garde." Newsweek, February 9, 1970, pp. 60-63.

_____. "Video Obscura." Artforum 10 (April 1972): 64-71.

Gosling, Nigel. "The Critical Tightrope." Twentieth Century, no. 1032 (1967): 11-12.

Greenberg, Bradley S. , and Thomas F. Gordon. "Critics' and Public Perception of Violence in Television Programs." Journal of Broadcasting 15 (Winter 1970-71): 29-43.

Hazard, Patrick D. "TV Criticism—A Prehistory." Television Quarterly 2 (Fall 1963): 52-60.

Kaplan, Abraham. "The Aesthetics of the Popular Arts." The Journal of Aesthetics and Art Criticism 24 (Spring 1966): 351-64.

Kitross, John. "Criticism." Journal of Broadcasting 11 (Winter 1966-67): 1-2.

Kostelanetz, Richard. "The Compleat Critic." Twentieth Century, no. 1032 (1967): 17-19.

Kreiling, Ernie. "The Kreiling Thesis." The Bulletin of the American Society of Newspaper Editors, September 1, 1965, p. 1.

Krutch, Joseph Wood. "Is Our Common Man Too Common?" Saturday Review, January 10, 1953, pp. 8-9, 35-37.

Kurtz, Bruce. "Artists' Video at the Crossroads." Art in America, January/February 1977, pp. 36-40.

Laurent, Lawrence. "A Critic Looks at Reviewing." Journal of Broadcasting 11 (Winter 1966-67): 16.

Levine, Richard M. "The Medium of Record Finally Catches On." New Times, August 7, 1978, p. 57.

Lichty, Lawrence. "What Does A Television Critic Write About?" Journal of Broadcasting 7 (Fall 1963): 353-58.

Mayeux, Peter E. "Three Television Critics; Stated vs. Manifest Functions." Journal of Broadcasting 14 (Winter 1969-70): 25-36.

"Out of the Blue." Time, August 20, 1956, p. 71.

Paik, Nam June, and Paul Schimmel. "Abstract Time." Arts Magazine, December 1974, pp. 52-53.

Rintels, David W. "Not for Bread Alone." Performance, no. 3 (July/ August 1972): 49–55.

Ross, David. "Douglas Davis: Video Against Video." Arts Magazine, December 1974, pp. 60–62.

Rossman, Jules. "The TV Critic Column: Is It Influential?" Journal of Broadcasting 19 (Fall 1975): 401–11.

_____. "What Do Reviewers Actually Review?" Journal of Broadcasting 9 (Spring 1965): 167–75.

Scher, Saul N. "The Role of the Television Critic: Four Approaches." Today's Speech 22 (Summer 1974): 1–6.

Shelby, Maurice E., Jr. "Criticism and Longevity of Television Programs." Journal of Broadcasting 17 (Summer 1973): 277–86.

Shils, Edward. "Mass Society and Its Culture." Daedalus 89 (Spring 1960): 288–314.

Sitney, P. Adams. "The Idea of Abstraction." Film Culture, nos. 63–64 (1976): 1–24.

_____, ed. "Metaphors on Vision by Stan Brakhage." Film Culture, no. 30 (1963): n. p.

Smith, Cecil. "Changing Portrait of the TV Critic." Television Quarterly 11 (Winter 1974): 29–30.

Steinberg, Charles. "The Compleat Television Critic." Television Quarterly 11 (Winter 1974): 5–11.

Tyler, Parker. "A Preface to the Problems of the Experimental Film." Film Culture 4 (February 1958): 5–8.

_____. "Stan Brakhage." Film Culture 4 (April 1958): 23–25.

Wardle, Irving. "Growth of a Critic." Twentieth Century, no. 1032 (1967): 12–14.

Wright, John L. "The Focus of Television Criticism." Journal of Popular Culture 7 (Spring 1974): 887–94.

NEWSPAPER COLUMNS

Crosby, John. "Hail and Farewell." New York Herald-Tribune, October 28, 1960.

Harrison, Bernie. "Everybody Wants Eaton's Stations." Washington Evening Star, September 2, 1966, p. A12.

_____. "90-Minute Era Lies Ahead." Washington Sunday Star, September 2, 1956, p. A30.

_____. "Old Gags and Tricks Still Working for Berle." Washington Evening Star, September 12, 1966, p. D8.

_____. "On The Air: A Year of Hope, Susskind Says." Washington Evening Star, September 14, 1966, p. D13.

_____. "On The Air: Drama Leads the Special Lists." Washington Evening Star, September 7, 1966, p. D15.

_____. "On The Air: Languid History, Fine Photography." Washington Evening Star, January 26, 1972, p. C16.

_____. "On The Air: On Cutting Costs." Washington Sunday Star, January 23, 1972, "TV Magazine," p. 2.

_____. "On the Air: 'Queen of Spades' Operatic Mishmash." Washington Evening Star, January 5, 1972, p. B13.

_____. "An The Air: Should Schools Select TV Shows?" Washington Evening Star, September 9, 1966, p. D15.

_____. "On The Air: 'The Monkees' Hits New Numbing Low." Washington Evening Star, September 8, 1966, p. A20.

_____. "On The Air: The Return of David Susskind." Washington Evening Star, September 8, 1966, p. C18.

_____. "On The Air: The Year of the Specials." Washington Evening Star, September 6, 1966, p. A21.

_____. "'That Girl' Looks Good." Washington Evening Star, September 9, 1966, p. D15.

____. "TV Tonight: More Musketeers, and Sure Delight." Washington Star, December 2, 1977, p. C7.

____. "TV Tonight: Trio of Specials Under CBS's Tree." Washington Star, November 30, 1977, p. D1.

____. "Van Dyke's Last Stand." Washington Star, December 4, 1977, p. H5.

Hearst, Stephen. "Writing About Television." Times (London) Literary Supplement, November 12, 1971, p. 1418.

Newcomb, Horace. "The Audience Is Crucial as Television Begins to Grow Up." Baltimore Sun, May 31, 1974, p. B5.

____. "Television Big and Unwieldy, But It's Changed Our Lives." Baltimore Sun, March 26, 1973, p. B5.

O'Connor, John J. "Blowing the Whistle on Dramatic License." New York Times, October 24, 1976, sec. 2, p. D31.

____. "Competition Makes Networks Go Rigid." New York Times, September 26, 1976, sec. 2, p. D29.

____. "A Conference Asks: Can Television Be Trusted?" New York Times, July 14, 1974, sec. 2, p. D31.

____. "The Granddaddy of 'Em All, 'The Forsyte Saga,' Returns." New York Times, July 3, 1977, sec. 2, p. D21.

____. "Has Archie Run His Course?" New York Times, September 23, 1979, sec. 2, p. D35.

____. "The Importance of the Independent." New York Times, February 19, 1978, sec. 2, p. D31.

____. "'Live From Lincoln Center' Has Found Its Focus." New York Times, July 11, 1976, sec. 2, p. D21.

____. "New Play Series Long on Talent, Short on Funds." New York Times, October 17, 1976, sec. 2, p. D31.

____. "Public TV and Independents—Wary Partners." New York Times, January 27, 1980, sec. 2, p. D31.

_____. "Scandinavian TV Argues Well for Imported Fare." New York Times, July 17, 1977, sec. 2, p. D25.

_____. "Should Public Television Be Playing It Safe?" New York Times, March 23, 1980, sec. 2, pp. D35, D38.

_____. "The Squeeze on Independents." New York Times, November 4, 1979, sec. 2, p. D39.

_____. "There's Gold in That There Trash." New York Times, March 28, 1971, sec. 2, p. D21.

_____. "Trollope's Novels Stylishly Serialized." New York Times, January 30, 1977, sec. 2, p. D29.

_____. "TV: Divine Miss M, Boundless Energy." New York Times, December 7, 1977, p. C30.

_____. "TV: 'Pilobolus and Joan' Solid Visual Achievement." New York Times, July 1, 1974, p. 59.

_____. "TV: Violence." New York Times, December 5, 1977, p. 76.

_____. "Why Can't the Networks Help Support PBS?" New York Times, October 30, 1977, sec. 2, p. D35.

Rose, Reginald. "TV's Age of Innocence—What Became of It?" New York Times, December 3, 1967, sec. 2, p. 21.

Wiegand, Ingrid. "Three Silent and Secret Acts." Soho Weekly News, February 19, 1976, p. 36.

UNPUBLISHED MATERIALS

Greenberg, Daniel A. "Television—Its Critics and Criticism (A Survey and Analysis)." Ph. D. dissertation, Wayne State University, 1965.

Newcomb, Horace. "Fiction as Anthropology: Images of the South in Popular Television Series." Paper presented at the University of South Carolina Conference on Visual Anthropology and the American South, Columbia, S.C., October 1977.

____. "Popular Television and Experimental Video: The Aesthetic Overlap." Paper presented at the Symposium on Film/Theater/ Video, Center for Twentieth Century Studies, University of Wisconsin, Milwaukee, February 1977.

____. "Television and Cultural Theory." Paper presented at the Conference on Postindustrial Culture: Technology and the Public Sphere, Center for Twentieth Century Studies, University of Wisconsin, Milwaukee, February 1977.

____. "Toward Television History: The Growth of Styles." Paper presented at the American Studies Association Convention, Boston, Mass., October 1977.

Shackelford, Wendell C. "The Critic of Public Media: A Discussion of the Dynamics of Appreciation and Critical Reasoning with a Detailed Analysis of Broadway Reviews in New York Newspapers." Ph. D. dissertation, University of Illinois at Urbana-Champaign, 1969.

Smith, Ralph L. "A Study of Professional Criticism of Broadcasting in the United States 1920-1955." Ph. D. dissertation, University of Wisconsin, 1959.

Thorburn, David. "The Evolution of the Television Detective." Paper presented at the American Studies Association Convention, October 1977, Boston, Mass.

INTERVIEWS

Davis, Douglas. New York City. Interview March 18, 1978.

Harrison, Bernie. Washington Star, Washington, D. C. Interview February 8, 1978.

Newcomb, Horace. University of Maryland–Baltimore County, Baltimore, Maryland. Interview February 9, 1978.

O'Connor, John J. New York Times, New York City. Interview December 7, 1977.

Ross, David. Washington, D. C. Interview March 15, 1978.

INDEX

Abe, Shuya, 141
"Abide With Me," 48
abstract imagery, 149; form, 158
academic critic (see critic)
access, 55-56; artists ability to gain unrestricted channels, 127; controversy surrounding, 56-57; problems, 55; visible, 80
"Adventures of a Nurse," 123
advertising on television, 1, 81-82, 84, 98; aesthetic characteristics of, 90; magazine concept of, 67; and mythology, 14
advocacy journalism, 84
Aeschylus, 101
"Age of Kings," 77
agent: art, 24, 114
alienation, 26
Alka-Seltzer, 90
all-channel receiver bill, 76
Alley, Robert, 36
"All in the Family," 50-51, 61, 75, 99, 100-01, 110
Alloway, Lawrence, 137, 138-39
Alpert, Hollis, 32
Alpert, John, 17, 59
American Ballet Theater, 45
American Broadcasting Company, 42, 48, 71-72, 75-76
American Film Institute Journal, 143
American Scholar, 143
"American Short Story," 56
American University, 143-44
"An American Family," 157, 160
anthologist: art, 24, 114
Anthology Film and Video Ar-
chives, 58, 165
Antin, Eleanor, 123-24
"Archie Bunker's Place," 50
architecture, 118
Arlen, Michael, 29, 32, 35, 41
art: and chance, 145-46; coexistence of traditional and avant garde, 118; on commercial television, 156; conceptual, 145; and cultural and social systems, 172; definition of public, 160; elements of, 46; into everyday life through video, 145; growing portability of, 126; and ideas, 145; as a human endeavor, 167; making, 149; and metaphysics, 145; as model of behavior, 138; in museum and gallery context, 168; narrative structures of, 116; Pop, 144; popular, 2, 10, 17, 90, 103, 174; popular and high, 103, 110; post-modern, 155, 157, 158; and relationship to life, 167, 168; returning to content, 155; salesmanship in contemporary world of, 23; use of everyday activity in, 146; worth in, 13
Art in America, 143
Art and the Future (Davis), 143
Artculture: Essays on the Post-Modern (Davis), 143
Artforum, 143, 167
Arthur, Robert Alan, 5, 172
artist, 20, 114; as commentator on current values, 138; conceptual, 144; independent film, 116; and the interview, 138;

and the statement, 138; and
use of popular mediums, 167
artistic process: romantic view
of, 162
artists' video, 36, 91, 114, 142,
158, 160, 168, 171-72, 175;
as alternative to traditional
television, 28, 128-29, 141;
and broadcast television programming, 159; definition of,
27; development since mid-
1960s, 159; interactive, 115;
nonnarrative, 115; personalized, 115
art museum (see museum)
"Art Now '74, A Celebration of
the American Arts," 120
Art/Tapes/22, 120
Arts Magazine, 120, 143
Arts in Society, 143
Atlanta Journal, 71
Atlantic Monthly, 31
audience, 20, 46, 51; appeal, 44;
existential equality of artist
and, 165; home viewing, 45;
live versus home viewers, 165;
loyalty, 99-100; minority, 58;
nature of, 165; participative,
149; process of direct video
interaction with, 145; symbol
systems in relation to, 110;
for specialized video performance, 166; theater, 45; value
of, 166; viewing habits, 47
"Austrian Tapes," 149-50, 162,
167; viewer reaction to, 150
Austrian Television Network
(O. R. F.), 149
avant-garde, 25, 159; fine arts
status of, 90

Baltimore Sun, 91, 105, 108-09
"Batman," 72
Bellows, Jim, 71
Belson, Jordan, 5

Benjamin, Walter, 126
Bergman, Ingmar, 90
"Best of Families," 52
"Beverly Hillbillies," 15, 16,
77, 93, 95-96, 97, 99; in a
cultural context, 94; image
of shiftlessness on, 95; im-
ages of massive social isola-
tion on, 95
bigotry, 51; as a comedic device, 50
"Black Journal," 61-62
Blue Book (Federal Communications Commission), 67
Bolshoi Ballet, 46
Boorstin, Daniel, 32
Boston Museum of Fine Arts, 117
Brandeis University, 117
"Brecht—On the Run from My
Fellow Countrymen," 49
Brecht, Bertolt, 49, 126, 152
154
Brecht, George, 144, 145, 152
British Broadcasting Corporation, 32-33, 39, 49, 73, 77,
78, 88, 109
Broadcast Education Association,
34
broadcast license renewal: and
problems with minority groups,
80
broadcasters: executive decision
making of, 79; internal activi-
ties of, 77; role as cultural
translator for society, 127;
and promotion of one-way communication, 173; and television
criticism, 176
Broadway, 62
Brokaw, Tom, 20
Brown, Tony, 61-62
Browning, Kirk, 45, 74
bureaucratic protectionism, 56
Burgheim, Richard, 30
Burton, Richard, 73

"Bus to Nowhere," 140

Cable Soho, 163, 165
cable television, 116-17, 128,
    132, 155, 173; access channels,
    18, 58-59, 161, 167; individual
    artists and access to, 128; live
    performance on, 151; as per-
    sonal art form, 151; and spe-
    cialized audiences, 160; tech-
    nology, 126; unlimited chan-
    nel capacity of, 127; used to
    buy and sell goods, 161
Caesar, Sid, 100
Cage, John, 137, 141, 145
"Camera Three," 56
Campus, Peter, 120, 122-23
capitalism, 98
Carey, James W. , 3, 89, 98
Carnegie Commission Report, 55
Carter, Jimmy, 15
Cashill, John, 14, 15, 16
catalogues: museum exhibition,
    120
Cavett, Dick, 45
Cawelti, John, 91, 92
"CBS Playhouse," 140
centralization: of institutions in
    society, 26
chance imagery, 148
Chaplin, Charlie, 101
character generator, 125
character representation, 50
Chayefsky, Paddy, 5, 141, 172
Chicago Daily News, 71
Chicago Sun-Times, 35
Chicago Tribune, 35
Chieftans, 56
choice: variety of personal ex-
    perience, 5
Christianity, 62
cinema (see film)
Cinema, 12, 59
City College of New York, 40
Cliburn, Van, 45

Cocteau, Jean, 5
Coleridge, Samuel Taylor, 174
Columbia Broadcasting System
    (CBS), 33, 42, 46, 50, 75-76,
    140, 146; CBS News, 59
column: characteristics of style
    in newspaper television, 71;
    function of newspaper, 71
"Comedy in Six Unnatural Acts,"
    57
comedic styles, 110; extension
    into social issues, 99, 101
commercial television (see tele-
    vision)
commercials (see advertising on
    television)
communication: forms of, 89; a
    ritual view of, 98
Communications Act (see Federal
    Communications Act of 1934)
communications technology: and
    broadcast satellites, 153; and
    relationship to culture, 88
Como, Perry, 76
Compton, Neil, 32
Congressional Record, 60
Connor, Russell, 115, 117-18,
    175
Connors, Bruton, 21
consumption: television advertis-
    ing's promotion of, 26
contemporary art (see art)
"Continuing Story of Carel and
    Ferd," 58
Corcoran Gallery, 146-47
Cornell College, 91
Corporation for Public Broad-
    casting, 55, 61
Country Time Lemonade, 15
Cousteau, Jaques, 72
crafts, 118
critic: academic, 23-24, 33, 88,
    175; applied, 21; artist as,
    137, 139, 141, 151, 159, 162,
    163, 167, 175-76; conservative,

23-24; consumer guide function of, 42, 45, 46; definition of, 20-24; definition of television, 25-33; drama, 32-33; evaluating contributions of television, 172-75; film, 32-33, 66; ideal television, 105; intellectual television, 32-33; journalist as, 41-42, 45, 88; literary, 32-33; as middleman between artist and audience, 22; pre-reviewing function of, 41-45, 69, 82-83; pseudo-, 23; radical, 23-24, 114-15, 134, 161, 175; reviewing function of, 22, 24, 45, 62, 66, 69, 73; role of, 107; as teacher, 33, 81, 99, 106, 111; television, 58, 63, 69, 80; television practitioner as, 32-33; television writing for syndication, 29

criticism, 111; approaches to television and video, 171-77; assumed influence of television, 29; climate of, 177; comprehensive, 47; deadline pressures of, 22; distancing factor of, 23; distributive function of, 22; film and theater, 66; formula, 107; as moral process, 103; new directions in television and video, 33-36, 171-77; "outback" television, 29; practical, 24; sophisticated audience-oriented, 111; survey of television, 31; of television in newspapers and magazines, 28-32, 107-08

Crockett, Davey, 14
Crosby, John, 30, 39, 66, 107
Cuesta, Mike, 90
culture, 51; brutal, 6-7; elitist stance toward, 4, 63, 110; forms of, 88; gallery and museum, 24; and institutions, 134; levels of, 6-7; mainstream in, 161; mass and high, 3-8; mediocre, 6-7; minority subgroups within, 80; popular, 3, 87, 91, 103, 105; superior or refined, 6
Culture Against Man (Henry), 67

Dallas Morning News, 34
dance, 118
"Danger," 140
Dann, Michael, 76
Davis, Douglas, 120, 124-25, 126, 137, 141, 142-68, 173, 175
"Dear Friends," 140
death and life: television's treatment of, 49
decentralization: television and social, 26
Deeb, Gary, 35
"Defenders," 100, 140
Democratic Convention (1976), 58
Dietrich, Marlene, 56
docudrama, 73
documentaries: on television, 59, 79; reasons behind decline of, 78
Dokumenta Exhibition, 153
Donatello, Donato, 23
Douglass College, 144
downtown community television, 18, 59
"Do You Know," 127
drama, 48, 75; aesthetic of, 63; and comedy forms, 110; criticism, 108; elements of quality, 48; live network, 78; serious television, 26, 140; writing, 49
"Drip Music," 145
Du Brow, Rick, 29

eclecticism, 155; in art and writing, 144
editor, 23; arts, 40; control of journalists' essays by, 23
Eisenstein, Sergei, 5, 137
electronic communication: technological potential of, 167
"Electronic Hokkadim," 126, 147, 152
Eliot, T. S. , 137
elitist art community, 164, 167
Emshwiller, Ed, 58
energy: relationship between people and, 142
entertainment, 26; ethic of, 160; forms of, 110; specials, 76
Everson Museum of Art, 118-19, 149
"Execution of Private Slovik," 42
existentialism, 157
experiential time, 157
experimental theater, 49

"Family," 61
family: in television melodrama, 96-97
Family Viewing Hour, 140
fantasy: and realism on television, 110
Farnsworth, Philo T. , 25
"Father Knows Best," 99
Federal Communications Act of 1934, 53, 161
Federal Communications Commission, 67, 79, 130, 140, 161
Felciano, Richard, 158
Fielding, Henry, 23
film, 118, 155; avant-garde, 59; companies in Hollywood, 53; silent in a performance context, 155
Financial Times (London), 40
fine arts, 90, 100
"Five Day Bicycle Race," 58

Flander, Judy, 83
Fluxus, 144
formula: television, 13; theory, 110
"Forsyte Saga," 48
foundations, 52; grants, 53
"Four Places Two Figures One Ghost," 152
Friends of Black Journal, 62
funding: for independent producers, 161
"Future of Communication Studies," 88

Gaines, Ernest J. , 56
gallery: curators, 144; video installations, 134
General Motors Corporation, 129
genre, 48; analysis of, 44; characteristics of, 49; comedic, 50, 51; imagery within, 89; importance of, 162; study of, 47
Gerbner, George, 104
Gillette, Frank, 120, 123
"Gilligan's Island," 72
"Girl From U. N. C. L. E. ," 72
Global Village, 54, 59, 161
Goldberg, Leonard, 76
Golden Age of Television, 140, 172; myth of, 116
Gomer, 100
Goodman, Julian, 78
Goodman, Paul, 32
Gosling, Nigel, 22, 23
gossip column, 107
Gould, Jack, 30, 39, 40, 42, 62, 66, 107
Grand Ole Opry, 56
Great Britain: television introduced in, 25
"Green Acres," 15, 77
"Green Hornet," 71
Greenberg, Clement, 144; on mass culture, 3-4

Gustafson, Julie, 54

Hagerfors, Anna-Maria, 49
Haigh, Kenneth, 73
"Hallmark Hall of Fame," 76
Hamner, Earl, 96, 106
Hanhardt, John, 115-16; 175
Happening, 144; and event move-
    ment, 145-46
"Happy Days," 99
Harithas, James, 119
Harper's, 30
Harris, Harry, 66
Harris poll, 76
Harrison, Bernie, 30, 66-85,
    106, 172, 174
Harrison, Noel, 72
Hartwick College, 88
Hawkeye, 51
Hazam, Lou, 79
Hearst, Stephen, 32
Henry, Jules, 67
Henson, Jim, 82
Hentoff, Nat, 32
Higgins, Dick, 145
hillbilly: as inferior native
    ethic, 16
Hoggart, Richard, 32
Hollywood, 54; journalist-critics,
    semiannual visit to, 34; tele-
    vision film production com-
    panies, 78
"Home," 54
"Home Show," 67
Hope, Bob, 76, 109
Houston Astrodome, 153
"How to Make Love to Your Tel-
    evision Set," 126, 154
Hush Puppies, 15

Ibsen, Henrik, 22
"I, Claudius," 48
ideas: and sense of context in
    art, 163
Image Union, 58

independent artists: access to
    broadcast television distribu-
    tion, 51, 173; works in the
    cultural mainstream, 172
independent community video
    documentary, 171-75
"Independent Focus," 56
information network, 126
intensifiers of meaning: televi-
    sion programs as, 99
International Network for the
    Arts, 143
"It Happened One Christmas,"
    43

John Boy, 96
Johnson & Johnson, 145
Johnson, Ray, 127
Jonsson, Gun, 49
Journal of Broadcasting, 30
Journal of Popular Culture, 69
journalists: pre-reviewing
    function of, 174

Kael, Pauline, 32
Kansas City Star, 71
Kaplan, Abraham, 9-12, 90
Kaprow, Allan, 144
Katz, Elihu, 109
KCET-TV, 55
Kennedy, John F., 77
kiddievid programs, 48
"King Tut," 79
Kitchen Center for Video and
    Music, 58, 151, 153, 165,
    167
Kitross, John, 30
kitsch: and high culture, 4
Kolodin, Irving, 32
Kostelanetz, Richard, 23-24, 114
KQED-TV, 160
Kreiling, Albert, 3
Kreiling, Ernie, 30
Kurtz, Bruce, 88, 90
KVST-TV, 119, 129, 131, 175

Laurent, Lawrence, 28, 30, 36, 39, 66, 107
Lear, Norman, 50, 53, 77, 104, 140
Leonard, John, 30, 40, 174
lesbianism, 57
Levine, Richard M. , 34
Levinson, Richard, 105
Lichtenstein, Roy, 144
Lincoln Center, 46
Link, William, 105
"Listener," 88
listener-supported radio, 130
"Little House on the Prairie," 15
Littlejohn, David, 27, 31-32, 62, 90
"Live from Lincoln Center," 45-46, 74
"Live from Lincoln Center," 45-46, 74
"Live Your Life," 49
Living Room War (Arlen), 174
Long Beach Museum of Art, 119, 120, 129-30
"Lookout," 146
Los Angeles County Museum, 145
Los Angeles Herald-Examiner, 71
"Lou Grant," 99
Lowenberg, Richard, 158
Lumet, Sidney, 140

Macdonald, Dwight, 3-6, 9, 32
magazines: general circulation, 44
Makarova, Natalia, 45
malapropism: as device in situation comedy, 95
"Man from U. N. C. L. E. ," 72
Manhattan Cable, 58, 152; access channels C and D, 151
Markle Foundation, 35
Martin, Quinn, 53
Marxism, 88
Mary Hartman, 104

"Mary Tyler Moore Show," 75, 99
"M*A*S*H," 51, 99, 101
Mason, James, 78
mass audience, 49; aesthetic reception and expression, 6; incorporated into society, 5; and plebian tastes, 4; societal significance of taste in, 6
mass communication, 88, 126
mass culture (see popular culture)
mass magazines: and editors of, 164
Massachusetts Institute of Technology, 88
"Masterpiece Theater," 52, 129
"Maude," 51, 101
MCA/Universal, 53
McCleery, Albert, 78
"McCloud," 14
McGovern, George: campaign, 79
McLuhan, Marshall, 26, 155, 159
medical care, 59
medium: as art form, 155; product and idea-related use of, 129
melodrama: aesthetic of reassurance in, 13; as television form, 13, 16
Metro-Goldwyn-Mayer (MGM), 53
Midler, Bette, 43-44
Mills, C. Wright, 3, 8-9
mind-to-mind communication, 149, 167-68
minority programming: on television, 129
Miss America Beauty Pageant, 76
Mississippi College, 91
"Monkees," 72, 75, 77
Moore, Mary Tyler, 46
moral superiority of rural wis-

dom, 95
motion picture (see film)
MTM Enterprises, 50
multiplicity principle: of plot development in television melodrama, 14, 89, 101
"Muppets," 82
Murrow, Edward R. , 68
museum; as alternative for viewer, 132; and cable television, 120; communities and the, 119-20; contemporary art forms and the, 119-20; curators, 114, 118; as forum for artistic interchange, 132; and informational programming, 132; interaction with television, 132; as producer of art programming, 131-32; program interchange via communication satellite, 175; video department, 119-20
Museum of Broadcasting, New York, 33, 59
Museum of Modern Art, New York, 41
"Museum Open House," 117
museum without walls, 132; and cablecasting, 173
music, 118
myth on television, 14, 26; of American South, 16; of cleanliness, 14; of distrust and resentment of anything intellectual, 15; of the frontier, 14; of individualism, 15; of manifest destiny, 14; of the middle landscape, 14, 16; as ordering mechanism in society, 15; of the puritan ethic, 15; as series of beliefs, 14

Naficy, Hamid, 158
narcotizing dysfunction, 87
Nation, 31

National Broadcasting Company, 25, 43, 67, 71-72, 73, 75-76, 78, 82, 104, 129
National Geographic documentaries, 76
National Observer, 143
National Public Radio: satellite service, 154
"NBC Opera," 67
Neo-Dada, 144
Nesbitt, Cathleen, 48
networking, 154
networks: commercial television, 60
"New Frontier," 77
New Leader, 31
New Republic, 32
New Television: A Public/Private Art (Davis and Simmons), 143
New Times, 34
New York Arts Journal, 143, 167
New York Daily News, 47
New York Herald-Tribune, 30, 39
New York Philharmonic, 45
New York State Council on the Arts, 117
New York Times, 29-30, 39, 40-41, 42, 43, 47, 50, 60-61, 140, 143; News Service, 47, 60
New Yorker, 29, 31, 35, 174
Newcomb, Horace, 15-16, 36, 51, 87-111, 172, 175, 176-77
newspaper: general circulation, 58; immediacy pressure of column, 107; impact of columns, 108; role of columnist, 107-08
Newsweek, 143, 161, 163, 167, 176
Newton, Dwight, 66
Nixon, Richard, 15
Nixon, Tricia, 147

Observer, 21
O'Connor, Carroll, 50-51
O'Connor, John J. , 29, 39-64,
    69, 74, 105, 106-07, 108,
    172, 174
"Oklahoma," 44
O'Neill, Eugene, 22
Open to Criticism (Shayon), 174
opera: aesthetic structures and
    relationship to television, 74;
    production, 46
Oxford English Dictionary, 20

Paik, Nam June, 115, 117, 120,
    127, 141, 142, 149, 158
painting, 118
Paley, William S. , 33, 60, 68
"Pallisers," 49
Paramount, 53
pecuniary philosophy, 67
Pederson, Rena, 34
Performance, 139
"Petticoat Junction," 15
Philadelphia Inquirer, 66
"Pilobolus and Joan," 58
Pitts, Fred, 146
plot: formulaic structuring of, 14
plug-in drug, 87
poetry, 118
"Police Tapes," 54
political conventions, 54
popular art (see art: popular)
popular culture (see culture;
    popular)
portapak, 115; cultural signifi-
    cance of, 17-18
post-modern art (see art: post-
    modern)
Powers, Ron, 35
Powers, Stephanie, 72
Presley, Elvis, 61
"Prisoner," 100
"Project '74 in Koln," 120
public access cable television
    (see cable television)

Public Broadcasting Service, 39,
    45, 48, 52, 55, 74, 139, 143,
    160; funding mechanisms, 52;
public television: 28, 39, 41, 48,
    52, 55, 57, 61, 63, 68, 76,
    79, 172; acquisition series,
    57; experimental facilities,
    160; funding of, 52-53; future
    in U.S. , 55, 77; independent
    producers' limited access to,
    57; and video performance,
    167
Pushkin, Aleksander, 74

QUBE (see Warner Communica-
    tions)
"Queen of Spades," 74
Quentin, John, 73

Radical Software, 143
radio, 67, 81; and audience par-
    ticipation, 155; use of the
    medium, 154
Radio Corporation of America
    (RCA), 25
rating services, 140
Raymond, Alan and Susan, 54-55
readership, 20; critic's percep-
    tion of, 47, 83-84; nature of
    for newspaper column, 109;
    popular culture audience, 108
Reilly, John, 54-55, 158
Republican Party, 129
review: format, 46; impact on
    success of program, 61; of
    new series episodes, 70; pat-
    tern of longer, 72; program,
    69
reviewer (see critic)
"Rhoda," 100
"Rime of the Ancient Mariner,"
    174
Rintels, David, 139, 176
"River Nile," 78
Rockefeller Foundation, 143

"Romeo and Juliet," 45
Ronald Feldman Gallery, 155,
  163, 167
Rose Art Museum, 117
Rose, Reginald, 139-40, 172,
  176
Ross, David, 114, 115, 118-35,
  173, 175
Rossini, Gioacchino, 23
"Rowan and Martin's Laugh-In,"
  100
run-on recording, 156
Russell, Charles, 140
Rutgers State University, 143,
  144-45

Saginaw Valley College, 91
Sahlins, Marshall, 98
Salisbury, Harrison, 59
San Francisco Chronicle, 66
Sarnoff, David, 25-26, 67
satellite: communications, 152-
  53; "secret" communications
  by, 153; transmission and
  privacy, 153
Saturday Review, 32, 174
scarcity: principle of broadcast
  channels, 130
Schaeffer, Pierre, 150
Schickel, Richard, 32
Schultz, Barbara, 55
script writing, 48
sculpture, 118; works containing
  TV monitors and play back
  self-images, 159
"Search for the Nile," 73, 78
Seawright, James, 158
Segal, George, 144
"Senator," 139
Serling, Rod, 172
"Seven Thoughts," 153
Seventh Seal, 90
"Shadow," 153-54
"Shadow Shadowed," 153
Shakespeare, 77, 101

Shales, Tom, 30, 35
Shamberg, Michael, 59
Shatner, Bill, 71
Shayon, Robert Lewis, 32, 107
Shear, Barry, 73
Shils, Edward, 3, 5-9
"Silver Screen," 154-55
Silverman, Fred, 75
Simmons, Allison, 27, 143
Simon, John, 21
situation comedy (see television)
"Sky is Gray," 56
Smith, Carlton, 82
"Soap," 104
social criticism, 104
social decentralization, 142
Socialist Alliance, 129
Soho Weekly News, 151
Something Else Press, 145
Sony, 159
"Southland Video Anthology,"
  119, 120, 129
space: personal or private, 26
special effects, 159
spectator participation: use of
  mediums to achieve, 167
spin-offs, 99
Spots (Kurtz), 90
Stanford University, 88
"Star Trek," 71, 100
Steinberg, Charles, 30-31
"Storyteller," 104
Streisand, Barbra, 44
"Studies in Color II," 156
"Studies in Myself II," 124
"Studio One," 140
subliminal seduction, 87
"Swan Lake," 45-46
symbol: definition of, 97
symbol systems: television's
  exploration of cultural, 26
synaptic function, 98
Syracuse University, 118-19

"Tales of Hoffman," 74

"Talk Out!," 126, 149
TCA Newsletter, 35
Tchaikovsky, Pëtr, 74
telecommunications technologies, 152
telephone: and perceptions of reality, 121-22
teleplay, 49, 55, 140, 141; concepts in, 48; writers, 139, 140, 176
television: 47, 60, 83, 140, 149, 152, 160, 176-77; as adaptor of existing works of art, 75, 175; adventure, 13; aesthetics, 48, 49, 73, 74, 88, 92, 94, 98, 101, 103, 110, 114, 159, 176; alternatives to, 80, 153, 175; anthropological approach to, 12, 175; audience, 90, 99, 100, 104, 105, 110, 116, 127, 149, 166, 168; cable (see cable television); censorship, 140; and children, 105-06, 171; and controversial ideas, 140, 173, 176; courses, 105-06; and culture, 12, 15, 47, 63, 69, 77, 84, 87-88, 90, 92, 95, 97, 98-99, 100, 103, 108, 172, 177; definition of, 1, 18; domestic comedy, 50-51, 110; drama, 48-49, 89, 140, 172; as dream, 12-13; as an educator, 172; effects of, 99, 149; fantasy and realism on, 94, 121; fictional lawyers and doctors programs, 13; formula, 92, 99-100, 105, 110; genre analysis of, 26, 36, 63, 72, 87, 90-91, 97, 98-99, 110, 111, 116, 175; history of, 66, 67, 84, 92, 98, 100, 110; and impact on artists' video, 159; and independent producers, 15, 53-54, 63, 168, 172, 173, independent stations, 41; innovative forms of, 114, 175; institutional economic strictures of, 1, 42-42, 47, 51-52, 68-69, 84, 89, 92, 98, 102, 114, 117, 140, 176; live telecast, 116-17; melodrama, 12, 13-14, 72; minority interest programming on, 118; minority-owned and -operated stations, 80; and minority subcultures, 1; movies made for, 13; mysteries, 13; network, 43, 76, 139; and the novel, 101; opera on, 74; performance on, 45-46; production financing, 55; programming, 46, 57, 68, 69-70, 75-77, 84, 131, 141, 161, 172, 175; programs about, 104; public (see public television); regulatory issues, 39; serial, 77; series, 44, 75, 77, 100, 110; sex on, 98; situation comedy, 17, 50-51, 75, 93, 95-96, 100-101; soap opera, 13; specials, 76; sports on, 109; station license renewals, 70; and symbol systems, 17, 111; technology, 76, 88, 152, 167, 172, 173; as a threat to civilization, 162; time signature of, 1, 124, 156-57; and values, 93, 96, 104, 173; and violence, 104; Westerns, 13
Television: The Critical View (Newcomb), 105-06, 109, 177
Television Critics Association, 33-35
Television: Technology and Cultural Form (Williams), 88
theater, 81
"Then Came Bronson," 100
"Theory of Radio," 126, 154
This Pen For Hire (Leonard), 174
Thomas, Marlo, 43

Thorburn, David, 13, 16, 36, 88, 89-90, 101, 109, 175
"Three Silent and Secret Acts," 151
time: as an element in art forms, 157
Times (London), 22
"Today Show," 67, 166
Tolstoy, Leo, 103
"Tom Jones," 72
"Tonight Show," 67, 82
Top Value Television (TVTV), 55, 59
"Track/Trace," 123
travel: as method of communication, 142
Tsuno, Keiko, 18
Tucker, Sophie, 44
TV Guide, 69
TV Magazine, 36, 116
TV: The Most Popular Art (Newcomb), 87, 90, 92, 94, 103, 106, 108, 110, 111, 175
Twentieth Century-Fox, 53
"Twilight Zone," 71
Tynan, Kenneth, 32

UHF: allocations, 76-77, 79
underwriters: corporate, 53, 56
United Artists, 53
United Broadcasting Company, 79
United Press International, 29
United States: Army, 140; House of Representatives Communications Committee, 53; Supreme Court, 161
University of California Art Museum-Berkeley, 119
University of Chicago, 91
University of Maryland, 91
University of Texas at Austin, 88, 90, 91
University of Tokyo, 141

value conflicts, 14; of urban and rural social systems, 16
value systems: of bourgeois culture, 13; legitimizing society's central institutions, 5
Vanderbeek, Stan, 117, 158
vast wasteland, 87
Vidal, Gore, 5, 32
video: 12, 58, 60, 143, 157-58, 171, 175; anthologies of works in, 118; audience for works, 164; characteristics of, 17; compared with television, 17, 161, 172; development as art form, 134-35; distorting broadcast images through, 141; distribution of works of, 173; and dominant television structures, 125; and elements of chance, 146; evaluation of works of, 17, 63, 158; experimental production in, 41, 58, 63, 91, 146; and film, 157; first principles of, 121; form versus content in, 157; immediacy and unpredictability of, 125, 147; installations, 115-16, 122-23; as an interactive tool in performance, 123-24, 149, 152, 158; intimacy of, 121, 158; live performances using, 143, 151, 157, 167; in museum context, 117; new narrative, 124; as personal expression, 117; and production values, 18; readership for writing about, 164; real-time or unedited, 121, 124-25; relationship of realism and illusion to, 121; on sociopolitical level, 125; spatial and temporal illusions of, 121, 122-23; statements by artists on, 40, 134, 142-43; synthesizer, 117, 142; two-way capabilities of, 27, 121, 125-26, 143, 147, 173; work-

shops, 143
Video Free America, 58
Video Freex, 146
video games, 142
video gallery/theaters, 58, 159
video home computer terminal, 142
video wallpaper, 142
"Video Visionaries," 27
videosphere, 147
videotape, 153; editing, 125
Vietnam: war in, 15
View From Highway 1 (Arlen), 174
viewer: as active information processor, 142; awareness, 45; behavior, 87; control of information, 152; and critical skills, 172; dehumanizing view of, 165; as existential, 164; in an interactive situation, 154; loyalty, 62; mind-to-mind intimacy with, 149; opinion, 44; relationship to television, 154; statistics on, for producers, 165; and value systems, 141; supported television, 130
Village Voice, 143
"Vision and Television" exhibition, 117
"Visions," 55
"VTR: Video and Television Review," 117

Wall Street Journal, 40
"Waltons," 15, 16, 96-97, 99, 106, 108
Wardle, Irving, 22
Warner Brothers, 53
Warner Communications QUBE, 127; two-way interactive cable-casting
"Washington: Behind Closed Doors," 139

Washington Civic Television, Inc. , 79
Washington Community Broadcasting Co. , 79
Washington Daily-News, 66
Washington Evening Star, 66, 70, 80
Washington Morning Herald, 66
Washington Post, 28, 30, 35, 66, 81
Washington Star, 30, 66, 69, 70-71, 81-84
Washington Times-Herald, 66
WCNY-TV, 149
Weaver, Pat, 68
Weiss, Marc, 57
Werner, Mort, 76
West, Don, 146
WGBH-TV, 117, 160
Whitney Museum of American Art, 115, 152, 165, 167
Whittemore, Reed, 32
Wiegand, Ingrid, 151
Wiener, Norbert, 142
Wilkens coffee, 82
Williams, Raymond, 88, 90, 175
Wilson Teachers College, 66
WNET-TV, 39, 54, 57-58, 160; TV lab, 117
Wood, Peter H. , 13-14, 15, 16
Woodrow Wilson Fellowship, 91
WOOK-TV, 79-80
work of art: criteria for evaluating, 9-11; form, 10; formal structure of, 4; origin and destination of, 9; relationship with spectator, 11; social functions, 11; ways of organizing, 92
World War II, 25
World's Fair: 1939, 25-26
Wright, John L. , 69
Writer's Guild of America, West, 139-40

WTOP-TV, 209

Yale University, 40, 88
Young Socialist's Alliance, 130
"Your Show of Shows," 100

Zionist, 62

ABOUT THE AUTHOR

HAL HIMMELSTEIN is Assistant Professor of Radio-Television at Ohio University, Athens. From 1978-79 he was Assistant Professor of Radio-Television-Film at the University of Kansas, Lawrence.

Dr. Himmelstein has published in the areas of popular television, artists' video, and the social environment. His articles and interviews with artists have appeared in <u>Access</u> and <u>Wide Angle.</u>

Dr. Himmelstein holds a B. A. and M. A. from the University of Kansas and a Ph. D. from Ohio University.